To Alaine
With Best Wishes
Joe Patent

Pilot

Pilot

A Tale of High Adventure

By Joe Patient

LEO COOPER
LONDON

First published in Great Britain in 1997 by
LEO COOPER
190 Shaftesbury Avenue, London, WC2H 8JL
an imprint of
Pen & Sword Books Ltd,
47 Church Street,
Barnsley, South Yorkshire S70 2AS
© Joe Patient 1997
A CIP record for this book is available from the British Library
ISBN 0 85052 544 6
Typeset by Phoenix Typesetting, Ilkley, West Yorkshire
Printed in England by
Redwood Books Ltd,
Trowbridge, Wilts.

Contents

Preface

In the Second World War many brave airmen 'failed to return'. I am very conscious of the fact that the incidents I have described could be duplicated a hundred times. Often, greater dangers and more nightmarish conditions were endured. Severe injury and the possibility of imprisonment or death were faced daily.

Everybody knew that the odds were against bomber pilots surviving a tour of operations. I was one of the lucky ones. I tell my story humbly, mindful of the heroism of many of my comrades.

I owe a great debt of gratitude to many of my wartime colleagues and friends who have encouraged me to write this book, in particular to John Diamond. His interest and enthusiasm spurred me on in the first place, and his practical advice, help and support, together with the financial assistance of my friend Brian Anton, have enabled me to complete my extensive research. I also wish to thank John Raison and Angela Marsden whose suggestions have improved the reading.

I dedicate this book to the memory of my mother who loved and had faith in me, to my dear wife Lucy who has loved me so unselfishly for over fifty years, and to Norry Gilroy without whose help I most certainly would not have survived.

Glossary of Abbreviations

AC	Aircraft
AC2	Aircraftsman Second Class
ACDC	Aircrew Dispatch Centre
ACM	Air Chief Marshal
ACRC	Aircrew Reception Centre
A/CDRE	Air Commodore
AFU	Advanced Flying Unit
AOC	Air Officer Commanding
ARB	Air Registration Board
ASI	Air Speed Indicator
ATA	Air Transport Auxiliary
AVM	Air Vice-Marshal
BAT	Beam Approach Training
BOT	Board of Transport
BSAA	British South American Airways
BSDM	British Stores Disposal Mission
C of A	Certificate of Airworthiness
Cb	Cumulo-Nimbus
CFI	Chief Flying Instructor
CO	Commanding Officer
DA	Delayed Action
DO	District Officer
DR	Dead Reckoning (navigation)
DZ	Dropping Zone
EAE	Egyptian Aircraft Engineering
EFTS	Elementary Flying Training School
ETA	Estimated Time of Arrival
FE	Flight Engineer
F/LT	Flight Lieutenant
F/O	Flying Officer
F/SGT	Flight Sergeant
FW	Focke-Wulf
GAF	Greek Air Force
G/CAPT	Group Captain
GOC	General Officer Commanding

GPR	Glider Pilot Regiment
GTS	Glider Training School
HCU	Heavy Conversion Unit
HGCU	Heavy Glider Conversion Unit
IFF	Identification Friend or Foe
ITW	Initial Training Wing
LAC	Leading Aircraftsman
L/COL	Lieutenant Colonel
LDV	Local Defence Volunteers
MCU	Mosquito Conversion Unit
MEDME	Mediterranean and Middle East
MTU	Mosquito Training Unit
NF	Night Flying
OTU	Operational Training Unit
PDC	Personnel Dispatch Centre
PFF	Path Finder Force
PMC	President of the Mess committee
P/O	Pilot Officer
POW	Prisoner of War
PRC	Personnel Reception Centre
PRU	Photographic Reconnaissance Unit
QDM	Course to Steer
RCAF	Royal Canadian Air Force
RDF	Radio Direction Finding
REAF	Royal Egyptian Air Force
RT	Radio Telephony
SBA	Standard Beam Approach
SFTS	Service Flying Training School
SGT	Sergeant
SLST	Sierra Leone Selection Trust
St Cu and Al Cu	Strato-Cumulus and Alto-Cumulus
STOL	Short Take-off and Landing
TI	Target Indicator
UTA	*Union Transport Arien*
UT	Under Training
US	Unserviceable
USAAF	United States Army Air Force
VHF	Very High Frequency
W/CDR	Wing Commander
W Op	Wireless Operator
WO	Warrant Officer

1

Beginnings

Everything seemed peaceful and calm as we flew through the dark, silent skies of that mid-September night in 1943. We were apprehensive, well aware of the possible dangers ahead. When I opened the bomb doors near the target exactly on time all hell broke loose. Dozens of searchlights blazed up in a great wall of blinding light; flak exploded all about us. We had to fly through this deadly barrier for only two or three minutes but it seemed like an eternity. Never again was I so tempted to jettison my bombs and get the hell out. Berlin was throwing the lot at us.

The crash of flak smashing into us was almost drowned by the roar of the engines. Direct hits disabled the starboard engine. In the turmoil I accidentally feathered the wrong propellor. We were plummeting to earth before I could restart the port engine. Petrol was now so low that our only way back to base would have to be across the heavily defended Ruhr. We might never make it.

Searchlights trapped us near Münster and two Focke-Wulf 190s scored direct hits on wings and fuselage. They failed to finish us off but the plane was in a bad way. Norry was clutching at his neck in pain where a bullet or cannon shell had scorched it. Another FW attacked. No way was I going to get out of this alive, so I tried to take him with me. He managed to give me the slip but I can still see his white staring face. He was very close. We struggled on towards Manston, prepared to bail out or ditch if necessary. Our petrol gauges showed empty five minutes before we crash landed on the airfield. Before we had time to breathe a sigh of relief there was an almighty bang and another aircraft crashed into us. Both planes were a complete write off. How the crews managed to escape almost unhurt we shall never know. I was told later that I was laughing hysterically as I staggered from the wreckage.

*　*　*

The nightmare of that night (only briefly described here) and of many others are indelibly engraved on my mind. Fifty years later the memories are just as vivid.

After flying some eighty Marks of aeroplanes and gliders between 1941 and 1973, I can hardly believe that in my schooldays, what are now everyday occurrences used to give us such pleasure and excitement. In the early thirties an aeroplane in the sky would be met with the yell 'Airy plane. Airy plane!' One and all would stop whatever games they were playing to gaze in wonderment, craning their necks to watch it until it vanished from sight. The multi-horse-drawn fire wagons racing along over cobbled or tar-blocked roads, their bells clanging, their firemen resplendent in gleaming brass helmets, were vastly more exciting than the blaring motor fire engines of today. Even holes in the road were a source of pleasure. Today's fence with flashing warning lights cannot be compared with the old watchman in his simple shelter, the cheerful glow and distinctive smell of a coke brazier with the tin of water heating for a brew-up, and paraffin hurricane lamps marking the danger. What cheery men they almost always seemed to be (mostly ex-service and often disabled), and what a fund of stories they had.

I could write whole chapters about my childhood, but this is not an autobiography. However, a brief outline of my background may add interest to the subsequent account of my experiences in the Royal Air Force and post-war operations in the Middle East and Africa.

Born in Southwark on 9 June, 1917, I was the tenth child of hardworking parents. My mother took in washing as well as lodgers and also fostered children; my father worked at the nearby brewery.

We lived very plainly and had to watch every penny, but we were luckier than many children in the area who often went hungry and barefoot because one or both parents spent many nights in the local pubs.

As soon as I was old enough I went to Rockingham Street Elementary School. I enjoyed it and by working hard eventually qualified for St Olive's Grammar School; but after an interview and consideration of my background, I was sent to West Square Central school. This was alongside what is now the site of the Imperial War Museum in St George's Road and from our classroom windows we could look over high walls into the grounds. Ironically it was then Bedlam Mad House, where King George III was housed for a time. We often watched the bizarre antics of the inmates, but I was sympathetic to the sick and elderly and sometimes got involved in brawls with those who derided them.

When my brother Jim left school at fourteen and started work, I took over his lunchtime and weekend job helping the milkman on his rounds. I pushed the milk barrow with its highly polished brass, copper churn and metal canisters and measured out pints and half pints into jugs and basins on doorsteps. I was allowed to keep any money I earned, but was expected to save it for outings and holidays. In my case these were the annual camps of the Boys' Brigade and Church Lads' Brigade to which I belonged in turn. There were two evening meetings each week, one social with ping-pong, boxing and games, the other with drill, including arms drill with rifles. I played the bugle at their weekly church parades and for some time sang in the choir of Trinity Church. This meant morning and evening services as well as afternoon Sunday School. I occasionally missed the odd service preferring to play with pals around Bankside, by London Bridge, and Borough Market where sometimes one of us would keep watch while others pilfered some fruit. On Sundays I was given two pennies by my father, a penny for me and a penny for the church. More often than not when the collection was taken, I would either pretend to put something in or, having changed the penny into two halfpennies, put one of these in.

3

I enjoyed West Square school until my second year, but I then began to resent cruel punishments from the French master which I considered to be totally unjust. I was so disgusted by this that when a French lesson was scheduled for the afternoon, I would skip school after the lunch break. Shortly before my fourteenth birthday I was wandering round Bermondsey on one of these afternoons off when I saw an advertisement for woodworking hands at a firm in Jamaica Road. I went in, told them I was fourteen, and was given a week's trial starting the following Monday. I had been to woodworking classes at school and could handle tools very well for my age. The job involved a great deal of deception at home about the long hours I was away each day and hiding my earnings as well as the tools I bought with them. It could not last. When I arrived home one evening, Mum asked me what I had done that day. I had scarcely begun to tell her when she accused me of being a deceitful little bugger and well and truly boxed my ears. That morning the man from the school board had called to find out why I had not been to school for the past few weeks. The reckoning with Pop still had to be faced when he came back from work. 'What else did you expect from the little bugger. Nothing but deceit.' He calmed down when I explained that I had spent most of my wages on tools, and the thrashing I had expected was avoided when I showed them to him.

By now I had passed my fourteenth birthday, so I was allowed to keep the job. I soon found that working from home caused friction and I managed to get a live-in job as a page boy at a block of luxury flats in the West End. Many famous people lived there or came to visit their friends. I remember being called a fool by Sir Thomas Beecham when I inadvertently tripped over his feet. I opened the door to the Duke of Gloucester who was visiting his friend Sir Henry Birkin, the racing driver. I was especially intrigued by a beautiful Argentinian woman who had received several visits from the Prince of Wales, later Edward VIII. This was, you might say, my further education. I was always eager to improve myself and tried hard to learn as much as I could. I was, perhaps, aping my betters, but seeing how the other half lived later helped me to be at home in any company.

At about that time my father died. When his few personal belongings were distributed, I upset my brothers by begging Mum to give me the gold buttonhole badge which had been presented to him inscribed 'For forty years meritorious service'. When asked why I so particularly wanted it, I replied that it would remind me what *not* to do. I vowed that I would never stay in a job for more than one year, a vow I kept until the war.

Through the generosity of a Mr Tucker I was able to attend a course at the Gravesend Sea School where, after three months' intensive and highly disciplined training as a steward, I joined the Orient Line on their luxury (for the passengers) cruise to Australia on their flagship the SS *Oronsay*. Gibraltar, Palma, Naples, Aden, the Indian Ocean, Ceylon and the long sea voyage to Fremantle – all were englightening in their different ways. I learned about the sleazy life ashore enjoyed by some of the visiting sailors and listened wide-eyed to their boasts about the brothels and exhibitions they had visited. It seemed to me that their collective view about anyone other than ourselves was that they were 'wops', 'wogs', or 'niggers'. When I protested about this, I was told, 'Wait till you get a bit older, sonny, you'll learn.' Thank God I never did. In all my travels I have found just as much good and bad in all ethnic groups as among my own.

Out of a job when I got home, I took one as a greengrocer's delivery boy. I learnt very quickly and was soon allowed to serve customers, becoming adept at presenting the good bits and hiding the others, and, when alone, practising how to scoop up and judge the weights. I watched very carefully how the greengrocer handled his wholesalers with their bargain offers. Amazed at his refusal of a whole unopened box of grapes for one shilling, I asked if he would mind if I bought one. 'If you want to,' he replied with a grin. The wood of the case turned out to be better value as firewood than the few grapes I was able to salvage from the whole box. 'You can sometimes buy things cheap, but never buy anything that is too cheap,' was his advice, a lesson well worth the shilling.

Despite that good advice, I was later to regret a short period when

I set up on my own, thinking that I knew it all. I soon had trouble with wholesalers who stopped dealing with me. They told me that their big customers (like the Co-op) had threatened to withdraw their business because I was undercutting them. A disastrous Christmas followed. I managed to get some large orders for all the extras associated with the festive season and even felt it worthwhile to go to the Borough market myself to make certain of getting the very best of everything. I worked night and day, boxing up and delivering the orders on time, but I was in for one of the biggest letdowns of my life. Almost half the customers who had made big orders made excuses for delaying payment and then did not pay. And I thought some of them were my friends. Angry and disillusioned, I sold up and looked for another job.

Regardless of the fact that there was high unemployment in the thirties, I always managed to get work quickly because I was willing to take anything. There followed a series of short jobs in West End clubs and restaurants. I was switchboard and cloakroom attendant at L'Ecu de France in Jermyn Street, commis waiter at Au Jardin des Gourmets in Greek Street, commis again at the Waldorf Hotel. A short period at the English Speaking Union gave me insights into another world, with its quiet air of gentility in slightly run-down surroundings. The mostly middle-aged or elderly members were understanding and considerate and, although the wages were meagre, the treatment of staff was better than in many a West End club or hotel. By the time I was twenty-one I had had twenty jobs.

To broaden my experience, I moved on to the Oriental Club in Hanover Square where I was employed as an assistant billiards marker and assistant wine waiter. I was soon able to move on to a similar job at the Arts Club in Dover Street where the wages were better. It was in fact more rewarding in every way. The head marker in the billiards room was a much older and well respected man who, when the tables were vacant, taught me some of the finer points of play. Not only that, the members were interesting and friendly. I could write whole chapters about some of those I served with drinks or played at billiards. Vociferous and animated discussions were to be heard throughout the building, an almost unique occurrence in London club life. The voices of Russell Flint, Alfred Munnings, Adrian Stokes, Augustus John and Sir William Reid Dick were just a few of the distinguished members we were privileged to hear and serve. It was a world apart. The diversity of the members, many of them outspoken and a few outlandish in appearance, was all the more noticeable to me after the staid conformity of the Oriental Club. However, when the head marker's job at the Oriental Club was offered to me I accepted. Not only was the pay better, enabling me to live out for the first time, but at last I was able to marry my sweet-heart Lucy.

I played cricket for the club in the West End inter-club matches, usually at the Paddington Recreation Grounds. On my way there one afternoon I walked through Woolworth's back entrance, just opposite the Club resplendent in white cricket gear (borrowed), with my friend Bill (Peggy) Pearcey. As I was buying three penny-worth of broken biscuits, Bill was chatting up the very attractive sales girl, whose even teeth, although slightly prominent, were extremely white. Bill seemed to be getting on well with the girl when I reminded him about the cricket match. Imagine my surprise when I opened my bag of biscuits to find amongst the broken ones three pennyworth of unbroken, wrapped de Beukelaer chocolate wafers. When I next went to Woolworth's, alone this time, I received the same treatment, together with a beautiful smile. I was hooked. I had thought she was interested in Bill but I was the fish that was landed. It was thus that I was introduced to Lucy and my courtship of my wonderful wife-to-be had begun.

By now I was able to earn a moderate amount of money playing snooker in my spare time at a nearby club, but all activity came to an end when I was forced to have a severe mastoid operation. Although I eventually recovered, I was out of work again and in rather dire straits. I was lucky enough to have friends who advised me to try for work at De Havillands. One of them, who had previously worked there, lent me his tool kit which I had to have in order to hold down the job. I told the board at the interview that I had been working as a fitter for Frigidaire in Cricklewood. Inevitably this deceit was uncovered, but when I explained that I needed the job desperately because I had a pregnant wife and a child to support, I was allowed to stay on.

2

Royal Air Force

I was lucky to be working at De Havillands when war broke out. Together with two friends, Sid Plumb and Roy Collins, I had joined the Home Guard as soon as it was formed and then known as the Local Defence Volunteers. We became an armoured car team, one of our frequent assignments being to guard Salisbury Hall where experimental work on the Mosquito was being carried out. The job of an 'A' class fitter on aircraft production was a reserved occupation, but after Dunkirk I felt I had to do something. I volunteered for the RAF as an air gunner, but it was pointed out at the interview that because of my job I could only be a pilot or navigator, and that in any case my educational standard was not good enough. I was given a slip of paper showing the qualifications required and it was suggested that I might study and perhaps apply again later. I felt that I had been fobbed off.

I went through this paper with Roy Collins who was very bright, even if he was quite useless with his hands. I remember him breaking three hacksaw blades in half an hour once when he was trying to help me when I was working all night. 'Transposition of formula' seemed easy when Roy explained that you simply put the figure on the other side of the equation and change the sign; and I was able to master other relatively easy problems with his help while we were on Home Guard duty together.

About six months later I re-applied. Either I impressed them or more probably they had been forced to lower their standards, having lost so many pilots. I was given a date for a medical. My only worry was the mastoid operation I had had in 1938 behind my right ear. When I got there I found a long line of chaps moving as if on a conveyor belt from one booth to another. As I approached the ear section I overheard men in front of me say 'yes' when a tuning fork was held up to each ear in turn. When I reached the table, the doctor held a fork to my left ear, I heard the pitch and said 'yes'. He then brushed the fork and held it to my right ear. Hearing nothing I nearly panicked and was tempted to say 'yes'. Thank goodness I didn't. I shook my head, he brushed it again and I heard clearly. He had obviously stifled it the first time, trying to catch me out. Medically fit, I was attested on 28 May, 1941, and accepted for training as a pilot. I was told to return to my job and await my call up. This came some months later.

On your last day at work at De Havillands it was customary to have a few drinks with your workmates at the Comet, a pub across the road from the factory gates. I have a special reason for remembering that evening. I belonged to the De Havilland small bore rifle club and was a member of their competition team which had a match that night. The rifles we used had a six size aperture rear sight and a ring fore-sight. I always used the smallest aperture, but when I lay down on the firing point on this occasion I could not see the black of the bull's-eye. I enlarged the aperture one by one but still could not see the bull through the foresight, even with the largest aperture. This was obvi-ously the result of the farewell drinks I had consumed. I was wondering what to do when I noticed that the round protecting shield on the foresight fitted snugly round the square of the target, and I fired without ever having seen the bull's-eye. Surprisingly I finished with a score of ninety-eight, only slightly below my season's average.

RAF life began in earnest when I reported to Air Crew Reception Centre (ACRC) on 9 September, 1941. I was billeted in Avenue Road near the London Zoo. We were marched to one of the Zoo's restaurants for our meals and I decided to make use of the march to learn the morse code. To the left-right, left-right I muttered dit dah

A, dit dah A, and I did this all the way there and all the way back. It was a fairly long march, but by taking one letter at a time each day, I learnt the morse code thoroughly before I went to 8 ITW (Initial Training Wing) at Newquay on 30 September.

I dreaded failure, although in my case it would simply mean a return to my reserved occupation. I knew that I would have to work particularly hard to make the grade and that I had much to learn. Four months of intensive training followed, both physical and mental. The beauty of it was that each subject was taught from scratch. It was probably boring for some who had just left college, but for me, ten years after leaving school, it was ideal. I did well in the exams, particularly in navigation in which I broke all records by getting 195 out of 200. For the morse exam with the Aldis lamp we were lined up on the headland with the light flashing from the small island in the bay. Two friends who were not very good at morse stood either side of me while I whispered the letters as they came across so that they could copy them down. To my astonishment, when the results came out I had only 95 while my colleagues got 100 each. I had obviously whispered correctly but had written a letter down wrongly.

At ITW I made one particular friend, Jack Ralph, a very dark, good-looking and well-educated Welshman. We did many things together and he helped me in a number of ways, but we had to part company when we left ITW. About twenty months later we met again, by which time I was an officer and Jack Ralph a sergeant pilot. I was very surprised. The circumstances of our backgrounds and education would normally have reversed the situation. We arranged to have a week off together which I spent at his home near Cardiff. The bus we travelled on was from the Ralph Bus Company, his family business.

The CO gave us permission to put on a couple of shows for the local children in the village hall. I organized a crowd of us into rehearsing a mixture of gymnastics and slapstick comedy. I was the anchor man in the human pyramid which ended, intentionally of course, in collapsing, with me as the fall guy under the human jumble of arms and legs. It was all very amateurish, but the children loved it.

There were other diversions. The CO was an enthusiastic golfer and arranged a competition with a small prize over the Links golf course at Newquay. Not many of us bothered to enter, but I did, and won with a ridiculously high score. The CO was not amused, but, when I explained that I had never played before, he honoured his debt. I later got to know one of the daughters of the Links steward with the result that two of us were invited to have Xmas dinner with the family. This made a wonderful break from RAF catering, and similar invitations were much appreciated by many servicemen who were entertained by the kind families of Newquay. After the turkey and trimmings, the parents left us and I was highly amused when I invited the daughter to sit on my lap. She did, but placed a cushion on my knees before doing so – something that had never happened to me before.

We were encouraged to take part in debates on various topical issues and to give talks on subjects of our choice. On one occasion, with the CO present, and knowing that he had been on the Stock Exchange before the war, I gave a tongue-in-cheek talk about the similarity of the dog track to the Stock Exchange. I referred to such things as changing of odds, buying and selling, laying off, and reaction to rumour. He said it has been quite interesting, but could not resist pointing out to the assembly the difference in procedures between the two establishments. I am sure he knew that it was a bit of a send-up. One of the visiting speakers at ITW was Pilot Officer, acting Air Commodore, Billy Butlin who gave us a pep talk. A few of the younger men were impressed, but I thought he was rather pathetic.

My sense of justice was outraged on one occasion. We had a young pilot officer 'penguin' (as non-fliers were called) who was a drip, and the butt of much of our humour. On inspection one day he passed behind us and tapped almost every other man on the shoulder saying 'haircut'. As I had been shorn only the previous day I was most affronted and made application to see the CO on a 'redress of grievance'. Two days later I was marched in to see him and he seemed a little embarrassed. He walked round and examined my head and said, 'Well, perhaps a trim.' And that was that.

Wing Commander Bill Wheatley was the CO. I was then the lowest form of animal life, AC2. When we next met in Egypt in 1947, to my surprise we were both squadron leaders. I met him again after the war, when he entertained me and showed me round the Stock Exchange. This only confirmed my belief that it was very similar to a busy betting ring, but without the interval or the interest of the concluding race.

The excitement of flying followed when I moved to 21 EFTS (Elementary Flying Training School) Booker on 24 January, 1942. I remember asking my instructor to loop the loop and roll. He duly obliged although it was not normal practice. I found the aerobatics intensely thrilling but I think the flying we were given was more an aptitude test than anything else. After a short embarkation leave I was sent to the Air Crew Despatch Centre (ACDC) at Manchester where I was billeted with a very kind family and experienced the luxury of an electric blanket for the first time. They looked after me well, despite the strict rationing in force at that time. I found Manchester friendly but dull, apart from a few tea dances, where we were welcomed by ladies whose husbands were 'away to war'. This provided opportunities of relieving tensions in conducive surroundings. I was pleasantly surprised to find that the bus conductresses refused to accept fares from servicemen.

We were kept in the dark by the ACDC as to where we were going. My main memory is of the evening prior to our departure when, regardless of denomination, we were invited to take Holy Communion because we were embarking on a dangerous journey. This turned out to be a trip to New York on the USS *George Eliot*, embarking on 13 March, 1942, and arriving on 26 March. We travelled in convoy, but the journey was uneventful apart from two warning turn-outs when I manned a Lewis gun post. We only had a brief look at New York before entraining for 5 Manning Depot at Lachine, Montreal, where we arrived next day. A manning depot anywhere is usually a bore because of its continual ebb and flow of personnel. We anxiously studied the postings lists as they were put up, waiting and wondering where we were going next and with whom. Routine parades, physical training and marches were arranged to keep us out of mischief. However, unexpected events made Montreal a wonderful experience for me.

I wondered what I had done wrong when I was told to report to the CO at once. To my astonishment I was told to collect my toilet things and clothing for a week and return to his office within an hour. Puzzled as to what it was all about, I collected my gear and duly arrived back at the CO's office. While waiting to go in, I saw a man arrive who was shown in immediately. After a few minutes I was sent for and introduced to a Mr Thom. I was told that I was released from duties and would be the house guest of the Thom family until instructed to return. Some of my friends wondered what the devil was going on when I was driven out of the camp seated in the back of a chauffeur-driven limousine.

All was explained when I arrived at the Thom's beautiful home. It was lavish by my standards, but not as ostentatious as some of the places where I have worked. After meeting Mrs Thom and their children, I was taken into an adjoining room for a drink. Douglas Clark, professor of music at McGill University, was there. I knew Douglas well and had been his guest at weekends when I was working for the Arts Club. He explained that he was a great friend of the Thoms but had felt that Mr Thom would have greater pull in getting me released for a visit. Bunty and David Thom showed me round the city and in the evenings I was often invited with the family to dine with their friends. The highlight of my stay was a skiing weekend in the Laurentian Mountains as guest of Douglas Clark, along with a party of his students from McGill. I was worried that a sprained or broken ankle might affect my flying career but could hardly explain this to the youngsters who might have thought 'the Limey' was 'chicken'. So, ski I did, but with great care on the gentler slopes. We had a party and dance afterwards.

Although anxious to get on with my training, there were tears in my eyes when I bade farewell to the Thoms and Montreal. Never before or since have I received such sincere hospitality and friendship. I had become very fond of Bunty Ann in a brotherly way. She drove with me back to Lachine and I kissed her for the very first time in farewell.

When I got back I found that I had been posted to 6 EFTS at Prince Albert, Saskatchewan. Arriving there on 14 April, 1942, I was surprised to find that the flying instructors were civilians, while the admin and ground staff were Royal Canadian Air Force. I got down to work immediately and used every leisure moment I had for study. I did not leave camp until the night before the final exams, when I was ordered out.

In England I had bought myself a 'teach yourself to fly' book in which various manoeuvres were described, among them the stall turn which I thought particularly graceful.

After my solo flights I was sent off to the area reserved for aerobatics to practise stalls and spin recovery. I decided to try the stall turn for myself. Playing safe, I climbed another 1500 feet and began to dive, but when pulling up into the vertical I was too late applying the rudder. This should have rotated me to then pull out of the subsequent dive, having turned 180 degrees. All hell broke loose. The aircraft stalled and fell back on its tail. The stick flew out of my hand and then came back and hit me in the stomach. The aircraft went into a wicked spin. I was scared rigid. Recovering from the spin, I imagined all sorts of damage could have happened to the aircraft after such violent treatment and I stooged around until my time to return, making possibly the most gentle landing of my career, almost expecting bits to fall off. Well done Tiger Moth. I never tried another manoeuvre without first having it demonstrated and explained by an instructor.

When the exam results were published my hard work was rewarded. I had graduated 'honour student' and could hardly believe it. In a class of thirty-four, Canadian and British, many from universities, I became the first Englishman to win the 'Len Waite Trophy' inscribed 'The student attaining the highest proficiency in flying training'. Air Commodore Bonham-Carter presented me with a wrist watch suitably engraved. The occasion was attended by the press and photographers, who sent a copy of the trophy to my wife in England. This was a great boost to me as I had thought that I had to work hard just to get through. Only eighteen months before I had been told that my educational qualifications were not good enough to become a pilot.

I must mention the instructors. All of them made you feel comfortable and at home, in particular Mr Glass, who sent me solo after five hours dual, and Mr Boffa who gave me my final check. Anyone who had been at Prince Albert would remember Mr Boffa whether they had flown with him or not. An older man than most of the others, short and stocky with a perpetual grin, he had been a bush pilot with countless hours in remote regions. There were many stories of his exploits at 6 EFTS. If he had a diffident student, he would demonstrate how easy it was to fly by looking round at the pupil in the rear seat on the approach, and with occasional glances at the rear wheel, land while still looking backwards. Another trick was done with a spare joystick hidden in the front cockpit. When airborne, he would wave it aloft throw it out of the aircraft, telling his pupil, 'It's all yours'.

I was posted to 15 SFTS Claresholm, Alberta, on 21 June, 1942. This was an RCAF station with much more 'bull' than Prince Albert. Training was on Cessna Crane twin-engined aircraft, a big jump from the Tiger Moth. I managed to solo after five and a half hours dual with Pilot Officer Flowers. I began to think that all the emphasis on instrument flying and navigation meant that the streaming was towards Bomber Command. Although I still studied hard, it was not with the same intensity as at Prince Albert. I enjoyed myself socially as well. One of the Canadian pupils had a Buick and thought nothing of driving the eighty odd miles to Calgary just for a dance. Four of us would usually go with him sharing the petrol costs, but I still thought it crazy, although it seemed commonplace to the others.

A highlight of my time in Alberta was my friendship with Doreen. Claresholm was a tiny place with a single street, a popular feature of which was Bill's Koffee Shoppe, where Doreen worked as a waitress. She came with us to Calgary one evening and although she was quite a good dancer (the Canadian/American style of dancing was quite different to ours), she and I spent quite a bit of time in the car park, where we became very friendly. There is a restricted number of positions possible in the back of a car but a couple were added to my repertoire that Saturday evening.

Later on in the course I was worried that I might be considered unfit as I was very sick whenever I was a passenger. We had to make several cross-country navigation exercises and I was ill every time. I used to walk to the aircraft with a bucket and towel. During ten such trips as navigator, the only time I was not sick was during my final navigation exam.

It was the practice towards the end of the course to send two pupils off together for mutual instrument flying, sharing the allotted time. One acted as safety pilot and lookout while the other flew on instruments with the blind screen up on the pilot's side. In early September I was sent off with an LAC (Lofty) to act as safety pilot. After a while he got fed up with instrument flying and, as we were nearing the foothills of the Rockies, took the blind screen down and suggested some low flying. I did not want to appear stuffy and grudgingly agreed. It was nearly the last flight for both of us.

We flew into the foothills and entered quite a narrow ravine far too low. As we rounded a bend there seemed to be no exit. The Crane is not particularly powerful and I was sure that we would not be able to climb out. Lofty seemed to freeze. Taking over, I threw on full power, dived towards the side of the valley and then pulled up into a steep wing over and turned round, barely missing the other side. We were very shaken. I felt that I ought to tell the school on our return, but, realizing that this would probably mean both of us being grounded, I kept my mouth shut. My relationship with Lofty was never the same after that and I often wondered what he might do in an emergency when he eventually got into ops.

I had been at Claresholm about six weeks when I received a letter from my brother Jim, informing me of the birth of my fourth child Kathleen on 24 July. Somehow my wife's letters had been delayed. After describing what a lovely baby she was, he threatened upon my return to use a soldering iron on my reproductive parts.

One day, while on a solo flight, and low flying (unauthorized and not in the Rockies), I flew past an isolated farm house about fifteen

17

miles from the camp. A boy and girl standing by the door waved to me and were so obviously friendly that I did a quick turn round. I avoided flying low over animals, aware of the harm this can do and the resentment which is naturally felt by the owners.

The following weekend I persuaded my friend with the Buick to visit the farm with me. The occupants were a Canadian Indian family who made us very welcome. The daughter, who was only fifteen, was the most exquisitely beautiful girl I have ever seen. It was a very modest home, but spotlessly clean. They had never met an Englishman before and the whole time I was there I was plied with questions about England and the war. They seemed to think that everyone in the UK was starving. I was so impressed with their hospitality, considering they themselves had so little, that I returned shortly before I left Claresholm with goodies and a pretty dress for the girl.

The results of the final exams were published and I was glad to find that I had done well and was among the few to earn a commission. We were told to wear a distinctive white armband until we could get our officers' uniform. I was proud of the results of my efforts, although a little apprehensive of the future among the upper classes. Financially, I would probably have been better off as an NCO but the thought uppermost in my mind was that, as an officer, Lucy and the children would be better looked after if anything happened to me.

Rumours abound everywhere in the services. It was hinted that, as I was a little older than most, I was remaining in Canada to become a flying instructor. I was so perturbed at this that I sought out the station padre and told him that if this were so I would refuse my wings. He talked to me about the importance of instructors and obedience to authority, but I was adamant in my resolve to fight the enemy and considered that, as an alternative, my work building aeroplanes would be a greater contribution to the war effort. The knowledge that this opening was available to me gave me the courage to put my case forcibly. He suggested that perhaps I was jumping the gun by listening to the rumours, but I begged him to do whatever he could to avoid any possible confrontation. If anything transpired I will never know and, although there were postings to an instructors' course, to my intense relief my name was not among them.

The actual Wings Parade was a bit of an anticlimax, with the usual back-slapping and a celebration at the end. I went into town with friends armed with my Brownie box camera, and after a slap-up meal had a photo taken with Doreen outside Bill's Coffee Shoppe with my wings and white armband prominently displayed.

On 1 October, 1942, we arrived at 31 PDC Moncton, New Brunswick, after five days and four nights on a train – an experience I shall never forget. At least half the time between rising and going to bed was spent playing cards, mostly contract bridge. The train stopped occasionally and we were all pleased to stretch our legs, but after the first day a subtle change of attitude seemed to take place. This was uncomfortable. Many of us had been together as buddies from the UK through Montreal, EFTS and SFTS, yet on the train those of us who had been commissioned had first-class accommodation, the sergeants second. The first day or so we mixed and played cards together, yet by the time we arrived in Moncton there was an indefinable but distinct separation between us, which I regretted and disliked but could do nothing about. Moncton, when we finally got there, was only memorable for being the occasion of the first interview and questionnaire about preference for the future and our reasons.

We returned to England on the *Queen Elizabeth* after fifteen days in Moncton. We left on 28 October and arrived in Greenock on 5 November. The week spent at sea at high speed with frequent changes of course to reduce the risk of U-boat attention was in sharp contrast to the slow convoy of fourteen days in the other direction only seven months previously. Once again those packs of cards proved a boon and a blessing, leaving little time to dwell on the possibility of an unscheduled bathe in the icy Atlantic. At the Sunday Church parade the singing of one of my favourite hymns, 'Eternal Father, strong to save' had a special poignancy. The Canadians seemed to spend the whole journey in the lounge playing craps – a game of dice. I later made an extensive study of the mathematical chances of each throw, but at that time I could not afford to play.

On reaching Greenock, we were immediately sent to 7 Personnel Reception Centre (PRC) at Harrogate. There was little to do except explore the fleshpots of that lovely city. One particular haunt of service personnel was the Mucky Duck (Black Swan) pub where I met an attractive blonde. She was later to cause some amusement to me but distinct embarrassment to a distant relative when she turned up in London at the home of another Joe Patient.

The first thing we now did was to get measured for our officer's uniform. Many of the better-off chaps went to Gieves and the like, but my venue was Burton's where, being stock size, I was able to get one off the peg. Even so, it was difficult on the allowance, and I had to ask Lucy to help with a few pounds from her meagre savings. I was then given disembarkation leave and told to report to 3 PRC Bournemouth on 28 November.

At last I was reunited with my wife and four children, seeing the latest addition, now four months old, for the first time. Number three was only nine months old when I left, so he only knew me from the photographs which Lucy kept prominently displayed. It was a very strange experience getting to know them all over again.

Naturally I made the rounds, showing off my commission and pilot's wings. While visiting De Havillands I asked one of the test pilots, Squadron Leader Greenland, to take me up in a Mosquito during one of his test flights. This resulted in two flights in DZ 384, one of fifteen minutes, another of thirty, my first experience of that wonderful aircraft. Later, my old Home Guard friends at De Havilland joined me for a celebration drink at the Comet and our old Home Guard CO took a photograph of me. This is only of interest because, when compared with one taken fifteen months later, the change is so remarkable. When shown the two pictures and asked to guess the difference in age, people varied in their replies between five and ten years. My comment after the considerable surprise usually shown when told was, 'I was a boy there and a man then'.

The month spent in Bournemouth was a jolly, with a few lectures, PT on the sands and the inevitable questionnaire and interview. As I was housed in a first class hotel, an occasional tea dance provided a welcome opportunity for female company.

On 29 December I reported to 11 Advanced Flying Unit (AFU) Shawbury, near Shrewsbury, for training on Airspeed Oxford twin-engined aircraft. At last I felt that things were moving. After four hours and ten minutes I went solo. On 26 January, 1943, I was transferred to Condover, a satellite station under the administrative control of Shawbury, for continuation training. From 7–12 February I did a course on beam approach procedures lasting for eleven and a quarter hours, plus five hours and three-quarters as passenger, again on Oxfords with 1521 BAT flight, Stradishall, beginning flying again at Condover on 16 February. A few days later the flight was assembled for a talk by the group commander, Flight Lieutenant Speer AFC. There followed the inevitable questioning, but this time in front of the rest of the flight. I found it quite revealing to hear at first hand the feelings and desires of my fellow pupils. A few plumped for operations, either fighter or bomber, while some felt they needed further experience. One or two dithered, perhaps reluctant to reveal their choice in front of others.

I have never suffered fools gladly and I know that my career in the RAF was not always advanced by my direct manner. There is no way of being certain, but I feel that on this occasion what I had to say may have affected my whole service life. When my turn came, I told the CO that, with respect, I did not think that any preference we expressed would have the slightest effect on our future postings. If a certain fighter or bomber group required X number of pilots, with the Operational Training Units (OTUs) having the necessary vacancies, that number would be sent willy nilly, regardless of how well or badly they had performed up to now. 'That, Sir, is my considered opinion as all along the line we have answered the selfsame questions.'

I was told to report to Flight Lieutenant Speer on 24 January when he simply said, 'Patient, I want you to show me what you can do.' I was a little puzzled because our flying programmes were usually just posted on the notice board. We went through exercises lasting about an hour and I remember that I was pleased with the way I had flown. I had not been inhibited or nervous under the critical eye of the CO even when he unexpectedly cut a motor while doing some very low flying. On 10 March I was posted back to Shawbury into what was called a reserve flight, without the slightest inkling as to the reason. On 30 March I flew with a Sergeant Gilroy, Wireless Operator (WOp). Under rather unusual circumstances, I was to crew with him again later.

Training at that time was intensive, with as many as five flights a day and with emphasis on instrument, formation and low flying. On 3 April I was sent to Montford Bridge for a test in a mobile decompression chamber. This was the first hint that something rather out of the ordinary was in store for me. I came away with a certificate that I

1) had witnessed a demonstration of the effects of anoxia at high altitude
2) was rendered anoxic at a high altitude
3) had been subjected to an altitude of 37,000 feet for 61 minutes
4) had descended at the rate of 3,000 feet per minute and had been entirely unaffected.

The certificate also stated 'Fit PRU' (Photographic Reconnaissance Unit) which of course set me thinking that this was to be my future. In fact, an even greater surprise was shortly to be revealed.

The effects of anoxia are difficult to believe unless witnessed in person. It has been the cause of many accidents and deaths. Basically, it is the lack of oxygen in the blood stream which causes the most unusual hallucinatory effects. Continued lack or lessening of oxygen leads to unconsciousness. When flying in cloud or at night with no outside reference, it is a strange fact that your instruments can show you turning one way, yet you feel that you are turning the other, and often, in turbulence at high altitude with insufficient oxygen, these vestibular reactions can overcome your senses. One of the most impressive demonstrations in the decompression chamber is effected by repeatedly signing your name. When the oxygen is reduced, the writing deteriorates into a repetition of a few letters of the name and then an unreadable scrawl. It returns immediately to a normal signature when the oxygen supply is resumed, only for you to find that your shoes and socks, or perhaps tie and trousers, have been removed without you being aware of it while you were writing.

On 28 April back at Shawbury, I was given forty minutes dual on that grand old lady of aeroplanes the Anson, and immediately sent off with four passengers on a cross-country flight of 4 hours 25 minutes. I was then used as a staff pilot on both Ansons and Oxfords, flying over forty hours in seventeen days.

Shawbury was a permanent RAF station, with its share of brass and traditions. On one occasion I fell foul of them. A nearby American Airforce base at Atcham was having a party and sent four tickets which were fastened to the notice board in the mess. As two tickets were still there at the advertised time of the party, I took one and off I went. It was a crazy bash, with incredible amounts of food and drink. On my arrival I was slapped on the back and told to help myself, with a recommendation to try the 'purple passion'. This was served in a huge bowl which could only have been an inverted observation turret and consisted of grape juice and pure alcohol. I circulated a little, resisting the frequent 'Come on buddy have another'. It seemed that the whole idea of the shindig was to get plastered. Wending my way to the dance area, I found a Land Army girl being plied with this concoction by two American Sergeants with fairly obvious intent. I asked the girl to dance and offered a few words of advice to the effect that there is not always safety in numbers, particularly when associated with purple passion. I also suggested something to eat to soak up the mixture. This was readily agreed to and we regaled ourselves with all kinds of unexpected delicacies. The food, drink and companionship produced a pleasant warmth, and my suggestion of a little fresh air was agreed. It was in fact disastrous. No sooner had we got out into the cool night air than she passed out. Fortunately there were many nearby who witnessed her collapse, otherwise, had we got further afield, the situation might have been misunderstood. I returned the young lady after recovery to the friends she had arrived with and went back to Shawbury.

In the morning I was told to report to the Station Adjutant's office and was surprised and annoyed when he berated me for taking the ticket for the party. There were heated words. He said sharply that such invitations were intended for the permanent officers on the station and not for transients, and particularly not junior ones. I told him that the tickets were still there after the party had started and apparently would have been wasted. Also, there was no indication on the notice board or in the invitation to indicate the exclusion of other officers. I was aggrieved and felt that it was an unjust dressing down, but nevertheless thought it wise to let the matter drop.

At Shawbury and in fact at all stations where I served, I would spend hours in the billiard room. The station padre was a very good player; I was very much out of practice but was soon giving him a good game. I remarked that to play as well as he did generally meant a mis-spent youth; he said that in my case this was probably true, but that his skill came from time spent in boys' clubs.

*   *   *

I was then astounded to find myself posted to 13 Operational Training Unit (OTU) at Bicester where we attended lectures but did no flying. This lasted only two weeks. We then transferred to 1655 Mosquito Conversion Unit (MCU) at Finmere. There were eight pilots and eight specialist combined wireless operator/navigator/-bomb aimer/air gunners. All wore the coveted observer badge. We were there with the object of teaming up and learning to fly and operate the Mosquito which at that time was undoubtedly the crème de la crème of British aircraft. The normal requirement for flying it was a previous tour of operations, or having instructed with 1,000 hours as pilot. My total at that time was 455 hours.

There was a Royal Danish Air Force pilot, Captain Stene, and a Danish observer Lieutenant Lochen, so it was natural for them to crew up; then a flight lieutenant joined a flying officer. I was next in seniority, and as there were two pilot officer observers, it was expected that I would crew up with one of them. I did not, and surprised everyone. I had overheard a conversation hinting that Norry Gilroy, one of the observers, would be left to the last as he was a Jew. One has to volunteer for aircrew duties, and in view of the risk involved of flying over enemy occupied territories, it took more than the average man's courage for a Jew to do so. Knowing the probable end for him, should he have to bale out or force land in Germany and be captured, the pilot with him might, by association, be given the same treatment. At that time the pilots had no way of knowing the relative abilities of any of the observers. One who had earned a commission might be thought better than an NCO, but this was by no means certain. My sensibility to the unfairness of this implied discrimination compelled me to ask Sergeant Norry Gilroy to be my observer. It was a decision I never regretted. Norry turned out to be an ace among aces, not only for his all-round and well above average operational efficiency, but also as a companion and friend. Much more will be said about Norry as my story unfolds. Suffice it to say, at this stage, that he was later commissioned and went on to complete a record number of operations, earning a well-merited DFC and Bar.

I had my first dual on a Mosquito on 3 June, 1943. What a thrill to feel the power of those two Rolls Royce Merlins pressing into your back as you open up. It was a big step for me from two Cheetah Xs of 375 horsepower each to the surge of two Merlin 21s with a total of 2,500 horsepower. My instructor for the first five and three-quarter hours was Flight Lieutenant Costello-Bowen who sent me solo on 8 June. Three weeks later he was promoted to squadron leader with the usual drinks all round. On 10 June I had an hour with Flying Officer I.G. Broom DFC.

The flying Brooms were well known in Pathfinder circles in that pilot and observer had the same surname without being related. They had a distinguished career together. The next time I met them was forty-five years later. My eldest son, who has made a study of my RAF days and has traced the history of every Mosquito I flew (over forty different aircraft of ten various makes), phoned me to say that a Sir

Ivor Broom was giving a talk at Hendon RAF Museum. Out of curiosity I went and inquired of two men who were chatting if they knew the whereabouts of Sir Ivor and got the reply from one, 'I am he'. With apologies, and showing him my logbook, I asked if he had been the instructor at Finmere in 1943. He replied with a smile, 'Yes, but little did you realize that I had only a few hours on the Mossie myself at that time!' At the end of his lecture he showed some slides, the last being a photo of the 'Flying Brooms'. It was like hitting me in the stomach. There were the two young men I had known so long ago.

*　　*　　*

Whilst we were at Finmere Norry spent quite a lot of his spare time at a tennis club. He came to me one afternoon and asked if I would help him out of a jam as he had arranged to meet two girls from the club. Knowing Norry, I was sure that they would both be good lookers, so I agreed. It was the beginning of more than a very good friendship which lasted for a great number of years. I have more than one picture of Joy with 'destroy' written on the back, but under no circumstances could I ever destroy them. Norry later admitted that he chose the wrong one that evening.

We were given a few days' leave and told to take all our gear and report to Marham in Norfolk. 1655 MCU was being transferred there and redesignated 1655 Mosquito Training Unit (MTU). Marham was another permanent RAF station where, at that time, the hush-hush OBOE* squadrons 105 and 109 were stationed. Training for us was then of an operational kind, almost exclusively formation, low flying and night cross-country with full bomb load (unarmed). All this was done with Norry.

Early in July Captain Stene joined me to act as safety pilot during an instrument flying exercise. I never cease to be amazed at the excellent English spoken by all the Scandinavian people I have known.

---

* OBOE was a revolutionary target-finding aid, used against towns in the Ruhr from late 1942. It gave the bomber simple navigational information to the target and the precise moment to release the bombs.

Had Stene not been dressed in the uniform of the Royal Danish Air Force I would not have thought him a foreigner.

An air-sea rescue search was called for on 15 July. It was carried out by four aircraft over the North Sea and lasted for about three hours. Sadly there were no sightings. The next night I went on my first Mosquito dual night flying exercise with Squadron Leader Costello-Bowen for fifty minutes, followed by forty-five minutes of solo circuits and bumps. We then had another break until 5 August when I was saddened to hear on my return that on 18 July Captain Stene and Lieutenant Lochen (the two Danes) had taken off on a normal cross-country exercise and had crashed near Cranfield, both being killed. No other details were available other than that the aircraft was a total write-off. A week later another of our aircraft crashed on landing after a night exercise, but fortunately the crew escaped with minor injuries.

On 9 August a major upheaval was caused by the deaths of Squadron Leader Costello-Bowen, Flying Officer Abbott and Corporal Magson (all from Marham), in a Ventura aircraft of 487 Squadron which crashed at Larch Wood and burnt out. The grapevine rumoured they were on 'a jolly'. High-spirited antics were part and parcel of aircrew life, but it was ironic that these men who had survived the worst that Jerry could dish out should die in this way, but these tragedies were seldom allowed to interfere with the training programme.

I had a night flight check with the CO, Wing Commander R. Ralston DSO DFC on 10 August, the only time I had the pleasure of flying with that distinguished officer. A further night cross-country was the first real test of my ability when my ASI (Air Speed Indicator) became unserviceable. I was instructed to land at Shipton which I managed without a hiccup, much to our relief. We spent the night there and returned to base the next morning after the ASI (the most important instrument on the aircraft) had been changed. As a result of this incident I made a habit of noting the hands-off trimmer settings of each aircraft on the approach when I was later carrying out normal pre-operational air tests.

When we returned to Marham we had further bad news. Flying Officer Broom was in hospital with a serious injury to his back, while his Canadian pupil, Flight Lieutenant MacDonald, died shortly afterwards. This had happened during the last part of a final approach at night, when a malfunction of the propeller below safety speed with full flap had made an overshoot impossible.

1655 MTU was a small unit, with an establishment of only four Mark 3 (dual) and eight Mark 4 (bomber) Mosquitoes, yet in the six weeks that I was at Marham the unit lost three, a quarter of its aircraft. Six men were killed and three injured without any help from the enemy, clearly underlining the hazards involved, even during training.

After I had flown with Norry a few times and found him to be very competent, I played a little trick on him. While he was engrossed in his maps, I surreptitiously feathered the starboard propeller. The engine stopped with a characteristic jolt which quickly had Norry asking what the devil was wrong. I said that I didn't know, but that anyway the Mossie could fly very well on one engine. I got it going again but about five minutes later I repeated the performance with the other engine. Norry looked worried and suggested that we should look for an aerodrome to land and investigate the cause. I pointed out that we were only ten minutes from base so it would be better to get home. I then restarted the engine and made a normal landing back at base. As we were making our way to the debriefing he said that he had entered the failure in his log and asked me what I thought was wrong. I told him that I had stopped them just to test his reaction to an emergency. 'You lousy shit', he cried and looked as if he could have murdered me. Then with a laugh I jokingly said, 'Don't you dare strike an officer, I'll have you court-martialled'. After a few moments, he laughed too, so no harm was done. Furthermore, I now knew he wouldn't panic.

At the end of the course, on 16 August, Wing Commander Ralston gave us all a lecture and wished us the best of luck, advising us to treat every operation with the same care and attention to detail as our first operational flight. Impressed by this, we followed his advice, which was doubtless based on his own distinguished flying record. We were given a week's leave and told to report to B Flight 139 (Jamaica) Squadron of 8 Group Pathfinder at Wyton, Cambridgeshire on 25 August.

★　★　★

It was during that leave that I remember taking Joy out for an evening during which there was an air raid. The sirens had been going like mad but we had not heard bombs being dropped. Just as we were getting into my car a warden directed me to an air-raid shelter. I gave a questioning look at my companion, but as it was getting late we decided to get her home to avoid too many explanations. By now the searchlights were very active and there was a great deal of gunfire, with occasional loud thumps as bombs exploded in the distance. I imagined that the odd tinkling sounds on the roof of the car were fragments of exploded anti-aircraft shells, but I thought it safer to carry on and not stop to investigate. Later I found small splinters of shrapnel embedded in the roof and bonnet which I kept as souvenirs.

Norry and I got to know each other very well, spending so much time together. We found a great similarity in our early lives. We were both from poor but hard-working families, and both fourteen when our fathers died.

With a similar standard of education and in reserved occupations, we had both experienced and could not condone the restrictive practices of the trade unions in wartime. Both were fond of dancing and girls, and, dare I say it, we both had the same healthy attitude to sex. Norry had volunteered to be a pilot, but owing to an eye defect was offered training as an observer. At that time his name was Goldstein, but after a conference with his family, they changed it by deedpoll to Gilroy, a wise and fairly usual precaution taken by Jews during the Second World War.

I was never able to understand why Norry was so successful with the girls. He was a good dancer, but so was I, he was an NCO while I was an officer and he certainly was not better looking. Admittedly he was more extrovert and undoubtedly had charisma. On one occasion, at a dance, we were studying form, and there was an attractive

29

blonde with an American major. I remarked, 'Nice, Norry, but no chance'. 'Want to bet?' he rejoined. 'OK five bob'. Five shillings I lost. How he pulled it off on so many occasions is a mystery. He had one dance with the girl, who a few minutes later met him outside. Norry simply smiled and said, 'That's five bob you owe me. See you back at camp.'

While on leave I usually paid a visit to the factory at Hatfield. On this occasion I told John de Havilland that I had been posted to a Mosquito squadron and asked if he would take me up and show me what she could do. After I had signed a waiver of claim for accidents, he took me up in HJ 898, a Mark 6 on test. For forty-five minutes he did everything, including a terminal velocity dive. Looking backwards we could see the tailplane bending upwards with the increase in speed. My experience during that flight, different from anything shown me before, enabled me to make manoeuvres with confidence which I would otherwise have hesitated to perform. I was very sad when, a few days later, John de Havilland had collided with another Mosquito in bad weather near Hatfield. He was killed and the country had lost a very fine test pilot.

3

Operations

When the day came to report at Wyton I scrounged some petrol coupons and picked Norry up at his home, where I was amazed at the number of people there to see him off. He explained on the run up to Cambridgeshire that his mother held open house for relatives who lived in the East End of London. When visiting they were only too pleased to accept the crowded conditions, to get some respite from the terrific bombardment of the docks near their homes.

After settling into our quarters at Wyton we went to meet our flight commander, Squadron Leader D.A. Braithwaite. After a few words of welcome, an established member of the flight showed us round the various rooms allocated to our squadron. There was a shortage of lockers in which to keep our flying gear, but we were told that we would get one in due course. It was a chilling thought that this would only happen when an aircraft failed to return. I offered up a silent prayer, happy to wait for ever without a locker. My sensibilities were soon to harden. Regrettably I became quite callous about death, especially as the other resident squadron had had so many losses. Had I not done so, I should have been unable to carry on. I have to confess that my insensitivity even reached the stage at which I would make bets on the number of operations a newcomer might survive.

Wyton was a permanent RAF Station shared by 83 Squadron and 139 Squadron with more comfortable accommodation and facilities than those other hastily constructed wartime airfields. 139 Squadron had been adopted by the people of Jamaica who had contributed the furniture of the recreation room allotted to the Squadron. I was surprised to find that one of the observers was black.

Philip Louis Ulric Cross was undoubtedly one of the most interesting people I have ever met. His majestic good looks and stature were matched by his beautifully modulated voice and impeccable manners. It was only natural that he should have his leg pulled, but he was more than equal to our ribaldry. Ulric had been a member of a flying club in Trinidad when war broke out. He had volunteered and was accepted for aircrew, eventually graduating as an observer in November, 1942. He maintained that his maths was so good that he was too highly qualified to be a pilot. Being a one-off, he was a very popular member of the squadron. He completed many more than the normal number of operations, earning a DFC and DSO, both presented personally by the King at Buckingham Palace. An additional honour was the portrait of him by William Dring ARA which was commissioned by the War Office and exhibited in the National Portrait Gallery. Many years later our paths crossed in the unlikely and remote area of West Cameroon. But that is a story still to come.

Norry and I had been particularly friendly with two crews on our Mosquito conversion and training course, both of whom had preceded us to 139 Squadron. Flight Sergeant V.J.C. (Ginger) Miles with Sergeant E.R. (Ferdy) Perry had completed seven ops, and by that time Miles had been promoted to warrant officer, the highest non-commissioned rank. Flight Sergeant T.K. (Tommy) Forsyth and Sergeant L.C. (Jimmy) James had done six ops, four of which had been to Berlin. It was good to meet them again and to hear their experiences. It gave us some idea of what we might expect. At last I felt that I was at war. Now for the moment of truth – operations against the enemy.

* * *

The CO did not believe in allowing new crews time to get jittery.

32

On our very first day we were on the battle order and did a night flying air test. While I test-flew the aircraft, Norry tested the GEE* navigational equipment, radio, W/T and bomb sight. If everything was OK the armourers would set about bombing up and refuelling ready for the night's op. This particular one was cancelled, but repeated the following night, 27 August, 1943.

After briefing, I checked the route with Norry, who also checked the codes, while I made sure we knew and had the colours of the day. Our load included a photoflash which we were briefed to release after dropping our bombs. This automatically set the camera in motion. Norry surmised that this was to check how near we got to our target, as we were a new crew on our first operation. We then went off to our respective messes for our first ever operational meal. This was the traditional eggs, bacon, tomatoes and chips, a ritual for all bomber command crews both before and after an operation. We then collected our rations of chocolate and orange juice which were unobtainable in civvy street.

As we were about to get into our aircraft I noticed that Norry was carrying a parcel in addition to his navigation bag. I said 'What on earth have you got there?' 'A brick,' was the immediate reply. I laughed and remarked, 'Don't you think 1,500 lbs of high explosives enough?' 'Ah,' he said, 'but this brick is special. It's wrapped in the *Jewish Chronicle* and I'm going to drop it through the "window" shute hoping it will hit some Nazi bastard on the head.' I went along with his joke, but after a time I became a little superstitious about it. As we operated more than once a week and the *Chronicle* was a weekly publication, he had to ask his friends for back numbers.

On the way to the target, according to our GEE fix and further dead reckoning, we were four minutes ahead of our briefed time to bomb, so we did a forty-five degree dogleg which might also have

---

* GEE was the first of the radio-navigational systems introduced in 1942. It greatly assisted the work of the navigator, although its accuracy fell off with increased range. Most importantly, it made possible the streaming of bombers along pre-determined courses, making coordinated attacks possible and heralding the advent of Britain's principal initiative in the 1942 air war, the 1,000 bomber raid.

deceived the enemy. This put our ETA (estimated time of arrival) spot on. We noticed a lot of anti-aircraft fire to our right. With two minutes to go, Norry crawled into the nose to the bomb sight and requesting 'bomb doors open', called, 'Left, left.' I applied a little rudder and cross-controlled the aileron to stay level. 'Left, left' more urgently this time. I was almost fully cross-controlling by now, when Norry exploded, 'Left, you bloody fool, left.' I just had time to make a banked turn and straighten out. He called, 'Steady, steady, five degrees right, steady s-t-e-a-d-y, bombs gone, flash released, photo taken.'

I closed the bomb doors and banked away as Norry was clambering quickly back to the cockpit to drop his brick. We then returned to base on our predetermined route. Immediately after landing the 'photo' boys removed the camera magazine and rushed off to get it developed, while we ambled over to de-briefing and a mug of hot tea laced with rum (compliments of Jamaica). In a very few minutes our photos arrived and were examined by the intelligence officers. They showed an excellent result, quite near the target centre, so we were rather pleased with ourselves. Only four aircraft of 139 Squadron took off that night, one returning early through technical trouble. My logbook entry for that night reads:

> 27 August, Mosquito IV 'N' Op No. 1 Duisberg. 3 x 500 pound bombs
> + photoflash. Quiet.

Just a line in the logbook with the last word 'quiet'. The emotions felt before, during and after an operation were hardly that. As we went out to the dispersal, usually in a WAAF-driven lorry, some chatted merrily while others sat quietly with their own innermost thoughts and, perhaps, fears. Reaction no doubt was very much dependent upon relative experience of actual warfare up till then. I never heard anyone discuss fear, and I doubt if it was ever strongly felt. Apprehension, yes. With much fear, I don't think anyone would have lasted long.

When Norry and I met again after our first operation, I explained the difficulty of keeping the aircraft level with major changes of heading. We agreed that the inflexion of the voice helped, but we had to evolve a more positive method between us to avoid a repetition of the previous evening when we had narrowly avoided an abortive run up to the target. Going round again was not, repeat not, a good idea if it could be avoided. We decided that if our 'left' or 'right', as the case might be, was more than five degrees he would state the degree alteration required so that I would know whether I could make a flat turn or would have to bank to get the required heading. It worked wonderfully. Not once did we have to make a second bombing run up to the target through misunderstanding. We always tried to bomb our target on the exact time or sight, without any pre-anticipation or release, regardless of the opposition we were receiving from fighters or ack ack.

Whenever I flew I would walk round the aircraft making a visual check that all panels were securely fastened, pitot head uncovered, undercarriage locks removed and so forth. All this would have been carried out by the ground crew, but it is a foolhardy pilot who did not make a personal check before signing for the aircraft on the form 700. Just before entering it for an operation, a feeling of apprehension almost always came over me which lasted while I strapped myself in and checked oxygen and radio. When I pressed the booster and starter buttons and had both engines running and tested, it seemed that I lost all feelings of tension and completely relaxed, my only thought being to get the job done and done well. But on no account must I minimize the dangers which were faced every other night or so, from which so many of my friends failed to return.

Between 27 August and 3 October, 1943, we were scheduled for operations on nineteen occasions. However, for reasons best known to the authorities only ten were carried out. Most cancellations at that time were due to heavy icing, fog, or other unfavourable weather conditions over the targets. There were two main reasons for the frequency of our operations. The German war effort had to be disrupted by sending their workers into air-raid shelters night after night, but the propaganda value of such raids was just as important back in the UK. Day after day the home news radio services would announce, 'Our bombers again attacked the heart of the Ruhr last night', sometimes substituting Berlin or Cologne or other large targets. 'All our aircraft returned safely.' What sighs of relief our wives, mothers and sweethearts gave but what anxiety when they added a postscript that one or more of our aircraft had failed to return. When this happened, I used to phone a friend near my home who would pass the news of my safety round to my wife. These nuisance raids were introduced without authority by Air Vice-Marshal Bennett and approved by his Commander-in-Chief, Air Chief Marshal Harris, later.

'One of our aircraft failed to return.' People little thought, could not know and were certainly never told, that this often meant a large percentage loss when only a few of us were out. To us, knowing who had failed to return could mean many things, depending on how well you knew the victim. He might be a close friend. Unless he was, one didn't think too much about it. His room mate would collect his personal belongings to be sent back to his wife or parents. Care would be taken to examine the backs of any photographs of girls, the word 'destroy' meaning what it said. After all these years I still have and occasionally look at more than one photograph with this annotation, despite being happily married.

For some reason I was often given the task of 'doing the honours'. When someone was lost, his wife or parents would be invited to visit the station to be shown round, with lunch arranged in an anteroom to avoid embarrassment. Often this went well, but at other times it could be a very tearful occasion. Naturally they were all told what a wonderful chap and good pilot or navigator he was.

On one of these unfortunate occasions the widow was a very attractive lady called Brenda. After 'doing the honours' she was returning to London. It so happened that I was free for the weekend and offered to drive her home. I kept in touch with her and a couple of months later began an association that was fine for both of us. I didn't feel badly about this as I hardly knew the unfortunate chap who had been killed. However, I was surprised how quickly some could forget or overcome their grief, while others mourned for years. I still have an occasional look at the photograph she gave me with 'God Bless You, Joe' written on the back.

*   *   *

At the briefing for our second operation, we noticed that our bomb load was all HEs, so we assumed that our previous target photograph had been satisfactory. The target was the same, but we had to cross the enemy coast near Zeebrugge, much lower down than previously. On the way out to the plane I could see that Norry had his wrapped brick and I had a little chuckle. It never failed to amuse me. It was a clear night. After passing just north of Antwerp Norry drew my attention to a series of lights lined up to form an arrow head which appeared to be pointing at us. We had not been briefed that these lights existed and were concerned that when we altered course the arrows moved too, keeping us in the apex.

During the early part of any operation I concentrated on good instrument flying, giving the navigator a better chance of accuracy while leaving him free to do most of the looking out. We did not have an auto-pilot in the Mosquitos. The lights were undoubtedly an indication to night fighters, so I did a little jinking every couple of minutes, keeping a sharp eye open for other aircraft and Norry informed of changes in course. As we moved out of one set of arrows, another pair would appear. We had about a hundred miles of this. It was obviously radar-controlled and quite disturbing. Our necks ached with looking to our rear so much.

We arrived near our destination and Norry calculated that we should be one minute late on target. Considering the jinking we had done, this was not bad going. He gave me the final course to steer and went down to the bomb sight in the nose. Three minutes before our ETA at the target a host of searchlights and flak started up in front of us. Norry called for bomb doors open. Because of our agreement on a modified method of calling for altering heading, I was never called a bloody fool again, at least not for the same reason, and we made a fine run up to the target. After we had dropped our two-pennyworth, and while raising the bomb door, we were caught in a searchlight. I

37

was diving and turning when four other searchlights moved on to us forming a cone with us in the middle. Flak started snaking up the centre. I knew I couldn't fly out of it easily, so I quickly changed height, up and down. Because of these violent manoeuvres Norry was having difficulty getting back to the cockpit. When we eventually escaped the lights, we settled down to the task of getting home. Norry had to be satisfied this time with dropping his brick on an unknown spot. All the ten bombing operations I carried out in 139 Squadron were made with Sergeant Norry Gilroy.

30 August, Mosquito IV 'N' Op No. 2 Duisberg. 3 x 500 pound + 1 x 250 pound. Medium flak. Coned 3 mins.

'Coned three minutes.' Every boxer knows just how long three minutes can be. Being coned, which means being in the centre of an apex of three or more powerful searchlights, is more than a little unnerving. You feel naked. It is almost blindingly bright and you are aware that night fighters could well be homing in on you. If you were on your way to the target with your bombs on board there was little you could do except hope and pray. Coming away from the target was a different matter. With a lighter aircraft there were a few tricks you could try with a reasonable chance of success.

Six aircraft of 139 Squadron had taken off to bomb Germany that night. Mosquito DK 337 with Pilot Officer I.A. Isfield and Sergeant J.C.B. Strang did not return. Just one aircraft, but it represented a 16.6 per cent loss. Norry and I had only had to wait five days for our lockers.

2 September. Mosquito IV 'W'. Op No 2½ Duisberg. VHF-1/C-GEE u/s. Bombed Walcheren. 3 x 500 pound. 1 x 250 pound delayed action. Light flak.

Target Duisberg and bombing Walcheren needs explanation. If the weather men were a little uncertain, we would make our climb to operational height on a fixed triangular course so as to arrive back at base from where a narrow vertical beam of light would be sent up. Depending on our position relative to the light, we could determine the accuracy or otherwise of the wind forecast. This would allow the navigator to make an adjustment to the next course to steer, if necessary. On this particular night it was spot on, so we set off for the target. Over the North Sea I went to say something to Norry but got no response. I had to release the oxygen mask and shout. He then indicated that both the GEE and VHF were *kaput*. We discussed aborting the trip, but agreed that, as the winds had been accurate, we would press on and do a timed drop, or perhaps with luck see someone else's bombs explode.

It was not to be. Suddenly a searchlight was probing for us and we were subjected to a certain amount of flak. Because of the equipment failures, I told Norry to make a bombing run on to the searchlight. Whether we hit anything we shall never know, but the searchlight went out. Returning to base, I reported the failures and proceeded to de-briefing. Naturally our early return was met with raised eyebrows. Once I had explained the reasons we were praised for carrying on. I then received what can best be called a bollocking for bombing friendly territory. I was very put out and said that if they could throw stuff up at me, I felt no compunction about throwing something back. We were awarded a half op for our efforts. I had an inkling that the de-briefing officer secretly endorsed my action, but those orders and instructions from above had, of course, to be seen to be carried out. Naughty boy, don't do it again. Bullshit! If there was a next time, I just wouldn't tell them.

It was perhaps indicative of the friendly relationship I had with my ground crew that the sergeant later took me aside and quietly told me that the VHF intercom and GEE were in fact OK. As the cockpit was so small I must somehow have dislodged a plug which had then eased from its socket. Had I been more experienced, the loss of all three facilities would have suggested such a likelihood. I might then have been able to rectify matters. The kindness of the ground crew in covering up for me probably prevented a 'black' being recorded against me. I spent the next hour with the sergeant going over all the reachable parts of the aircraft, carefully noting the function of each and every plug and socket.

After several air tests, a fuel consumption test and several cancelled operations, we were back in action on 14 September. Meanwhile the Lancaster Squadron had organized a party to which we were invited. The ground staff arranged a fountain and waterfall ablaze with coloured lights, and the catering boys put on a slap-up running buffet with unlimited free drinks. The station WAAFs were invited and the medical officer unofficially sent off ambulances to the local hospitals to collect any off-duty nurses. The excellent station band was laid on for dancing. The host squadron had borrowed a huge astro-dome from stores and filled it with punch which I suspect was largely pure alcohol. I didn't even chance a sip. Norry did and pronounced it foul. As it was a dance to which so much local talent had been invited, Norry and I, knowing the secluded spots around the camp, found all the ingredients for a wonderful evening. I suppose there was a universal feeling that if it was going to be a short life, let it be a happy one.

Joy had given me a woollen teddy bear about eight inches long for luck. I used to hang it on the undercarriage level whenever I was flying. Over the years it got a little tatty, but I would never think of flying without it. Most of the aircrew had some form of rabbit's foot, and even today I have a small teddy which I hang on one of the knobs on the dashboard of my car.

When we went to briefing on 14 September we found that this was to be our first Berlin raid. With mixed feelings, we followed and noted our instructions. Afterwards, while we were studying our route, I told Norry, 'This is just another operation, a bit further to go but just the same.' We went off and had our eggs and bacon and at the appointed time eight crews went to their aircraft. It never bothered me which one was allocated to me, although I did like to have the one in which I had done the NF test.

We climbed to 30,000 feet before crossing the enemy coast and saw the same sort of arrows as we had on our second op and I carried out similar evasive action, keeping a watchful eye for fighters. Norry told me later that there had been a speck of dirt on the outside of his observation blister, which every now and again caught his eye. For one tense moment he had thought it was a night fighter. After out-flying the arrows, we encountered spasmodic searchlights. Having been routed round the known heavily defended areas, we had little trouble. After an hour and a quarter our GEE blips faded out, so for the rest of the way we flew by DR (dead reckoning).

The weather was clear enough on the approach for us to confirm our position by a bend in the Rhine which showed us to be only three miles off track. Norry gave a correction of heading and went to the bomb sight. With about three minutes to go, I opened the bomb doors and started the run up to the target wondering where all the action was. As we were sure of our position, we realized that a 'target' about fifteen miles to our right was an obvious spoof. The Germans often lit up fields a few miles from built-up areas in the hope that crews unsure of their position would think others had bombed there and would do likewise.

At zero hour, exactly on time, our bombs went down on Berlin. Norry, getting back as fast as he could from the bomb aiming position, determined to let the heart of anti-Semitism have the joy of reading the *Jewish Chronicle*, with the brick as a bonus. He was particularly elated and seemed fulfilled as we turned for home. I was beginning to think this was a piece of cake when we heard the familiar sound of close ack ack and almost immediately we were coned by (it seemed) every searchlight for miles. Thank goodness our bombs had gone and with almost half of our petrol used up we were light and manoeuvrable yet, regardless of what I did, we were passed from one batch of lights to another.

The weather had deteriorated and we entered the ghostly combination of searchlights and thundercloud which was soon throwing us about. Then that other enemy, icing, started to build up. We had obviously hit a cold front, but at least we had lost the searchlights. Apart from a considerable amount of icing and discomfort from turbulence, the remainder of our return was uneventful. We were airborne for nearly five and a half hours and were gratified that other crews had also reported the spoof target, thus confirming our own position.

14 September, Mosquito IV 'P'. Op No. 3½ Berlin. 3 x 500 pound. 1 x 250 pound DA (delayed action). Medium flak. Coned 6 mins. V heavy Cb and icing.

As I have already described the experience of being coned for three minutes, I can leave to the imagination the same ordeal lasting for six minutes. Cb or Charlie Bravo is the meteorological code name for cumulo-nimbus, that great anvil-topped thundercloud which can vary in intensity from mild to wickedly uncontrollable turbulence. When Norry and I were later transferred as a crew to a specialist meteorological flight within 8 PFF Group, we had more frightening experiences with Charlie Bravo than any we endured at the hands of Goering's Luftwaffe or the evil ack ack. I was later to learn that eight Lancasters went out that night, but owing to adverse weather conditions returned before reaching the enemy coast. Eight Mosquitos of 139 Squadron went to Berlin. With no one else operating, we faced the full might of the German defences. A senior crew, Flight Lieutenant M.W. Colledge and Flying Officer G.L. Marshall, failed to return. A 12½ per cent loss.

On my way to briefing two days later I met Tommy Forsyth, an Aussie chum of mine with whom I shared many relaxing hours and reminiscences. I remarked, 'At least we know the target.' If Tommy was on the battle order the target seemed to be invariably Berlin or the Big City as we called it. Of anyone I knew, other than Norry, who I would have loved to see survive, it was Tommy. I will later devote more than a few words to this cheery and goodhearted friend, who unfortunately was not finally to return. I have often wondered at the complexity of my make-up, so often hard and relentless and at other times ridiculously soft. Perhaps, after all, there is some significance in one's birth sign. I am writing this in my kitchen after breakfast, over 46 years later. Lucy has just come in and noticed the tears in my eyes.

It turned out that Berlin was indeed the target, but in view of our relatively easy trip of two days previously, I felt a little less trepidation. However, heedful of Wing Commander Ralston's advice, I paid careful attention to the briefing and preparation for the flight.

After the traditional meal and good luck shouts from other crews, we flew uneventfully at 28,000 feet. Eighty miles from the target we found that we were five minutes early. A dogleg put us right for time and we prepared for the run in as Norry went to the bomb sight. I opened the bomb doors. All hell broke loose. Obviously someone had arrived a few minutes early and had started up a hornet's nest of anti-aircraft defences. Dozens of searchlights lit up the sky as flak exploded everywhere. I don't think they were firing at any particular aircraft, but just saturating the air space. We had never seen anything like it. Though we had to fly through this for only two or three minutes it seemed an age. If ever I had been tempted to jettison my bombs and get the hell out of it it was then. As things turned out perhaps I should have. However, we pressed on with the same system of alteration of heading previously agreed, and bombed right on target.

As he scrambled back Norry shouted, 'Flak to starboard; turn to port.' 'I've got it on my port wing too,' I yelled, then the starboard engine had a direct hit and failed. In my haste, and looking out for other trouble, I inadvertently pushed the wrong feathering button and stopped the good engine, realizing immediately what I had done. I knew that to save accumulated power I must restart my port engine before feathering the damaged starboard, despite the vibration caused by the windmilling engine. Meanwhile I was losing height at an enormous rate, which however, took us out of the terrible barrage above. I restarted the port, feathered the starboard propeller and taking stock of the situation asked Norry to give me a direct course for home. He told me that this would take us across the Ruhr, but I knew that it was unlikely that we should have enough petrol to take any other route. Fifty minutes later, on our way home and by this time down to 17,000 feet near Münster, we were coned and given a helping of flak. I eluded these searchlights but only at the expense of another 5,000 feet. ~~Me 109s~~

Two ~~FW 190s~~ attacked us almost immediately and scored cannon hits on the port wing and nacelle of our good engine and port outer fuel tank, flaps, elevators and ailerons. Bullets flew through the

43

narrow space between our heads. I instinctively pushed hard forward and the rest of the fusillade passed overhead. Norry was clutching his neck where a bullet or cannon shell had scorched it. From the variance of the hits, the fighters must have synchronized their attack from different angles but mercifully they did no vital damage. Aware now of their presence, when one of them made a further attack I turned into him. He broke off and must have wondered how we could still be flying after so many hits. He drew up alongside, close enough for me to see the pilot clearly. I thought no way was I going to get out of this, so deciding to take him with me, I went straight for him. His reaction was quick and I just missed him. He must have got the message or lost me, or probably low of fuel returned to his base. No doubt he was pleased with his night's work and probably claimed a kill. But it still wasn't over for later over Woensdrecht I was picked up by searchlights again and given a large helping of light flak, fortunately causing no damage. I dived out of it down to 200 feet and crossed the coast at this height. Nursing the aircraft up to 4,000 feet, I told Norry that if the engine failed he was to jump and I would try to ditch as close to him as I could.

My fuel gauges were showing empty but I could dimly see land ahead. The radio was not working, so I told Norry to fire off an emergency Very cartridge. Within a few seconds a flare path was lit almost directly ahead. With the hydraulics shot out of action, I couldn't get the flaps or undercarriage down. Without a moments hesitation I cut the motor and went straight in, making a smooth belly landing. We slewed round about 45 degrees as we came to a stop and while we were unfastening our safety harness there was an almighty bang and an aircraft hit and bounced over us. As we were climbing out I thought 'Christ! We came through that lot only to kill one of our own chaps.' We rushed over and tried to get the pilot out, with petrol running all over the place, when the crash crew arrived and relieved us of the job. I was told later that, as I walked away with Norry, I was laughing and staggering like a drunk. Manston had not seen our Very light but had lit up the runway for a Typhoon returning from a strike. This knocked the rear section of our aircraft completely off. What an end to a night, or rather a nightmare.

We were taken by ambulance to the medical quarters and the MO insisted that we should stay the night in the station hospital. Norry told me that the duty officer had complained to him that we had made the runway unserviceable by tearing up some of the steel mesh. In his naturally disturbed state, Norry told him in no uncertain terms what he could do with his runway. I was told some weeks later that the fighter boys had put up a plaque in their mess 'To the boys who ruined Manston'.

In the morning the MO asked us how we felt and was told 'As right as rain.' He reported this to Wyton and Flight Lieutenant Moore came and picked us up in an Oxford. Meanwhile we had managed to scrounge a couple of photos of our crashed Mosquito. As if to emphasize our good fortune, we were told that our tanks were all virtually dry. The Mosquito was, of course, a complete write off.

Back at base I had to write a full report which I composed with Norry's assistance, giving the facts without embellishment on the events of the previous night. But I considered it wise to omit two facts: feathering the wrong propeller and my intention to ram the FW. When the CO read it he said he was taking us off flying for a time. We protested most strongly, so he said he would refer it to Group Headquarters. It went to Air Vice Marshal D.C.T. Bennett who congratulated us on our miraculous escape, but felt we should cease operational flying for a time and proposed to send us to an OTU as instructors. We emphasized the fact that we felt OK and sincerely wished to carry on. Bennett rarely changed his mind, but we must have impressed him because he allowed us to return to operations.

In the excitement Norry had forgotten to drop his brick.

My logbook entry was,

16 September, Mosquito IV 'T', Op No 5 Berlin, 3 x 500 pound 1 x 250 pound. Hit by flak and lost starboard engine 10 mins N of target. Coned 3 times and hit. Attacked and hit by 2 FW 190s; result 8 cannon holes 5 bullet holes. Crash landed at Manston with no petrol. Typhoon landed on top and crashed. A/C cat[egory] E. No injuries.

Similar incidents happened in subsequent operations, but thank goodness, not all at the same time. I was told a few days later that my previous half op had been upgraded and that I was to be credited with the other half, hence my logbook entries now moved from 3½ to 5. I was a little puzzled about this until I heard a rumour that I had been put forward for an award. Perhaps the upgrading came about because the number of sorties has to be stated in a recommendation and the half might have been tedious to explain. Obviously the entry in my logbook was not the full story. Many variations of that night's activities have been printed, some condensed, some expanded, but I have yet to read the full account, never having been asked to write it. The following reports from other sources may be of interest.

Extract from Manston Ops Record.

16 September 1943 Flight Lieutenant Sinclair 3 Squadron toured round from Dieppe – Péronne – Boulogne but found no targets. He saved the excitement for his landing at Manston, where he ran into a Pathfinder Mosquito which had just belly-landed on the runway. One Typhoon Cat B and one Mosquito written off. The Mosquito (of 139 Squadron) had returned from Berlin on one engine and had been attacked by an FW 190 which scored hits on its way back.

Pathfinder Force by Gordon Musgrave

16 September F/O Joe Patient was hit by flak over Berlin and the starboard engine had to be feathered. On the homeward route he was coned twice and reduced height to escape searchlights and flak. Manoeuvring was not easy on one engine so it was not surprising that his Mosquito received further damage when two FW 190s jumped it over Holland. The FWs scored hits on the wings and the fuselage and the navigator, Sergeant N. Gilroy, was wounded. The crippled Mosquito staggered into Manston where it crash landed five minutes after the petrol gauges had been reading zero. Before Patient had time to breathe a sigh of relief, a Typhoon nipped up behind him and removed the whole of the tailplane.

Pathfinder 8 Group Records

16 September 1943. 5 aircraft took off, anti-morale on Berlin. Four reached target bombing through 10/10ths on ETA. Position – flight flares were observed on approach to and over target area – flak was reported as negligible although one aircraft was hit in the port engine and crash landed at Manston on return. The remaining aircraft returned early with technical trouble.

The way that reads it was nothing to get excited about. But it was a nightmare. When I read it I wonder whether we or the others had been to different places.

139 Squadron Operations Record Book

Night 16/17 September 1943. The main excitement, however, was experienced by Flying Officer Patient. He was hit over the target and had to feather his starboard engine. On the long stooge home he was coned twice and lost a lot of height each time. Over Holland he was attacked by two FW 190s which pumped a good deal of cannon shells and machine gun bullets into his wings and fuselage. Eventually he staggered at low level to Manston where he made a good crash landing, five minutes after his petrol had registered zero. Just as he came to a stop, a Typhoon nipped up behind him and removed the whole of his tailplane. Both aircraft were written off. Fortunately nobody was hurt.

★   ★   ★

We were given two days off, so dashed home for a return to sanity. When we got back on 20 September I made an air test on DZ 483 X. At 1,000 feet there was a bang and the starboard engine started racing with severe vibration. I feathered – this time the correct one. Whereas the Mosquito normally flew beautifully on one engine, on this aircraft I was unable to maintain height. I radioed control to keep the runways clear and at the same time told Norry to fire off an emergency Very cartridge. It was obvious to me that I had insufficient height to get back if I lowered my undercarriage, so I unfeathered the engine which immediately started to overspeed. However, this gave me a little more height until the vibration was such that I had to feather again. By repeating this performance, I managed to land downwind with my wheels down. After this hairy episode I was beginning to think that I had a charmed life. That night eight of us crammed into one car and had a merry booze up at the George Hotel in Huntingdon, one of the aircrews' favourite haunts.

Oldenburg was to be our next target, a city not far from Bremen in the north of Germany. We were to take with us (excluding the brick) three 500 pound GPs (general purpose bombs) and one green TI (target indicator) which was to be dropped on the target at an exactly specified time. We were proud to be selected for this special job of marking.

On the night of 22 September, after the routine preparations, we climbed to 28,000 feet. Norry then found that something seemed to be wrong with his navigation. The estimated wind he had been given at briefing was almost the reverse of that he had calculated. I told him I would rather trust his calculation and to use it and check on our next fix. As usual, he turned out to be right. A little past Amsterdam the GEE blips faded and we continued on DR. As we were nearing our ETA we could see five separate fires blazing on the ground about twenty miles apart. These were obviously spoof targets, so we proceeded strictly on DR. Three minutes before our ETA we started to run up on a dark area about five miles from one of the fires and dropped the three 500 pounders. As there were five minutes to go until zero hour for our TI, I did a carefully timed instrument flight circuit to arrive over the spot we had bombed, exactly on time. There were some searchlights and flak but not enough to alarm us. Shortly after pulling away from the target, we saw large flashes on the ground where some of the heavies were bombing our green TI.

The trip home was uneventful. At debriefing we found that owing to the large variance in the winds given, many others had been hopelessly off course and had bombed alternative targets. When the heavies returned, some having taken photoflash records of their attack, we were reassured to find that we had marked the correct target. This gave Norry and I a great boost to our morale and added to our confidence in each other. The trip was recorded as a very successful diversionary raid (with no loss of aircraft) while the main force bombed Hanover. This involved 711 aircraft, of which 26 were lost, or 3.7 per cent. These losses were lower than the recent average and credit was given to the Oldenburg diversion for this result. My logbook reads:

> *22 September, Mosquito Mark IV 'Q' Op No 6 Oldenburg. 3 x 500, 1 x 250 TI at 30,000 feet. Heavies recorded pasting below. Diversionary raid. 32 Lancasters 8 Mosquitos.*

A note in the 139 Squadron operations record stated that 'Sergeant Parlato was not content with the small fires at Oldenburg and went on to bomb Hanover with the main force. It was his first trip.'

After a day off and two NF tests with Sergeant J.C. Baker, Norry and I flew our 7th op, this time back to Duisberg with the usual load. It proved to be a very run-of-the-mill sortie. We reported half-hearted ack ack with just an occasional searchlight and were back at base in just under three hours after a successful bombing run. I was later to find out that the four Mosquitos from 139 Squadron were the only Bomber Command aircraft to be over Germany that night.

> *24 September, Mosquito IV 'W' Op No 7 Duisburg. 3 x 500, 1 x 250 (36 hr DA). Quiet trip. Slight flak and searchlights behind.*

★　　★　　★

Sergeant Baker was a very pleasant chap with a quiet manner. He was later posted at the same time as Norry and I to 1409 Met Flight where he had a distinguished career, earning a commission and a DFC. Eighteen months later he flew on a goodwill tour of Canada with Flight Lieutenant M. Briggs DSO, DFC, DFM in the Mosquito LR 503. This aircraft had flown 213 sorties, the most recorded for a Mosquito in any command. Briggs had been a LAC air gunner at the beginning of the war, before the time when all aircrew had to be at least a sergeant. He then went on a pilots' course followed by numerous operations. This crew, who had for so long faced and survived against the might of Germany's forces, were killed giving a display at Calgary with LR 503 on 10 May, 1945. What a terrible end for two gallant men, made doubly tragic because the war in Europe had just ended. Oh! fickle finger of fate.

★   ★   ★

Hamborn was our next target. As we were taxiing round the perimeter on our way to the end of the runway, I suddenly lost brake pressure and found myself heading straight for a trolley load of bombs. I knew that even if I opened up my inside motor I would only have increased speed, so I cut both engine switches just before trundling over the bombs and scattering them in all directions. Norry had seen what was going to happen and had the door open. We knew that most of the bombs usually had ten-second fuses. We shot out of the aircraft, creating Olympic sprint records and dived to the ground. The ground staff did likewise. We did not know if the bombs were fused and we certainly did not wait to find out. After lying low for a few minutes, we gingerly went back to collect our gear from the aircraft and returned to the flight office. We were allocated another aircraft and half an hour later we were on course for the target. This trip was only a little less routine than the last one.

> *26 September, Mosquito IV 'L', Op No 8 Hamborn. 3 x 500, 1 x 250.*
> *Moderate flak coned 2 mins. Fighter co-op close.*

I made a note that Sergeant Parlato had been hit in the knee by flak at 30,000 feet on the same target.

There was an enquiry the next day about the bombs incident. Had they exploded with so many aircraft near it would have been very serious. I was cleared of any carelessness, but the armaments officer was hauled over the coals for leaving the trolleys on the edge of the narrow taxi-way. Fortunately the bombs had not been fused, so all was forgiven. I was greatly relieved and went out with Norry to celebrate.

We had set off before midnight on all our previous operations, but on 28 September our miserable take-off time was 0315 hours. Not only that, we were going to the heavily defended Ruhr target, Cologne. After climbing to 26,000 feet we broke cloud at last but could still see cumulo-nimbus tops around us. Continuing to 30,000 feet we were able to skirt round isolated anvil tops way above this height. Even so, we met severe turbulence which, with a bomb load aboard, was most unpleasant. As we made our way round with Norry noting our course alterations, the cloud thinned towards the target. Searchlights and flak showed clearly. After bombing through cloud on ETA, we turned for home, seeing land for the first time below 1,000 feet some twenty miles from base. At debriefing we found out we were the only aircraft from 139 Squadron to get through that night, the remainder returning or bombing alternative targets owing to the severe weather.

After this trip we were given four days off. I stayed a night with my mother before going home to St Albans. One of the many wonderful things about Lucy was that she never resented the visits I made to my mother. This I have always appreciated and during this short leave I actually baby-sat for one evening to give her a break. Imagine my surprise when she returned with a young RAF lad with the U/T aircrew white flash in his forage cap who she found wandering in the lane. I pulled her leg about this for ages but made the boy welcome. Of course I was plied with questions well into the night by this would-be pilot.

*　　*　　*

Unknowingly our last operation with 139 Squadron awaited us when we got back to Wyton. My logbook entry:

> *3 October Mosquito IV Q, Op No 10 Hanover. 2 x 500, 2 x green TIs (window). Numerous searchlights. Fighter co-operation. Track marker flares. Very successful diversionary. Heavies turned off to Kassel.*

On this occasion TIs were dropped to make the Germans think that the main target was Hanover. We circled dropping bunches of window (strips of metallized paper) which had the effect of saturating their radar screen and giving the impression of a large force raiding Hanover. This deceived them into focusing their fighters to that area (unpleasant for those of us who were there) but allowed our main force of heavies a safer run into their main target area, Kassel.

Later that day we were summoned to the CO's office and asked if we would be agreeable to a transfer to the specialist Met Flight at

Oakington. This was considered to be an elite unit within the PFF. Norry and I exchanged glances and said yes. We were immediately given leave and instructed to report on 21 October to 1409 Met Flight, Oakington, under Flight Commander George Hatton.

*   *   *

Lucy was most surprised to see me again so soon and looked very concerned until I told her about the transfer. During this long leave I visited my friend Sid Plumb and his wife, Maud. I have mentioned Sid before, when we were at De Havilland, and in the Home Guard together. He will certainly appear again in subsequent pages. He was tall, well built and rosy faced, and had done some quite astonishing things in his time. Before the war he had held various motor cycling sidecar records and as a lad had swum for his country. On this occasion Sid and I went over to the Four Hammers in the Watford Road for a drink, but had hardly sat down when Maud rushed in shouting, 'Joe, Joe, you've been awarded the Distinguished Flying Cross.' Lucy had just received a telegram from the C-in-C Bomber Command, 'Bomber' Harris, congratulating me on the award of an immediate DFC. She was so excited that, knowing where I had gone, she got friends nearby to phone through the news. This, of course, resulted in drinks all round.

I feel very strongly about the inconsistency of awards, and this was a case in point. I had been awarded a DFC for my fifth operation. Norry's part in that night's flying was of equal importance and without him I probably would not have survived, yet nothing was done about his invaluable contribution, not even a mention in despatches. I was an officer, Norry an NCO. There was much criticism of the American system of granting medals for almost everything. At that time I wore two ribbons; had I been in the US Air Force I would have qualified for several more. There was no inconsistency in their acknowledgement of operations carried out and in this regard their system was the fairer one. Also their decorations were the same for officers and other ranks, unlike the RAF. After five of their operations, the whole crew qualified for an Air Medal, and for each following five a bronze oak leaf cluster was put on the medal.

When five of these clusters had been earned they were replaced by a single silver one. Normally, in the USAAF, a DFC was awarded after thirty operations. They were also awarded for acts of individual gallantry or special operations. These awards were automatic, not dependent upon the whims or antipathies of the CO.

The first medal I wore was the 1939–43 star, but that did not reveal very much. The wearer could have fought in the Battle of Britain or, as in my case, commenced operations in August, 1943. This became an even greater anomaly when they changed the same medal into the 1939–45 star. The Victorians were a little more imaginative. Their general service medal carried bars showing the various campaigns engaged in.

It is not generally understood that there are only two military awards that can be made posthumously – the highest, the Victoria Cross, and the lowest, a Mention in Despatches. The most disgraceful case of injustice revealed during my research was that of a Captain who had finished a distinguished tour of operations but had volunteered to extend it so that he could finish it with his crew, who still had two more operations to complete. Tragically, this gallant officer and his whole crew were killed, so that the DFC which he had already earned was cancelled. I cannot imagine a more shameful situation. For the Captain the loss was meaningless but for his parents, wife and children it meant the deprivation of something infinitely precious to them and some small consolation in their grief at his death. There should be a committee to examine and rectify such injustices.

A titled flight commander carried out nine sorties without serious difficulties and was awarded a DFC and, after another nine, a bar to the DFC. During the same period and in the same flight, there were several pilots who had carried out many more sorties and, in some cases, had returned badly damaged and on one engine, yet received no recognition of any kind.

It was generally recognized that in Bomber Command, after carrying out a successful tour of thirty operations, you would leave for your rest with a DFC. The award was usually presented by the Air Officer Commanding the group at a parade held specifically for the presentation of decorations. In the case of an immediate award, however, the recipient had the honour of having it pinned on by the King or his representative at Buckingham Palace. I received my award from the late King George VI, while my wife and mother looked on. At the briefing it had been pointed out that we should shake hands with him very gently, otherwise he would finish up with a very sore hand in view of the numbers who were receiving awards.

After the investiture we had our photographs taken, then we strolled through the park and went into a pub in Grafton Street where I knew the manager and his wife very well. Mickey greeted me with, 'Where have you been?' 'I've just come from the Palace,' I replied. 'Damn good show, isn't it?' he remarked thinking that I had come from the Victoria Palace Theatre. It was a good laugh when I explained, and he bought drinks all round. We had arranged to meet other members of my family, Sid Plumb, and of course Norry at the Boulogne restaurant in Soho for a celebration lunch, followed by a matinée at the Prince of Wales where Sid Field was starring in the show and giving his celebrated golfing lesson with his stooge Gerry Desmond.

My sister was heard to remark 'Good God' when the main male dancer in a ballet sequence neared the edge of the stage. Under his tights he either had an oversized codpiece or his dancing had 'accentuated the positive'.

*   *   *

When I picked up Norry to return to Wyton, he told me he had spent a week at Bournemouth in the Palace Court Hotel and had had a wonderful time. I asked him what bank he had robbed and was told that the stay was free. Apparently Lord Nuffield had instituted a scheme whereby aircrew could stay at several top hotels in the British Isles as guests of the Nuffield Trust. It was a pity that Norry hadn't told me about this. I could just imagine the fun and games we could have got up to together.

When we got back, I was concerned to hear that Tommy Forsyth was in the station sick quarters. I was allowed to see him for a few minutes and thankful to find it was only a minor ailment. He pulled my leg about the bit of ribbon I was sporting below my pilot's wings. He knew that I had been transferred to Oakington but that was near enough for us to be able to get together easily. We arranged to keep in touch and I left with a flippant cheerio, but it was to be goodbye.

Two days later, as I was leaving for Oakington, I was numbed to hear that he and Jimmy James had not come back that night. Flight Sergeant T.K. Forsyth and Sergeant L.C. James took off in Mosquito DZ 597, target Berlin. The squadron records read, FAILED TO RETURN.

Although one grew callous about losses, Tommy's hit me harder than any other up to that point. When I later reported to Oakington, George Hatton could see that I was under strain. Mercifully he did not put me on ops until the 27th. This gave me time to settle down, it seemed strange that I felt no great anger towards the enemy, just great sorrow at the loss. For a while I hoped and prayed that he had been taken prisoner, but unfortunately that was not to be.

Tommy Forsyth had carried out seventeen operations with 139 Squadron, eight of which were on Berlin. Being so far into Germany and so heavily defended this was undoubtedly the most dangerous target. It seemed inevitable that his luck would run out. He was a great teller of stories. One he told me over a pint in St Ives was typical. 'There we were, Joe, bloody flak all around and tossing us about like a cork being pissed on. My arsehole, threepenny bit halfcrown – threepenny bit halfcrown. When I looked round at Jimmy he was laughing his head off and shouting at me to look at the pretty lights. I thought he had flipped but then I noticed that his oxygen tube had unfastened. I managed to get it plugged in and turned the oxygen on full. Jimmy shook his head, took one look, and fainted.'

Tommy admitted that he had put up a few blacks and done two tours in the naughty boys' school. He didn't have much to say about it except that they had tried to make it unpleasant, with emphasis on strict regimentation, very early morning drill, PT on the sands and early bedtime. He felt that this might have discouraged bad behaviour had it been conducted on Dartmoor under canvas, but in Blackpool it was all a bit of a lark. The authorities eventually realized this and changed it to Bournemouth. There he did his second tour with the same old early morning drill on the beach. One morning the drill corporal was yelling at the squad of naughty boys when an elderly lady came along and shouted at him, 'You leave those poor boys alone.' At the same time she set about him with her umbrella, while they kept marching along pretending not to hear the command to halt.

On one occasion when Tommy and I were drinking together, I jokingly suggested that we ought to start a 'Single Engine Club' with him as president having made two single-engined returns from ops, and me as chairman having (at that time) only made one. Returning on one engine was the subject of much discussion. The concensus of opinion was that it was better to make for a neutral country if that was nearer. It was an exaggeration, but I often said that I would rather fly the Mossie on one engine than most twins on two. Even so, she was a lame duck on one engine compared with the German fighters. I discussed this with Norry and we agreed that in view of the extreme luck (or divine intervention) we had enjoyed on our fifth operation, should we lose another engine on the Big City we would definitely head for Sweden, and had planned a route should the occasion arise.

Ten weeks later I lost an engine just north of Berlin, but changed my mind and returned to base, possibly because my observer on that occasion was Pilot Officer Bernstein. This was one of the few ops I flew without Norry. I told him that I had come back because I knew he would be lost without me.

Many of us made the most of the odd things which happened to us. This was known as shooting a line, and usually took place in front of new arrivals. Those coming to PFF, however, had often seen operations themselves and had their own stories to tell. One night Tommy Forsyth lost an engine and, because of severe damage, found the aircraft difficult to control. As he put it, 'The bugger just wouldn't fly straight, so I thought it better to make Jimmy jump and told him to bale out. He snapped on his chest parachute, kicked the door away, took one look and the next minute was up on my shoulders begging me not to make him jump and telling me what a good pilot I was and that I would get them back. Well, Joe, what else could I do? We got back, just, but I made the little bugger sit in the hole all the way back and then he blamed me for his frostbitten arse.'

Another incident happened as we were returning from the Ruhr one night. Our squadron call was 'Booklet', each pilot had a number, in my case 'Booklet 21', and our homing station call was 'Roseleaf'. Except in emergencies everyone kept radio silence until nearly home. We were all on our way back when we heard faintly but clearly 'Hello Roseleaf, Roseleaf this is Booklet 23, vector – vector' (asking for a home-coming course to steer). Tommy was obviously in trouble again. Back came a gentle, cultured WAAF voice, 'Hello Booklet 23, are you in trouble?' 'Am I in f...ing trouble,' came the quick reply. Unfortunately use of profane language is more or less accepted today but in 1943 it was almost unheard of. I was sure that there would be repercussions. Many senior officers of the old school failed to take into account the tension an ops crew was under, and this is how it affected him. No wonder he never received honours or promotion, but to me he was a better man by far than many of the mealy-mouthed hangers-on round the brass who received both.

Tommy's courage was well illustrated on 7 October when he took off at 2155 hours for Munich. While climbing on track, he had his rudder virtually knocked off by another Mosquito flown by Flight Sergeant Izatt. Most of the nose of Izatt's aircraft was smashed so it was forced to return early because of the intense cold. Much was made of this incident by reference to the accuracy of navigation in the PFF, in that they were both climbing on the same track. Tommy pressed on, which must have been very difficult with a full bomb load, and succeeded in making a good landing at 0031 hours. Many a less dedicated pilot would have jettisoned his bombs and returned home with no blame attached. The skill and tenacity he displayed was clearly a case for decoration, had he not been a naughty boy.

While in Bournemouth Tommy became attached to the daughter of a local publican. She came up to St Ives and stayed there while he was operating from Wyton. When he went missing I had the unpleasant task of taking a photograph he had of them together to give to her when I told her the news. When she saw me I didn't have to say anything. There were tears in my eyes as I gave her the photograph, she came into my arms and I hugged her as she wept. As she calmed, she admitted that she felt it was bound to happen and shortly after returned to Bournemouth.

It was strange to have been friendly with a man and not know much about him, except that he was Australian, with the normal young Australian's use of bad language. On 16 October, 1943, he entered the station sick quarters at Wyton and was discharged on the 18th.

Flight Sergeant T.K. Forsyth and Sergeant L.C. James are now just two names among thousands inscribed on the Runnymede Memorial to those who died with unknown graves.

4

The Met Flight

Harrowing experiences and a very different routine awaited us with 1409 Met Flight at Oakington. Norry and I were introduced to the crews and it was explained to us that all crews were placed on a flying duty roster. When you were on the top, you were on duty twenty-four hours a day and night until called for an operation. You had to keep flying control informed of your exact whereabouts during that period so that you could be contacted at a moment's notice. After your sortie, you went to the bottom and were not required to be on duty again until you were third from the top of the roster. It was essential that crews were always available to report weather conditions over intended targets before any bomber force set out.

In his memoirs Air Vice-Marshal D.C.T. Bennett described the part played by 1409 Met Flight with its handful of crews and navigators specially trained in weather recognition:

'When a flight was called for, the code name Pampa was used and normally came from Bomber Command, although we flew Pampas specially for other commands when they required it and for other services occasionally. No 1409 Flight flew by day or by night as and when required. Sometimes there might be one aircraft out, sometimes there might be three or four. Their total time in the air often covered most of the twenty-four hours in the day. Their penetrations into Germany were quite deep, even in broad daylight in clear weather. Naturally they flew high and fast, but the danger was extreme, and it was a most nervewracking job for the crews concerned. Admittedly, in the final

59

analysis, their losses were extremely low, although not quite so low as the rest of the Pathfinder Force Mosquitos and the Light Night Strikers.'

Routes had to be carefully planned and a full record of the weather taken at appropriate positions.

'They had no guns of any sort and nothing offensive' Bennett continued.
'I often wondered if it was appreciated at HQ Bomber Command, or for that matter by any other senior officers who called for a Pampa, that in doing so they were asking for an unarmed aircraft to proceed deep into the heart of enemy territory, often in broad daylight, without any cloud cover. The ease with which they called for Pampas was sometimes quite frightening.'

Shortly after we had joined the Met Flight George Hatton gave me some advice about daylight operations over Germany which were new to me. We discussed condensation trails (contrails) which occur at different levels, depending on the relative humidity and temperature. Not noticeable at night, except by moonlight, they are of course obvious on a clear day and are caused by the moisture emitted by the aircraft engines. When this exceeds the saturation point it turns into cloud. From our point of view there was both advantage and disadvantage in this phenomenon. If we began to make contrails below our operational flight for best performance, our ploy was to fly well into the contrail level so that any enemy fighters intercepting us would also make trails and therefore be seen, enabling us to take evasive action. Even so, it was disturbing. You feel highly vulnerable, aware that you are alone and yet on view to millions of hostile eyes.

We were always on the lookout for banks of cloud into which we could disappear should we encounter 'unfriendly natives' in the form of the Luftwaffe fighters. I had good reason to respect their ability. George Hatton also reminded me that the mark IX Mosquito had 900 horsepower more than the Mark IV and was therefore much faster than the IVs we had flown before. By 'going through the gate' we could at our best operational height outrun the FW190s, so that if they were chasing us we could wait until they were almost within range before opening up. I wasn't aware of it at the time but George had been caught napping by two German fighters as he neared Cromer on return from a Pampa and had been forced to bale out over the sea. This showed that you could not relax for one moment until you got out of the aircraft.

Norry and I were both sent off with experienced partners on our first two sorties. This seemed a little unnecessary in view of our operational experience, but we needed a refresher on our meteorology. On 2 November we were asked to test a new fighter warning device called Monica. This was a radar system emitting a signal from the rear of the aircraft which would be reflected back on striking any solid object behind us. It was an excellent idea, which gave warning of a fighter attack by pips in the earphones, the frequency of the pips giving an indication of the range. It was designed to start at about 2,000 feet with a slow pip-pip, increasing as the object came nearer. If successful this would give the rear gunners of the heavies a valuable warning, particularly at night, and for unarmed aircraft a warning of being attacked.

We arranged for other aircraft to 'attack' us to evaluate the invention. After nearly two hours testing we landed and reported satisfactory warning of the attacking aircraft. Very good, we thought. It was arranged that we should test it on our next Pampa, which happened to be the next day. We took off at 0515 to investigate weather at a specific point out over the North Sea to about sixty miles off the coast, level with Esbjerg in Denmark.

Everything went well to our turning point and until about five minutes on our way back. We were feeling fairly relaxed as it was most unlikely that fighters would be so far out over the North Sea. All of a sudden there was a loud pip-pip, pip-pip, so fast that according to theory something had to be on our tail. I reacted with immediate evasive action so violent that it would have taken a genius to stay with me. The pips stopped so I resumed my course but the warning was shortly repeated. After three or four times, I was sure that no fighters could be in the area and concluded that the insulation had broken down so I switched the damn thing off to avoid further shocks to my system. I nevertheless kept a good lookout behind, with an occasional weave in case I was wrong. After making our Met report we discussed the events with the boffins. Norry put forward the theory that the gubbins was too sensitive and reacted to cloud. Off we went to check this. Clever Norry. That was what it turned out to be. The equipment was desensitized and we did a further air test with the same result. So back it went to the experimental establishment for modification.

On our next Pampa we could have done with a serviceable Monica because we finished up with an aircraft resembling a sieve. Well, nearly. It was all a bit embarrassing for me. On our way back from the Pampa deep into Germany we were aware of three sets of contrails far behind us. I told Norry to keep an eye on them and to tell me when they were about 2,000 yards astern when I would apply full throttle but not go 'through the gate'. When he told me 2,000 yards (and later admitted it was more like 3,000) I duly opened up with further instruction to report if they closed to 1,000 yards, when I would go 'through the gate'. All the time Norry was saying, 'closing, still closing'.

Everyone who has anything to do with engines and respects them dislikes pushing them to their maximum power for other than a few moments. I am no exception and was only prepared to do so in an emergency. I then made probably the most stupid remark of my life. As I was applying full power, I said, 'George Hatton told me they can't catch us.' I had barely got the words out of my mouth when we were peppered. I had been heading towards a bank of cloud where I thought we could lose them. (I nearly wrote 'the Bastards' but after all, like myself, they were just doing their job.) Taking a downward action with the engines at full power, with Norry shouting 'He's still on our tail,' I tightened my turn and the enemy 'flipped' trying to follow. This action resulted in a screaming dive and increase in speed which, when I hit cloud, really had me in trouble. All the gyro instruments were spinning like tops and my teddy bear was all over the place. I had throttled back as soon as the FW broke away and was thankful for my earlier concentration on basic instrument flying: needle – ball – airspeed, needle – ball – airspeed. Norry told me later that I was mouthing these words into the intercom as I was trying to get the aircraft level and under control. That all those bits of balsa, plywood and fabric held together with glue managed to stay in one piece after such violent handling is a great tribute to De Havillands and the Mosquito.

I knew the 190s had scored several hits, but where? Only a little could be seen from the cockpit. My main concern was whether the fuel tanks had been holed. The gyro instruments had not recovered so I was still flying on basics. Norry gave me an approximate course and we decided to stay in cloud as long as it lasted. As soon as I felt we were over the North Sea I called for a Vector, depressed my transmitter for a fix, and was pleased to get a course to steer for home which was only ten degrees different from that estimated by Norry. I was RT controlled down to within sight of base, when I thanked them for their help. We seldom had to rely on Vectors, but I had had enough that day and was content to have the responsibility taken off my shoulders.

Aware that the unseen damage might result in an unorthodox landing, I asked flying control to examine my undercarriage closely as I flew slowly past the tower. There appeared to be nothing amiss, so I made a normal approach and landed. As my tail wheel touched the ground there was a wobble, but not enough to concern me unduly. As soon as Norry had sent his Met report through and I had spoken to the intelligence chaps, we went to have a good look at the damage. The tail wheel had been hit and the tyre punctured which explained the wobble. There were cannon holes in both elevators, port flap and starboard aileron. There was even a clean bullet hole through one of the propeller blades, making about a dozen in all. The following morning I was handed a board with a piece of 9-strand aileron cable fastened at the ends, with the middle showing 7 of the strands severed. As we levelled out of that rolling dive at a speed which Norry estimated to have been in excess of 600 mph, our lives had depended on two strands. Our guardian angel had been with us again.

Shortly after this incident intelligence reports came through that the Germans had devised some form of liquid injection into the engine of the FW 190 (G) which had the effect of increasing the compression ratio. Although it could only be used for a short time, it gave the aircraft a burst of speed to put it within firing range of the Mosquito.

It occurs to me that some of what I have written and have yet to write may be difficult to believe. I have therefore, wherever possible, referred to official documents. I am most anxious to avoid any error as there are many 'experts' who manage to disprove an incident, thus throwing the whole content in doubt. The official entry in 1409 Flight's record operations for 6 November, 1943, reads:

> '0935. Varying amounts of st cu and al cu and cirrus were found in the target area between 10,000 and 30,000 feet. The trip was not without excitement for the crew as the aircraft were attacked by 3 FW 190s and, although, cloud cover was eventually reached, it was not before the machine had been hit several times, including one through the port propeller and one in the petrol tank, which also nearly severed the aileron controls. The crew are to be congratulated on reaching base at 1300 hours without further incident.'

We were given two days off after this miraculous escape, but I did not feel I should go home in case I mentioned the episode and made Lucy worry. I always made out that what I was doing was not dangerous. I remember telling my elderly mother that I got the ribbon I wore for playing in the band. Also, as 83 Squadron was going to have a party the next evening, I felt that would be a good way of unwinding.

Norry invited his special girl friend from Harrogate who turned out to be very lovely. He was quite capable of fending off the mostly senior and well decorated horde of wolves at the party, so he was proud to show her off. Afterwards he drove her to Ely where she was staying the night. He had quite a story to tell me about it the next day. 'Having had a fair bit to drink, I lost my way in the town and drove through ever-narrowing streets, until my wide, square-backed Talbot got wedged between two ancient houses. I started trying to back out, but as I backed, the shutters on the downstairs windows began to be knocked off by the side of the car. They clattered to the ground with a frightful racket. Upstairs windows started opening. People in all shapes and sizes of night clothes and funny tasselled night caps (like those worn by the Seven Dwarfs) appeared and angrily demanded to know what I was doing damaging their property. After calming them down and saying that I would pay, some of the men came down and gave me directions on how to back out. I found this very difficult in my slightly inebriated state. All the time my girl friend and I could hardly stop giggling. It was just like a pantomime. Eventually they managed to back me out and I gave them £2 (a third of my weekly RAF pay) which they said would be enough to pay for the damage. They told me how to get to the hotel and still giggling we drove off.' This will explain why I never let Norry drive me.

I too enjoyed the party, although I had not invited a guest. I scrounged a couple of dances but was not in the mood for amorous adventures. This was rather out of character for me and I retired quite early.

On 9 November we had an uneventful trip to Abbeville-Reims-Metz-Mulhouse-Troyes–Dieppe. Our only real problem was where to drop Norry's brick. Nowhere in Germany did they need a brick; with so much unscheduled demolition courtesy of the RAF there must have been a surplus of bricks. In the end we decided that Metz could probably use some good reading or make other use of the paper. Many years later, when I was in the antiques trade, it occurred to me that Norry's bricks, complete with wrapping, would be collectors' items. As for this trip, it helped us regain our confidence. We reckoned we could not survive many more sorties like the last one. Another uneventful operation which followed next day reinforced this feeling as we flew to Sylt-Flensburg-Odense-Esbjerg. After the debriefing that day I had a pleasant surprise. I was told that a Captain John Thom was waiting to see me in the mess.

John was the eldest son of the Thom family who had been so kind to me in Montreal. He knew my whereabouts through his sister Bunty with whom I kept in touch. I had a quick word with the OC Flying and flew John round for about forty minutes in the aircraft I had just returned in. We had an enjoyable evening, I consumed a little more than my norm, safe in the knowledge that, having operated on the last two days in succession, I was most unlikely to be needed for a couple of days. His visit was too short although he night-stopped and we got a party going.

A trip for the Americans on 13 November took us to Wilhelmshaven-Ulzen-Osnabruck-Utrecht. We were airborne at 0100 hrs, arriving back at 0420, ready for an early breakfast. We decided to go home, taking our saved-up chocolate and orange juice. We would return early on the 15th having made arrangements for a substitute in the unlikely event of being needed before then. While we were away, Pilot Officer F. Clayton and Flying Officer W.F. John created a personal record of two sorties in one day, while the Flight had its record of five. This is why we were at the top of the roster when we returned. But there was bad news waiting for us, a reminder that the Met Flight still had its dangers apart from the weather. On 14 November those two gallant officers had failed to return and were believed to have been shot down in the Lille area.

Pilot Officer Clayton was one of the oldest members of the unit, having carried out his first Pampa in a Spitfire from Bircham Newton on 31 May, 1942. He had completed fifty-three sorties as well as many hours' work on the 'Thum' and 'Prata' ascents. ('Thums' were climbs to 24,000 feet three times a day by Gladiator aircraft taking meteorological measurements at every 50 milibars. 'Prata' were similar flights but by Spitfires operating up to 40,000 feet.) Flying Officer John also had considerable experience on Pampa and other flights. They were just one crew of so many lost every day, but one out of eight close associates brings the reality of it very near. I had then only done seven operations on the Met Flight, already with one very shaky do. It occurred to me forcibly that if a very experienced pilot like Clayton with fifty-three ops under his belt could get shot down, either I had been very good (in the flying sense) or, most probably, very lucky.

A trip to Stavanger (Norway) on 16 November coming back by Texel on the Dutch coast and taking just over three and a half hours had a special interest. Our weather information had to be reported

back in morse code. After all the months of training in wireless tech-
nology Norry had endured this was the only occasion in a long career
when he used morse. The following day we carried out a further test
of fifty minutes on the modified Monica which the boffins had sent
back. Alas, it was just as sensitive to cloud as before. This was the last
we saw of that particular boffin brain-child for seven months.

At 0400 hrs on 19 November we were telephoned to do a Pampa
to Rotterdam – Arnhem – Düren – Blankenburg and were airborne
at 0410 which must have been a record for speed from notification
to take-off. Shortly after setting course our GEE equipment became
unserviceable but as it was a fairly short trip we decided to carry on
using DR navigation. On our calculated return to the British coast
we found 10/10ths ground fog as far as we could see, as well as low
cloud. When I tried to contact base, we found to our dismay that our
VHF radio was also useless. We were up the proverbial creek without
a paddle. Norry suggested a square search as, without any fix for three
hours, on DR alone we could have been anywhere. The alternative
was to fly south-west until we were certain that we were over the
Atlantic, then to make the descent below the fog if possible, and
return north-east until we hit land. Our IFF (identification friend or
foe) was of course switched on. This enabled radar to track us
positively in case some over-zealous British ack ack gunner decided
to have a go at us.

After a further twenty minutes flying without seeing anything, we
made a square search. This involves flying in a continual square,
gradually increasing the length of each leg of the box. After about
fifteen minutes we came across a flashing beacon but could see no
clear ground. I circled and fired off the colours of the day from the
Very pistol but received no reply. We continued our square search
but after about fifteen minutes I had to tell Norry that we only had
about twenty-five minutes of fuel left and that as we were pretty
certain to be over land in view of the flashing beacon, we should
prepare to bale out rather than risk breaking through the fog into a
hill. After another five minutes searching we saw a searchlight which
started dipping towards the north-east. This led us to a cone of two

searchlights below which, between patches of cloud, we could see a runway already lit up. We landed thankfully and found that we were at RAF Pershore.

Naturally we were in a hurry to get the weather report to HQ and as we were rushing in with jackets undone and hatless we were called back by an officer. 'I will have you know that junior officers salute senior officers on this aerodrome,' he barked. 'Jolly good show, sir, very glad to hear it,' retorted Norry, grabbing his hand and pumping it up and down. It was all I could do to keep a straight face. 'What a prick. It must be a Training Command station,' said Norry as we went to find a telephone. On plotting back the route he calculated that if we had stayed on our course over the UK and continued into the Atlantic instead of starting our square search we might well have gone too far with the possibility of an unscheduled swim in the icy November sea.

After refuelling and raising eyebrows in the Mess by requesting eggs and bacon for breakfast, we thanked the ground staff for their help and took off for base, arriving at 1125 hrs. We reported the lack of response to our Very light at the beacon. We were then given leave, perhaps in recognition of another shaky do.

It was during this leave, while in London visiting my sister, or perhaps someone else's sister that I had my first close experience of a buzz bomb, or the V1 to use its official name. The distinctive sound of its engine seemed like a badly tuned two-stroke. Everybody listening to it was hoping that the engine would keep going at least until it had passed by. When it cut out there was an eerie silence or whine in the glide until I lost sight of it. Shortly afterwards came an awful explosion. I was near enough to see the cloud of dust billowing up. It was quite frightening. I was glad to get back to St Albans and later to Cambridgeshire where there were very few of these ghastly contraptions. My heart went out to the Londoners who were the chief recipients of these and the later V2 rockets.

During one of my leaves I met my friends at the Comet pub at Hatfield and met Barbara Harris. There was a highly publicized court case, as a result of which the Rector of Stiffkey was de-frocked because of his association with Barbara when she was a young girl. He later added to his notoriety by various unusual escapades and publicity stunts which received considerable coverage from the popular press. The lads decided to go to the Cherry Tree in Welwyn Garden City, an old dance haunt of mine. There were three of us in my old Austin Ruby Saloon for which I had paid the princely sum of £25 and I opened the sliding roof. All of a sudden the car was surrounded by fellows carrying Barbara and to my astonishment, they tipped her head first onto my lap, with her skirt over her head and revealing tiny briefs. It was quite chaotic and hilarious, but we had all been drinking and she more than most. She was bundled into the back onto the lap of my friend Roy Collins. When we arrived at the dance, Barbara was still out like a light, so we left her in the back. After the dance she was still flaked out and I was told she lived in Hatfield. Driving to a lay-by, I got into the back with her. She showed neither resistance nor enthusiasm, so I had second thoughts and took her home.

*　　*　　*

My logbook entry for Pampa 10 Op No 20. sounds very matter of fact.

> *Dammoshaved – Berlin – Lauenburg – Texel. Lost port engine at Waren. Searchlights and flak very heavy at Hamburg.*

I flew with Pilot Officer Bernstein as Norry was not yet back from leave. Shortly after turning for home just north of Berlin, I experienced my first runaway propeller which happened without any warning. The engine gave a sudden scream as it raced. I quickly feathered which fortunately happened according to the book. Earlier I mentioned my decision to divert to Sweden as I would have done had Norry been with me and thus saved the lives of two of my comrades (see page 70).

We had flown for one and a half hours in daylight but luckily it was now dark and this undoubtedly influenced my decision to return. I cannot imagine anyone getting back from Berlin in daylight on one engine unless there was cloud cover the whole way. As it was, we endured an unpleasant few minutes from searchlights and heavy flak over Hamburg. An added problem when losing the port engine was the loss of the GEE navigation aid. It was a relief when we arrived at base after receiving QDMs, and flying for some time in 10/10ths cloud.

Rather than risk burning the brakes out by taxiing to dispersal on one engine, I left the aircraft with the one propeller feathered just clear of the runway. After telling the NCO in charge of the duty ground crew about the runaway propeller, I returned to the Mess on the crew bus. I went to bed early after having something to eat.

The following morning we heard that Flight Sergeant 'Curly' Addis and Sergeant Johnny Sharpe had died. They had taken off within minutes of myself the previous day and, according to the records, had transmitted distress calls near Dieppe and eventually were homed to Exeter where sadly they crashed 600 yards short of the runway. 5 December was another black day. I had flown an Oxford communications aircraft to Feltwell to pick up the new CO, Flight Lieutenant V.S. Moore, a New Zealander and ex-Lancaster pilot. On my return I was told of another tragic accident. My friend Pilot Officer J. Burgess with whom I had made my second Pampa had been killed together with Flight Lieutenant H.F.M. Taylor, a newer member of the flight. Shortly after take off Taylor reported trouble with his port engine. As the weather was bad he was diverted to Marham where he attempted to overshoot on his approach to land. Instead, he spun into the ground.

When I was told that the aircraft in which they were killed was the one I had left in the middle of the airfield only 36 hours previously I was furious. As the group engineering officer, Wing Commander Sarsby, was at the bar I threw caution to the wind and used some very strong words about sending off unserviceable aircraft. He threatened to have me court-martialled as I had not put 'aircraft unserviceable' in the Form 700. This seemed to me a minor misdemeanour considering that I had left the aircraft out on the aerodrome. After the trauma of flying several hundred miles with the whole might of the German forces available to give me their undivided attention, the signing of a form was easily forgotten. I told him that he would be in bigger trouble than myself if all the facts were known.

It seems that the propeller had been unfeathered and the engine run without any immediate fault showing up. Obviously the test run had not been exhaustive enough to show the breakdown and so two colleagues were robbed of their most precious possession and two families plunged into mourning.

I had been with the Flight only forty-six days but already three out of the other seven crews had perished. It makes yer fink don't it? It also makes nonsense of the figures quoted in war diaries. A .4 per cent loss of Mosquitos may have been accurate for the whole period of the war, covering all commands. It was, however, very misleading for Pathfinder Force at that time.

It was bitterly cold on the morning of 11 December. Norry was back from leave and we set off at 0330 hrs for Texel-Hanover-Ulzen-Empen. Apart from moderate flak over Hanover it was an uneventful journey. When we got back we were glad to find that two of our old friends from 139 Squadron had joined us in the Met Flight. WO 'Ginger' Miles and Flight Sergeant Ferdie Perry had by now completed nineteen bombing ops, the last four of which were on Berlin. They too were living on borrowed time.

On 19 December we went on a very unpopular flight known as a stooge. This was usually an examination of a frontal system, often with severe weather conditions of turbulence and icing. Despite such hazards, if we did not cross enemy territory, the flight did not count as an operation, although the Met Flight had lost crews doing them.

I caught influenza at this time, the cause unknown. (Norry suggested 'getting out of a warm bed and going home'). However, it spoilt my Christmas. Meanwhile Norry initiated a new pilot into the mysteries of the Met Flight, a Flying Officer Powell-Wiffen who had an accent to match his name. He brought with him a greatly admired Lancia open tourer which we were never allowed to drive. This led to much leg-pulling of the newcomer whom we nicknamed Swiffle Piffin.

Thick fog enveloped the country for quite a time in January and all heavy bombing operations were called off. It was our luck to be at the bottom of the roster. Although we could not go home in case the weather cleared, we had a whale of a time locally with dances and dates. There grew a great bond of friendship between Norry and me. We could almost sense each other's thoughts and moods. I cannot ever recall a cross word between us, although, needless to say, we pulled each others legs on many occasions. Such friendships are rare and can only be developed through the sharing of great danger.

On occasions we were invited to give pep talks in factories to boost the war effort. After answering questions, I usually finished with 'My Observer was such a good meteorologist that he could look into a girl's eyes and tell whether'.

During an unexpected fourteen days leave I introduced Norry to dog racing at Park Royal. I often went there as I was friendly with two of the bookmakers, also a butcher who sometimes had the odd joint (without ration books) for his pals. We didn't do too well so Norry said 'never again' and, forty-five year later, he told me had never been to another dog race. During this leave 1409 Met Flight moved lock stock and barrel to Wyton. We had to return to Oakington to collect our personal bits and pieces before going to our new (old) station. We had been very comfortable at Oakington, especially as Cambridge was so near. However, Wyton had been our first operational home. We knew our way around there and fortunately had kept in touch with many old friends.

Ulric Cross was about the only one of our old 139 Squadron buddies left, although we were pleased to hear that some had managed to complete their tours. We made an air test on 19 January, the usual practice after a longish leave, and I had some beam approach practice on 21 January with Flight Lieutenant Berridge. Later that day I flew a sortie with Norry returning without incident other than a frequent surge and then loss of power on one of the engines which was duly reported.

One evening a whole party of us climbed into one of the cars to go to the George at Huntingdon which had always been one of our favourite pubs. After quite a few drinks we set off home. With so many squashed into the car, we didn't notice until we were well on our way that Norry was missing. Norry's tale of that night went the rounds of the RAF and was even told, slightly modified, on the stage by a comedian. This was his story. 'When I came out of the George I found the sods had gone off and left me to fend for myself, so I had no alternative but to walk back to camp. By now it was very foggy indeed. I could hardly see two feet in front of me. As the odd car crawled by I tried to get a lift, but to no avail. I became a bit cheesed off with this and when the next one came by I opened the rear door and got into the back without saying anything. I looked around the car and in my sozzled condition was about to make apologies for my intrusion, but found there was no one else in the car, not even a driver. When it came to a corner or a curve in the road, a white hand materialized from nowhere, turned the wheel and vanished. I was getting very jittery and nervous about this and tried to collect my addled thoughts together, but told myself that while it was going in the right direction, I might as well sit tight.

'After about twenty minutes of this ghostly journey, the car finally came to a halt at the gates of Wyton aerodrome. I got out and had retreated two or three yards from the car when a squadron leader and flight lieutenant came into sight. "I shay old chaps," I said with a drunken slur, "don't go near that car, it's haunted." "Haunted be buggered," said the squadron leader. "We've just pushed the bloody thing all the way from Huntingdon." '

On 23 January, 1944, we flew Sergeant Sabine, one of the newer Observers, to Exeter. I think he had talked the CO into it on compassionate grounds – or it may have been passionate. However, as the Mossie is a two-seater, he had to lie in the bomb aimer's position in the nose. It took an hour and ten minutes going and forty-five minutes coming back. I seem to remember that at his request I flew over the house he was visiting. After an air test on 25 January we were again at the top of the roster.

Norry was jittery when I saw him the next day. He had been called on to do a Pampa with the new CO to Cologne – Frankfurt –

Saarbrücken – Dieppe. I heard afterwards that at every turning point the CO had made murmuring sounds and had descended to the base of the clouds from 25,000 feet, sometimes down to 10,000 feet. Then he had climbed back up again and proceeded on to the next town where the whole thing was repeated. This was quite unnecessary and, as Norry was very experienced and a good judge of cloud heights, he quite rightly considered that the hazards were plenty enough without asking for trouble. He said it was no wonder that the CO was known as Flak Happy Moore. The Observers were greatly relieved when he was posted two days later and a new CO, Squadron Leader Mike Birkin AFC, took over the flight.

Mike Birkin was liked by everyone. He was an unassuming gentleman, with a quiet word of encouragement for any who needed it. I happened to mention that I had met Sir Henry Birkin when I was working as a page boy in the West End and it turned out they were cousins. He had not flown the Mark IX Mosquito and I had the pleasure of joining him on his first flight with out unit on 29 January. A short stooge on the 31st saw the month out.

On 2 February I was asked to take Flying Officer Mattock on DZ385 (a Mark XV) to Sherborne where I stayed the night. On my return journey, being alone, I decided to test its performance at height. This mark of mosquito was developed specifically to combat the enemy's high-flying JU 86s which would come over and drop the odd bomb with impunity as we had no aircraft which could reach them. Only a few XVs were made. About five feet was added to the wingspan. By fitting smaller wheels, removing the armour plating, reducing the petrol tankage and by generally reducing the weight of the aircraft by as much as one ton they managed to reach the height of the JU 86s and above, with ample speed to catch the intruders. De Havillands achieved this in a remarkably short time, whereupon the JUs stopped coming.

I was naturally anxious to try out this unusual aircraft and on my way back from Sherborne climbed higher than I had ever done before. My euphoria was short-lived. The elevators froze solid at the end of the climb and I had to throttle back and descend until they were usable again, having to make much use of trim on the way down – quite exciting.

More excitement happened on 25 February during another interesting trip. Norry (now a flight sergeant) and I set out on a gentle stooge over the North Sea. On our return to base fog had formed with visibility of only a couple of hundred yards. For the Met boys this was not a serious problem unless their beam approach equipment was unserviceable. I considered calling for a diversion but Norry reminded me that we had dates at St Ives that evening. He suggested that if I could find the beginning of the runway in use and say 'Now', he would take a fix with the GEE set. I was then to fly out as in a normal circuit and he would home me on to the fix on the heading of the runway, as in a bombing run. He would tell me about 1500 yards out to put the wheels down and part flap, to set the controls and descend as on a normal approach. He would tell me the distances to go as we neared the fix. With any other navigator I would not have done it, but Norry was a wizard with the GEE set so I agreed to give it a try, intending on the first attempt to stay a little high with flaps up and then overshoot. However, he brought me in so perfectly that when he said 'Now' I looked up from my instruments and there was the beginning of the runway, dead in line, so, slapping down the flaps I landed straight ahead. There was a lot of comment about us getting down safely in the fog, but we said little about it at the time. We felt we had justified getting the Met report through quickly and had earned our other diversion to St Ives.

We bandied this 'invention' about between ourselves. I felt that we should not wait until we were caught out in difficult landing conditions but should plan ahead by recording the coordinates of the end of all the runways and any other areas suitable for landing in an emergency. We would pay particular attention to heights of obstructions, with distances from the touch-down points and of course heading of landing run. We then discussed our theory with Mike Birkin who gave us permission to try it out in good visibility to discover any snags. On 28 February we practised for an hour and a half, taking a fix on all six ends of the three runways at Wyton. I religiously followed instructions, flying on instruments and only looking up when Norry said, 'Now'. On only one of the approaches would I have had any difficulty or danger in attempting to land. When I said this was no good, Norry re-examined the cathode and found the blips had wandered. So two things were learnt. One: The idea had a good emergency use; Two: The navigator had to be continually checking the line-up of the coordinates.

I began to wonder whether this was just an extremely good emergency reserve up our sleeve in view of Norry's particular expertise, or whether it had a wider application. We had approached in six directions, with successful downwind and crosswind approaches as well as the normal one into the wind. We duly reported to the CO. I was told to try it out the next day with a different Observer, Flight Sergeant Baines, who meanwhile was briefed by Norry on the procedures. We flew for an hour and although I felt there was not the same exactitude, (perhaps I was biased), I could have landed on all his approaches.

*　*　*

At about his time, Norry was told to report to Air Vice-Marshal D.C.T. Bennett at PFF Headquarters in Huntingdon. I was amused by his story when he returned. After pleasantries, he was asked how he liked the Met Flight and then the AVM said, 'Can you ride a horse?' 'Only so-so Sir,' Norry replied. 'I can't bear it if it tries to eat grass. I am liable to roll off the top of its head.' He was then asked if he could drive a car. 'Oh yes,' said Norry, lying through his teeth. Then the AVM said, 'Thank you Gilroy, that's all.' Norry returned in a bit of a daze thinking that the AVM was off his rocker. But the CO told him that he was to have five days' leave to purchase his uniform as he was now an officer and a gentleman. Of course, nothing else than Savile Row would do for Norry and I remember how disappointed he was at the poor fitting round the neck. Five days' leave did not give him time to have it altered and he was particularly upset because he had used £60 of his mother's hard-earned savings towards the cost. All the same, his family were all justifiably proud as Norry was the first of the Gilroy-cum-Goldstein clan to be awarded the

76

King's Commission. This, of course, made it so much more convenient, particularly when visiting other units, as we no longer had to separate to different messes and quarters.

I had a series of successful GEE approaches on 19 and 21 March with Flight Sergeant Ferdie Perry. We now felt confident enough to approach HQ with our findings. Mike Birkin was very pleased with our efforts and hoped to get all his crews to adopt the system as an emergency back-up. He allowed us as much flying time as possible for practise in order to perfect it.

A pre-dawn Pampa was ordered for the US Army Air Corps on 22 March. The logbook for the four hour op reads:

> *Mosquito XVI 'C' Pampa 25 Op No 29. Kapellen-Meyenburg-*
> *Stadskanaal-Antwerp. Searchlights and fighters very active. USA 9.*

My Observer on this occasion was Flight Sergeant Sabine. Fate is a very capricious thing. He had one more week to live and in a remote way, I was responsible for his death (see page 80).

Later that day I was woken up and told to report to the ops room. Up to that point I had never been asked to fly again the same day after an operation. I was then told to make a test flight with Flying Officer Green and Flight Sergeant Perry on Mosquito IX LR 509 S. This had been modified and fitted with long-range tanks, a third oxygen point and additional radio. I was told on no account to talk about it to anyone and was informed that I had been removed from the duty roster until further notice. The Mosquito is a tight fit for a pilot and observer in thick flying gear. There is only just enough room for the observer to crawl into the nose for the bombing run-up to the target. During this flight it meant someone lying down in the nose for the whole time, not a nice position in the event of a crash, forced, or wheels-up landing.

The normal air test was seldom more than fifteen to thirty minutes. This one lasted an hour and a quarter. Afterwards I was told to be ready for a special operation but given no details. The next day I made another test on the same aircraft with Corporal Millar (ground staff) lasting nearly an hour and a half, testing the transfer of fuel to the mains from the extra tanks which had been fitted. Two days later the purpose of all this was revealed. I was briefed to take Wing Commander E. William Anderson DFC (Group Navigation Officer) and Flying Officer N.W.F. (Gert) Green DFC to Berlin. 'Why the extra tanks?' I asked. 'Even with a bomb load we can do Berlin and back with an hour's fuel to spare, and why Flying Officer Green instead of my own Observer?' I was more or less told to mind my own business and just listen to the briefing. I was to fly to a point above a transmitter on the east coast and at an appointed time and height, set off without any deviation whatever on a straight track for Berlin. We were to arrive five minutes before the PFF markers and the main bomber force which was to be a big one. I didn't like the idea of a straight line at all and said so. They justified their decision as a navigational necessity to ensure being spot on at Berlin as by taking back-bearings on the transmitter they could in this way keep relatively accurately on track. I thought it crazy but realized that there was no point in arguing about it. The only concession made to me was that I could choose the route back.

This was to be my 30th operation. On a main force squadron it would have meant an end of tour op followed by a long rest, but on PFF there was still a long way to go. To become blasé about flying, regardless of how much you have done, would be asking for a quick reunion with those poor unfortunates who had gone before. I was perfectly aware that I had been living on borrowed time for some while, hoping that whoever held my overdraft was not yet ready to foreclose. The mere fact that I am writing this shows that some time or other I must have got out of the red! My logbook entry as usual understates the reality of that night.

> 25 March, Mosquito IX 'S' Pampa 26 special mission op No 30 Berlin. Circled for 35 minutes. 72 aircraft lost. (2,600 tons dropped). Belt of fire 6 miles wide. Searchlights and fighters very active. Coned and heavy flak at Hamburg.

A night scorched indelibly on my memory.

Despite my anxiety about the direct line to Berlin, we arrived much to my surprise, with very little attention from the Hun. While there, it was a different story. I was not briefed as to what was going to happen. Anderson told me to circle the city and watch for the PFF markers to go down. Almost to the second down went the flares and target indicators, followed shortly afterwards by bomb explosions. I imagined Anderson would then just act as Master Bomber, but that was not his function. He said, 'Patient, keep going round.' By this time a goodly number of the main force had dropped their calling cards and the air seemed so full of aircraft that the ack ack and fighters hardly needed to aim as they were bound to hit something by just letting loose. I had seen four big ones go down in flames and was thankful that we were a few thousand feet higher and that there were plenty of easier and larger targets below.

I was then startled by Anderson broadcasting on the main listening out frequency: 'Come on Canadians, remember Dieppe.' So this was why Anderson was there. Almost immediately it seemed that every searchlight in Berlin coned us and I spent nearly the whole time using every trick I knew trying to get out of the glare. To add insult to injury, the next transmission was: 'Say chaps, see those poor buggers up in the searchlights? That's us.' I could gladly have killed him. Twelve aircraft x seven aircrew = eighty-four good men I saw die that night and of course there were many more. The next broadcast was: 'Pity the poor Hun tonight.' Immediately someone else broke radio silence with 'Serve the bastards right.'

After thirty minutes' circling I suggested to Anderson that perhaps we had done enough, there was so much fire and smoke below. 'Just once more round,' was his reply, 'and its all yours,' and then trans-mitted, 'Well boys, let's go back to our bacon and eggs.' I nearly laughed when a faint voice came back saying, 'What about another marker?' I could visualize some 'press-on type' determined to drop his bombs as briefed but perhaps late owing to some mishap or other. After all that turmoil I received a further helping of flak near Hamburg on the way home.

The following day my attention was drawn to a blurb pinned to the notice board, which I later removed. It read: 'A great force of heavies attacked the German capital last night and dropped the largest bomb load ever. As far as is known the raid was a complete success although the TIs scattered towards the south at the close. The unusual part of the attack was the pep talk which was given to the crews over the target by Wing Commander Anderson of PFF HQ, flown there by that intrepid birdman Flying Officer Patient, who in his turn was navigated there by that other intrepid airman, Flying Officer Green. The result of the raid was of course sealed by the assistance of these three press-on types. With persuasive encouragement, the main force carried right on to the heart of the Third Reich with complete disregard for the intense opposition from flak and night fighters. Whether or not this method of attack will be repeated is, of course a military secret but without doubt great credit must be given to the tenacity of this crew.'

Although many more raids were made by Mosquitos, that was the last major raid on Berlin by Bomber Command. The extract from 1409 Op Records summed it up:

F/O J Patient (P) F/O N.W.F. Green (NAV/W) and W/C Anderson (NAV) took off in LR 509 on the fourth sortie of the day. This was a special mission to Coltishall – Berlin – Stendal – Cuxhaven – PSN 54 degrees 30'N 07 degrees 30' E – Coltishall – Base, with W/C A as MC. After circling the German capital for forty minutes, the a/c returned to base without incident, apart from being coned near Hamburg, landing at 0110 hrs. The total duration being 4.40 hrs.

Two days later I was OC Flying when Flight Sergeant G.W. Roberts, who had returned from a short leave, asked to have an air test. I sent him, together with his Observer, Flight Sergeant D.S. Sabine, off in LR 509. They were only airborne fifteen minutes when the aircraft blew up with no survivors. The cause was never ascertained with certainty, my own theory being that with the hasty modification of the aircraft for its previous flight, plus the throwing about it had received from myself and the enemy, an electrical wire to the fuel pumps had perhaps become chafed and caused a spark. Under war conditions one must become fatalistic. I had flown 'S' for 4 hours and 40 minutes on its penultimate flight. Why, oh why should

I be the one to survive? I have always been a gambler and know that there is always a luck factor. This must have been the equivalent of winning the Irish sweepstake, followed next day with a record pools win.

Extract 1409 Op Records, 27 March 1944:

> *F/Sgt G.W. Roberts (P) and F/Sgt W. Sabine (NAV/W) took off in Mosquito IX LR 509 on what proved to be a disastrous flight, as news was received that they had crashed into the ground at 1515, that the machine had exploded, and they had both been killed. There were also rumours of the a/c being seen on fire in the air. "George and Dicky" had only been with us since the beginning of the year, but both were very keen and were becoming very useful members of the flight. They will long be remembered by all who knew them.'*

I had lost friends whom I knew better than George and Dicky, yet it seemed that this loss disturbed me more. Although I was kept busy with eight flights (but only one sortie) until the end of March, I was glad to get away for a spot of leave and put it all behind me by other indulgences. Two rather routine flights on 30 March, 1944, must, however, be mentioned.

Norry and I took of at 1035 hrs to 5500° N. 0500°E., after which we reported 4/10ths cumulus cloud over the sea with cloudbase at 1,660 feet and tops at 9,000 feet. A large amount of cumulus was noted and reported to the north of our furthest position. Landed at 1235 hrs. A further Pampa deep into Germany was carried out by Flying Officer T. Oakes (P) and Flight Lieutenant R.G. Gale (NAV/W) taking off at 1200 hrs. They reported seeing only fair weather cumulus throughout their route. These rather mundane flights are mentioned because of their relation to what has been described as the greatest error of judgement in any operation of Bomber Command, resulting in its biggest single loss. It would seem that the two reports were discounted because the bombing raid on Nuremberg that night was carried out in full moonlight and with little cloud cover. The results were disastrous. Ninety-five aircraft (sixty-four Lancasters and thirty-one Halifaxes) were lost, with very little damage to the target.

Wyton was like a morgue. Never had I experienced such silence, although many other stations had suffered greater losses. It is difficult to appreciate that more fully trained aircrew died in that one night than the total killed in Fighter Command during the whole of the Battle of Britain. Following as it did, less than one week after the traumatic flight to Berlin, when seventy-two aircraft were lost, I was glad to get away from the gloom for twelve days' leave.

I spent a lot of time with my old friends Sid Plumb and Roy Collins of LDV and Home Guard days and really whooped it up in an effort to forget that disastrous week. The way I was feeling I had no thought for the future and very selfishly had little thought for my own family either. Towards the end of the leave I calmed down, probably due to my money running out or perhaps a little conscience creeping in.

Back at Wyton, I had a bit of a scare with my first Pampa. This just crossed enemy territory and therefore counted as an operation. It was fortunate that it was a short trip. The starboard engine developed an oil leak and I was unable to feather the propeller. On the way home the vibration became very severe and it was difficult to maintain height. I felt that, if it became worse, the vibration might fracture the engine mounting with disastrous results, so I reduced speed as much as I dared and made a forced landing at Rivenhall. I had to be right first time because no way would it have been possible to overshoot. We made our weather report from there, about an hour later, an Oxford flown by Flying Officer Lewis-Watts arrived to take us back to base.

On 17 April HQ sent a very experienced pilot, Squadron Leader Rees, to test our GEE approach system. Of course Norry was chosen to demonstrate while I watched with binoculars from the control tower. They were airborne for only fifteen minutes. I began to think that something was wrong but was relieved to find the only problem was that the VHF and intercom were unserviceable. After changing aircraft, they were airborne again twenty minutes later. They made approaches on both ends of the runways and on a few other spots chosen by Rees at random. We discussed all the implications of our system with him before he returned to make his report and he told us he could have landed comfortably on all the approaches. He congratulated us on having the idea and Norry in particular on his faultless demonstration. We were told later that, after evaluating all the information, Group HQ decided that GEE landings were fine for very experienced crews, but that the human error factor meant that they could not recommend it for teaching to the main force and would not include it in the training programme. I was given to understand that the method was passed on to Coastal Command to adopt as a standby. Presumably a slight miscalculation or unnoticed wander of a blip over water, with no obstructions, would not be disastrous.

We were naturally disappointed but you can't win 'em all. I have no doubt that, had 'a bit of brass' thought of the idea first, it would have had a better chance, with no doubt an OBE or suchlike as acknowledgement for the inventor.

Our next Pampa was to Ymuiden – Barnstorf – Mülhausen – Prün – Voorne. We met heavy flak crossing the enemy coast and sporadic flak at various places en route. We considered it inaccurate if we couldn't hear it crack and continued, hesitating to alter our height or direction in case we ran into it, thereby compensating for its inaccuracy.

We had most unusual instructions on our next sortie. On 21 April we were called at 0210 hrs and took off for Abbeville – Koblenz – Rüthen – Egmond. At our furthest point we were to call the Master Bomber on VHF radio, informing him of the height and base of cloud at Cloppenburg (south of Oldenburg). We called Master Bomber a couple of times without reply. So we called Deputy Master Bomber, again with no reply. In desperation we called 'Deputy Deputy Master Bomber, can you hear me?' 'Loud and clear' came the reply. We gave the information as briefed as quickly as possible. I was concerned that with so much RT transmission the likelihood of fighters being homed onto us was high. It amazed me that the radar-controlled searchlights had not picked us up on our extended radio transmission. We left in a hurry, with a change of height and a certain amount of jinking, wondering whether the Master Bomber and the Deputy had been shot down, or if their RT sets had become unserviceable. On our return we were shocked to find ourselves a hundred miles south of our intended track as we crossed the French coast. However, eventually we landed after one more trip with a slight difference, and with three and a quarter hours to add to our night flying totals.

In between operations Norry several times managed to persuade Flying Officer Skitch, who was the instructor on the SBA Oxford, to give him some dual, thinking that later he might apply for a pilot's course. He was showing promise and I was pleased. If I were injured it wouldn't be the first time a navigator assisted a pilot in landing.

A brilliantly clear morning on 23 April saw us making huge contrails at 8 degrees E along the coast of Denmark near Esbjerg. Just as we were about to turn for home Norry called my attention urgently to four contrails about three miles behind us, with the comment, 'I don't care a bugger what George told you, let's get the hell out of here.' I didn't need any encouragement. I eased the stick forward and increased speed, flying out of the contrail level as we now had them in sight. I could not head immediately for our next turning point as this was due west and the pursuers would have been able to cut the corner and intercept. I therefore eased round to my next leg. They closed to about a mile but gave up shortly after, presumably low on fuel. We were then able to resume our track. All rather exciting, but as we had noticed them in plenty of time there was little danger involved. It would not have been a good time to have engine trouble.

While Norry was on leave for a few days I flew two stooges with Flight Lieutenant Dale DFC and equalled the old record set by Flight Sergeant F.Clayton of two sorties in one day. There followed an operation with the so-called king pin of the navigators, Flying Officer Green DFC, on 26 April to Walcheren – Aachen – Magdeburg – Nienburg – the Hague. Owing to GEE unserviceability and, despite the king pin factor, we finished up eighty miles south of track, something Norry secretly gloated about later. On 27 April, again for the Americans and with Flight Lieutenant Dale, we had what was virtually a Cook's tour round southern France for nearly three and a half hours.

Norry having returned, we were called at 0150 hrs on 28 April for a short Pampa to Vassey – Soissons – Ghent. On crossing the coast we found the flak and searchlights very active. We were coned twice in a short period and had to take evasive action several times. We were relieved to get back without damage, but realized that even short trips were not necessarily sinecures. Although we had by now completed about forty-five sorties each, there were still more to be done and we were well aware that, according to statistics, the last few trips, like the first few, contained the highest percentage of losses.

During our next Pampa on 1 May Norry drew my attention to a lot of flashes and explosions on the ground, but with no visible bursts of flak, he decided to take a fix on the centre of activity before continuing our route. When we returned to base we found out from the intelligence chaps that intruder fighters had been attacking an enemy airfield. Bomber Command was not the only section of the RAF which was keeping busy.

We had to take off in a hurry on 4 May. An Observer, J.C. Baker, had been taken ill on a flight and the plane had to return. He handed the route maps to Norry and we were airborne in the same aircraft within fifteen minutes. We completed the sortie, a stooge out into the Atlantic. After debriefing on our return we had the welcome news of fourteen days' leave to recharge our batteries.

I spent the first few days with my mother, who remarked that I was looking much older and suggested that I was burning the candle at both ends! The rest of the time was spent at home with various reunions, often at nearby dances. My old car broke down towards the end of my leave, putting an end to gallivanting, so I went to De Havillands and managed to scrounge a lift with Squadron Leader Cox from Hatfield to Wyton on one of the very earliest Mosquitos, a Mark 2, W 4052. This prototype Mosquito, built as the F2 (fighter) had umpteen alterations and modified experiments during its lifetime, with various mixtures of guns, cannons and weird-looking airbrakes round the fuselage.

W 4051 and 4052 were built (for security reasons) at Salisbury Hall, a moated manor house where a hangar had been built and disguised as a barn. W 4051 when completed had been dismantled and then re-erected at Hatfield for the initial test flights by Geoffrey de Havilland jnr. These were so successful that he flew W 4052 on 15 May, 1941, from a short field only 450 yards long adjoining the 'barn' where it had been built, so saving valuable weeks. News of this development must have reached German intelligence because only a day or two previously a German spy, K.R. Richer, had parachuted into a nearby field. He was quickly apprehended and later executed.

★　　★　　★

Upon our return from leave we were, of course, on top of the roster, but there was a lull and, except for a couple of air tests, we were not called until 24 May when we carried out a short daylight sortie to Leiden – Helmond – Maastricht – Knokke without incident. The only time we ever had a recall was on 28 May after only being airborne for ten minutes. Then, on 29 May, we flew to Ijmuiden – Kassel – Berlin – Hamburg, all points heavily defended and reminding us of grave events. We took off at 0500 hrs. This meant it was daylight as we crossed the enemy coast. We found a contrail level at 25,000 feet passing Kassel and climbed 3,000 feet into it to enable us to have as much warning as possible. The Hun was very sensitive about Berlin and seldom did anyone venture near without a positive response of some sort. At that time anyone shooting down a Mosquito was credited with two kills.

Norry suggested doing a box round the Big City rather than over the top, which I was about to suggest myself. On the continual lookout for clouds (which weren't there) one felt stark naked while watching for the signs of life which could spell death. I would have felt more comfortable had we had guns, yet, strangely, I thought of a saying heard so often during my childhood: 'He who fights and runs away, lives to fight another day.' As there was virtually no weather in sight to report, it did not matter if we altered our route a little. We flew well north past Eberswalde before turning towards home, hoping that this move would make things difficult for fighters on the way to intercept. They would be using up valuable fuel waiting for us.

Shortly after turning 90 degrees to port on course towards Hamburg, we noticed to the right of us, on the edge of the Baltic, what appeared to be a huge runway, many times wider than a normal one. We wondered what it was used for. Norry asked me to fly over it while he took a line overlap photograph and plotted the position. We did this in perfectly clear conditions from 28,000 feet, keeping our eyes open all the time for unfriendly natives. We carried out the rest of our route to Hamburg and base without, to our intense relief, seeing any fighters and without any attention from the expected ack ack.

We arrived back at base after four hours and five minutes. By the time Norry had broadcast over the scrambler to the various intelligence commands, the photographic bods had brought the line overlap to the intelligence officers. There was a buzz of interest as they studied the prints. From the fix Norry had taken the position was found to be Peenemünde, a research station well tucked away off the beaten track. It was heavily involved in the development of Hitler's secret weapons with which he had hoped to alter the course of the war and to grasp victory by destroying cities and the morale of the British with doodle bugs and rockets. This V weapon development site had been put out of action in a massive raid by 596 aircraft during the night of 17/18 August, 1943, an operation which employed many novel features, later fully described in an excellent book by Martin Middlebrook, *The Peenemünde Raid*. The experts were obviously interested in the apparent recovery of the area shown clearly by our photographs.

From the sublime to the ridiculous. The next day we did a stooge over the North Sea. Norry was quite peeved at what he regarded as 'buckshee trips', but it was the luck of the draw. We were very busy this time with each crew flying Pampas almost every day. On 1 June we made one to St Brieuc – Savigny – Dreux – St Valery en Caux – Cap Gris Nez, with instructions to take photographs at Cap Gris Nez. The job was carried out to the letter and we landed after two hours and fifty minutes.

On 3 June we made a Pampa to Morlaix – Vièrge measuring cloud tops and base all the way round. We found it pretty solid from 18,000 feet down to 500 feet in most of the places. It was a bit dicey descending to 500 feet when not completely sure of our position, but it was required, so we did it thoroughly. Norry told me that it took over five minutes before all the groups, including the Army and Navy Headquarters, linked into his broadcast of this sortie. He had never before had so many questions thrown at him from so many quarters. We got the feeling that something dramatic was about to happen. Later we realized that it was probably this report which delayed the D-Day landings.

On the following evening an Ensa group gave a show at Wyton. One of the singers was Cherry Lynn, a pretty girl with a fine voice. An impromptu dance was arranged and Norry made a beeline for Cherry. He was dancing her out of the room and along the corridor, when the Station Commander popped his head out and called, 'Keep it on the island, Gilroy'. Sheepishly, he had to bring her back but not before he had arranged to meet her the following day.

On 6 June we were airborne at 1225 hrs to report on weather to the west of England down to the Scillies, then south-east to Guingamp in France. It was an unimaginable thrill as we flew over the English Channel to see hundreds of ships steaming towards the French coast. We realized that the promised invasion must have begun. Now that the fortunes of war had taken a complete turn, there was a feeling of elation and gratification that insignificant 'me' had taken a part in it. When we arrived back at base everyone from the lowest to the highest was thrilled and charged with emotion at what was now known as D-Day. After our debriefing and report, we joined in the jollifications, embracing all and sundry, and kissing every girl we met regardless of rank or beauty.

The following day, or I should say D-Day plus One, we did another operation to Voorne – Alost – Douai – Beauvais – Dieppe. On the way we saw RAF fighter aircraft crossing the enemy coast and felt sure that the ack ack and Luftwaffe had enough to contend with without bothering about one little Mosquito. Some of our fighter pilots were not very well up on their aircraft recognition, so there was an ever-present possibility of being shot down by one of our own in the general mayhem. This chance was reduced in the last few days

1. & 2. From boyhood to man-
hood. The author in 1942
and 1943.

3. 'But at last I was able to
marry my sweetheart Lucy'
(p. 7).

4. Mr and Mrs Thom, my hosts in Montreal. 'Never before or since have I received such hospitality and friendship' (p. 14).

5. 'I had become very fond of Bunty Ann in a brotherly way' (p.14).

6. 'A highlight of my time in Alberta was my friendship with Doreen' (p.16).

7. 'I have more than one picture of Joy with 'destroy' written on the back but under no circumstances could I destroy them' (p.26).

8. 'The Crew'. The author with Norry Gilroy.

9. Some of my buddies in 139 (Jamaica) Squadron (see p.29). L to
   R: Johnnie Ross, Ginger Hellyer, George Cash, Lenny James,
   Tommy Forsyth, Derek Scrase, 'Mac' McDonald, 'Curly' Addis,
   Johnnie Sharpe. (Ross, Hellyer, James, Forsyth, Addis and Sharpe
   were all killed in action.)

10. 1409 Met Flight - the Weather Boys - in early 1944 (see p.59). The author is seated third from the right.

11. 'I had barely got the words out of my mouth when we were peppered' (p.62). Norry and Joe, 6 November, 1943.

when all our aircraft had black and white stripes painted round their fuselages to help in recognition. The weather was still bad and the Navy were having difficulty in landing stores and munitions to supply the bridgeheads which had been established.

9 June was my birthday, and no one was more surprised than I to have reached the ripe old age of twenty-seven. The roster, being soul-less, celebrated it by sending us on an interesting trip to Le Treport – Bolbec – Le Mans – Granville with instructions to make a descent at Le Mans, ascertain the cloud base and so forth, and take photographs. Circling to make sure of our position before taking them, we came across a huge parade ground with what looked like troops lined up and ready for inspection. Without hesitation, opening my bomb doors I dived on the assembly. I had neither bombs nor guns but they did not know that. By putting the propellers into fine pitch which added to the scream of the engines, I must have made many of them soil their pants. When they saw the aircraft diving towards them, bomb doors open, they broke ranks and either threw themselves flat on their faces or ran like hell. I flew as low as I could and pulled up into the clouds before they could get a shot at us. I could see the funny side of it and had a good laugh on the way back. What a pity Norry hadn't got his brick ready but it was all over in a few minutes and I certainly wasn't going back.

Our deepest probe ever into the Atlantic was our next flight on 12 June, a round trip of 1,500 miles.

A feeling of anti-climax seemed to be creeping in as, on 15 June, we carried out what was to be our last operation together, although I didn't know it at the time. We flew to Flensburg – Stralsund – Salzwedel – the Hague, my 16th for the Americans. Our calm was rudely shaken on crossing the coast towards Flensburg as a ball of fire seemed to come up from the ground heading straight for us. Before I could take evasive action it veered away and up. We realized that we had seen the launching of a V2 rocket, on course for England. It gave us a few very uncomfortable moments. The rest of the trip of three and three-quarter hours was uneventful.

By this time I had completed altogether fifty-nine sorties,

forty-eight of which were with Norry as my observer. He had completed fifty-three, five with other pilots. I had expected to do one more operation and was prepared to carry on until Norry had completed his requirement, so I was quite surprised when we were informed on our return that we were both posted. After a long leave Norry was to go back to 1655 MTU as an instructor, I to Upwood as a test pilot. I was peeved not to be given leave at the same time as Norry. It would have been wonderful to have spent some time with each other to celebrate our survival after all we had been through together.

Before Norry left we had a celebration which was remembered for a long time. All the Met Flight (except the standby), plus many of the Lancaster crews of 83 Squadron, joined in. It was quite an event at that period of the war to survive an extended double tour with 8 Group Pathfinders. As Air Vice-Marshal Bennett said:

> *No. 1409 Flight never hesitated for one moment, and never failed to do their job with absolute reliability and consistency. In fact, even when aircraft unserviceability interrupted the flight it was only a matter of minutes before an alternative aircraft was in the air on the same job, or, alternatively, if the unserviceability occurred when the flight was well in hand, it would be completed in spite of the unserviceability. There were harrowing experiences for the crews of 1409 Flight when they were intercepted, particularly by the German jets just towards the end of the war, which could outpace them but not out-manoeuvre them. The anxiety to run for home had to be overcome whenever the enemy closed, so as to take advantage of the Mosquito's ability to out-turn the enemy.'*

As he said earlier, 'They flew high and fast, but the danger was extreme.'

5

Gliders

Being sent to Upwood as a test pilot was the last thing I had expected to happen.

Earlier, when I had done about forty-five sorties, I was told to report to the Senior Personnel Staff Officer (SPSO) Hamish Mahaddie, a well-known, highly decorated officer whose ability to tell stories was only surpassed by his smooth-tongued persuasiveness. He spoke in an attractive Scottish brogue, telling me that I had done a good job and that a posting awaited me which he thought I might like. I was to be instructing in Canada with the possibility of having my family with me. 'It's being organized over there but is not ready yet. How would you like to do another five trips meanwhile? Otherwise my only alternative at the moment would be Wellingtons.'

Being a simple soul, I was taken in by this approach. I was even more simple when another five trips were offered, then another five. At my third, I made it clear that there would be no more after that. He didn't let me finish the sixty trips that this last stint would have meant. I was pulled off at fifty-nine. No, not to Canada, but to Upwood nearby, testing broken-down, shot-up, patched-up Mosquitos. Also on test at Upwood were Canadian-built Mark XXs powered by Packard Merlins, made in the USA and all pansied up with chromium-plated nuts and the like, unlike our utility-built Rolls. Why precision engines built to the same specifications should be so different is beyond me, but, to pass those aircraft on as serviceable, we had to increase the normal permissible mag drop appreciably. For safety and efficiency, aircraft engines are fitted with two magnetos. When one is switched off, the RPM always drops a little and a maximum drop is specified for each type of engine. Provided that the drop is within this maximum, the engine is running smoothly and the RPM returns when switched on again, with each magneto tested in turn, the engine is serviceable.

When the Mark XXs arrived at Upwood they were then equipped to the requirements of the different squadrons, test-flown by me, and, like all the other marks, if satisfactory were delivered to their designated squadron without landing back at Upwood. This saved fuel as well as wear and tear. It also entailed a lot of travelling by road. However, there was occasionally another aircraft to pick up to be flown back to Upwood for repair or modification. Such was the case when I tested a Mark XX KB267 on 14 July, 1944, and delivered it to Woodhall Spa where I met the dynamic Wing Commander Guy Gibson VC DSO DFC. He was killed together with his Observer, Squadron Leader J.B. Warwick DFC, on that very aircraft, while acting as Master Bomber on the twin towns of Mönchengladbach/Rheydt on 19/20 September, 1944. They are buried in the Roman Catholic cemetery at Steenbergen-en-Kruisland, the only Allied servicemen to have graves there.

The squadrons were always screaming out for aircraft, so if there was only a minor fault I would deliver and explain what had to be done. Invariably they were only too glad to accept the aircraft. This practical consideration on my part was not the reason, but the excuse for my removal from 8 Group.

I only spent about four weeks at Upwood. During that time I made sixty-nine flights including forty-one 'test and deliver' flights. I had more than one hairy experience in patched-up aircraft but one of them frightened the life out of me. I was just airborne on a Mark 3 (HJ 971) when one engine vibrated like mad and threatened to shake the aircraft apart. The propeller refused to feather, but the shaking reduced a little when I throttled back. I made a wide circuit at only 100 feet or so, with one engine windmilling, struggling to maintain height. I breathed a sigh of relief when I got down. On investigation it was found that one of the blades was out of true, thus causing the vibration.

By this time I had become so familiar with the flying characteristics of the Mossie that often, when I was alone, I would take off, make a circuit and land with one hand on the throttles and the other on the elevator trimmer, not touching the control column except to apply the brakes. With practice it became easy. Co-ordination between throttle and sensitive use of trimmer were all that were needed. One of the ground crew was rather disliked (to put it mildly) and I was told that he hated flying. We could always insist that anyone who had worked on an aircraft should fly in it when on test. Before the next local air test, I told the man in question that I was going to show him how safe and easy it is to fly. He demurred but I insisted, while the others tried to hide their grins. I performed one of my hands-off circuits and in the end felt quite sorry for the white-faced passenger. He almost fell out of the plane when I switched off.

My relationship with ground crews was always very friendly. With petrol rationing, I would never have been able to dash off so often on short breaks home had my car not so frequently disappeared while I was flying, only to be mysteriously full of petrol when I later picked it up. I greatly admired the ground crews. Had it not been for my reserved occupation, I could easily have been one of them, so inadequately paid and without the glamour of wearing a brevet.

I never considered my period of testing as a rest from operations but enjoyed the challenge it presented. Consequently, I was furious when told that I had been posted to Silverstone as an instructor on Wellingtons. When I left the Met Flight and went to Upwood as the test pilot, I hadn't realized that I would then come directly under Sarsby (see page 70), who by that time had become a Group Captain. It did not need much imagination to see why I had been posted. He probably disliked me as much as I disliked him. When I asked Hamish the reason, he said that it had been reported that I had tested and delivered several aircraft substandard. So my earlier indignation had not done me any good. However, in a remote way, my posting to Silverstone led indirectly to my eventual promotion to squadron leader.

★ ★ ★

Silverstone (No. 17 OTU) placed great emphasis on tradition and bull. The friendly, relaxed attitude normally prevalent on operational stations was foreign to Training Command and those coming from ops were quickly reminded of the fact. For me, there was another marked difference. After the speed, power and manoeuvrability of the Mosquito, the Wellington was a wallowing old duck. I soon discovered this when I was given 45 minutes dual with Flight Lieutenant Hawkins DFM on 6 August, followed by solo circuits and landings. I had never operated with a large crew, always with a trained Observer. What could I teach them? Actions which I would take in a Mosquito under fire couldn't possibly be used in a heavy. It seemed to me that my function was more that of a safety pilot watching for signs of inefficiency than an instructor.

On one occasion when I thought I could teach them something I got one hell of a dressing down from the CO. I was OIC (Officer in Charge) of flying for that night. When the Met forecast came in I found it OK and sent the crews off on a cross-country, myself with Warrant Officer Bolter and crew. The flight was completed with just a little cloud, moderate turbulence and slight icing (or so it seemed to me). On my return I was astonished to find that, even with instructors on board, some of the flights had aborted. In the morning I was sent for by the OC Flying, acting Wing Commander G.D. Lyster DSO, DFC. 'Patient, how dare you send off crews in such appalling weather? Such irresponsibility is very reprehensible,' and so on. I reported that I had flown myself and that conditions certainly were not bad. If crews were not given experience of weather at that stage, there would be many aborted sorties and bomb loads jettisoned when they got to squadrons.

He was obviously taken aback at being spoken to in this way by a subordinate and suggested that my specialist experience in weather had clouded my judgement as to the requirements of inexperienced crews. I was to be more careful in the future. He continued, 'I noticed the other day that you did not take any steps to enforce discipline when a sergeant passed you without saluting. I am therefore going to delay your flight lieutenancy for three months.' What appalling self-righteousness. I felt like telling him just what I thought of him and his station but for once I managed to keep quiet. With a hint of sarcasm I simply said, 'Is that all Sir?'

I was sent to 92 Group Instructors' Flight on a course which lasted eighteen days. I flew twenty-seven times, rarely doing anything other than circuits and bumps, overshoots and single-engine flying. This was great stuff which would have been a real help had they sent me there first. I had, by that time, after only 45 minutes dual on a Wellington, already flown as an instructor on eleven occasions. How we managed to win the war with such obvious mismanagement is a mystery. It would be difficult to imagine such a thing happening in the Luftwaffe. I returned to Silverstone with not much more to show for it than another 31 hours and 15 minutes added to my total flying hours.

Back at Silverstone I met another pilot, Flying Officer T.A. Austin DFC, who had just completed a tour of ops. We naturally had much in common. We became friends and were usually together when our off-duty coincided. At the bar in the evenings we frequently overheard, 'If only we could get on ops.' The speakers were moaning that once in Training Command you were stuck there. I often felt a suspicion of hypocrisy and insincerity in all this, a feeling shared by my new friend. He too was disgusted when I told him the outcome of the up and down I'd had with the OC Flying. Many of the instructors had been there a considerable time and certainly did not welcome me with the warmth received in operational messes. They seemed to keep apart, but when the 'brass' came in, the deference and toadying up at the bar was obvious. For that reason we chose to do most of our drinking in nearby Towcester, where the atmosphere and the customers were more congenial.

A most unusual sequence of events then followed which only added to my suspicion of hypocrisy at Silverstone. After the catastrophe of Operation Market Garden (Arnhem), the Glider Pilot Regiment

(GPR) was decimated and the only feasible way to reconstitute it quickly was to enlist the aid of the RAF, who at the time had a surfeit of trained pilots.

Brigadier Chatterton was ordered to prepare a glider force large enough to fly 2,000 gliders across the Rhine. In desperation he went to see Air Chief Marshal Sir Peter Drummond (Director of Training RAF) who agreed to transfer RAF-trained pilots into the Glider Pilot Regiment. It was decided to re-form the GPR on an approximately fifty-fifty basis, Army and RAF. Each squadron would be formed alternately with either a Major as CO and Flight Lieutenant as second-in-command, or a Squadron Leader CO with a Captain as 2iC.

As the Army needed 5–600 RAF pilots, volunteers were sought from the newly-trained, who at that time had few prospects of being posted to squadrons. Not unexpectedly, the response was there. After a short course on light gliders, they were given a more comprehensive course on the Horsa and intensive infantry weapon training. But there remained a vacuum of leadership, for the vast majority of the volunteers had never experienced a shot fired in anger.

The Americans were also short of glider pilots and had to utilize power-trained pilots to make up the required numbers.

To this end, a remarkable signal was distributed through the various commands asking for volunteers from experienced pilots as leaders, with the reward of Flight Lieutenant rank and immediate release from current duties. Here was the moment of truth for those protesting 'if only we could get on ops'. There were only two volunteers from 17 OTU Silverstone who answered this urgent call – Flying Officer T.A. Austin and myself. It really tickled me that acting Wing Commander Lyster, DSO, DFC and later AFC, who only a few days before had held up my promotion, now had to recommend me for a Flight Lieutenant posting.

I am afraid that what I have written will offend many readers who may have served in Flying Training Command, but I have no intention of gilding lillies. Naturally, there are always exceptions.

I have already mentioned that I spent many weeks at the Public

Record Office at Kew and elsewhere, trying to confirm details of some of the many incidents I have described. In many cases details are incomplete or totally absent. According to the records of 17 OTU Silverstone, I never arrived there, but there is evidence that Flying Officer T.A. Austin and myself were posted from Silverstone to Bridgnorth.

⋆ ⋆ ⋆

On a lighter note, we had an ENSA show at Silverstone starring Pat Kirkwood. I got chatting to her in the Mess afterwards. She was a very attractive young woman who that night was wearing a dress with a crossover bodice of two different colours. This had the effect (to my eyes) of making one of her breasts appear lower than the other. While I was talking my eyes must have kept wandering, because she asked me what was the matter. So I told her! Fortunately the embarrassment of the moment was alleviated by a senior officer who joined us, but she was not amused.

An amusing coincidence occurred during my stint at Silverstone. It was my wont to ask pupil pilots where they had trained. One happened to have been to Claresholm. When I mentioned that I had trained there, he remarked that he intended to return after the war and marry a waitress from 'Bill's Coffee Shoppe' and proudly showed me a photo of himself and Doreen, taken outside. Amazingly, it was as though he had changed places with me at the same time and place just two years (yet it seemed a lifetime) earlier. What memories that photo recalled. I later showed him the picture of myself and Doreen, but refrained from any further comment.

I was sent to Bridgnorth for weapons training. We did little of that but a lot of PT. We were only there two weeks but I left feeling fitter though very little wiser. I certainly failed to learn anything from the sadists who, while you were struggling through an assault course, stood about nonchalantly throwing thunderflashes unpleasantly close.

When we arrived at No. 3 GTS (Glider Training School) Zeals, they were in process of transferring to Culmhead, and on 9 December, 1944, I was ferried between the two as a passenger in a

Hotspur glider. After an hour and a half dual I went solo, and experienced eleven tows (just over three hours in all).

Flying in gliders is an entirely different sensation from flying powered aircraft, the nearest to it being the throttled back approach and glide of a light aircraft. After release from the tug aircraft, the stillness, quiet and floating sensation is remarkable. There is very little time to appreciate it on a circuit, as you have to concentrate on getting down in the right spot. There is no going round again if you get it wrong. But, with a remote release high up, one can enjoy moments of pure ecstasy. The simplicity of instrumentation and the magnificent all-round view from a light glider are fantastic.

I went on to 22 Heavy Glider Conversion Unit (HGCU) Fairford. After 45 minutes dual on the Horsa with Flying Officer Blackman, I went solo on Christmas Eve. The glider training was intense, including just one snatch take off dual in the Hadrian, followed by one snatch solo. A snatch was used for the recovery of gliders from areas too small for a tug aircraft to take off. The towing rope was joined to a line suspended between two poles, then the tug would fly across low and pick up with a hook trailing from the underside of the aircraft. The consequent acceleration in the glider from a standing start was quite an experience. I also occasionally acted as a second pilot on that ridiculously under-powered apology of an aeroplane, the Albemarle, which was used for towing at Fairford. I ended the course with twenty-two tows between 22 December and 5 January, 1945.

My body was then subjected to the greatest humiliation and torture I have ever experienced at the hands of other 'humans'. I was posted to the Army's Fargo Camp on Salisbury Plain for weapons training. We were billeted in Nissen huts, the toilets and wash places conveniently well away from our quarters. The architect who designed the layout must have been extremely sadistic. I shiver now just to think about it. It was midwinter and bitterly cold.

The weapons training was thorough. We all wore the same denim-type clothing, with no insignia of rank, but the instructors knew who were the officers and seemed to delight in allocating the dirtier jobs to them. I could never understand why we had to crawl through mud and slime to learn how to use a Bren gun, throw a hand grenade or carry the mounting, the bombs or the mortar. This torture was always carried out miles away from the huts and wash houses.

Then there were the assault courses. These were far worse than any shown on television. At the end of a long and gruelling sequence of crawling, jumping and climbing, you were expected to walk along a large slippery tree trunk from which you had to jump down and across a mire of evil-smelling mud to a safe landing on terra firma. The only snag was that it would have taken an Olympic long jump champion with a running start to succeed. Even if he managed it, he would have broken his legs on landing. We, of course, landed right in the mud and would be lucky not to get a mouthful by falling forward. During the wade and climb out, a sadistic army corporal continually shouted derisively, 'Is that the best you flabby lot can do?' Then followed a long jog back to quarters, freezing in our singlets and shorts, where the water in the ablutions would be cold. If you complained you were simply told (lied to) that, had you made a decent time on the course, the water would have been hot.

There was one particularly nasty drill corporal who I am quite sure had never seen enemy action. In a raucous voice he was always yelling, 'Wait till yer git under fire', as he demonstrated with obvious relish how to stick a bayonet into the enemy's guts and how to remove it with a twist. It was as if he was experiencing an orgasm as he demonstrated.

At the end of the course, which seemed like an eternity but was just short of a month, we had the customary all ranks party to which we invited the instructors, despite our aversion to some of them. As I was the senior officer, it was my duty to welcome the guests on arrival and point them to the hastily prepared table which constituted the bar, with just beer and soft drinks, as spirits were not allowed on these courses. We were naturally resplendent in best blue with rank and service ribbons on view. After a while that particularly obnoxious corporal sidled up to me and, looking a little shamefaced remarked, 'Of course I didn't mean people like you, Sir.' I was in party mood and with a touch of hypocrisy replied, 'You were only doing your job.'

Until joining the GPR my service life with the squadrons had been spent on pre-war permanent stations where the officers' messes had every comfort and facility. I felt very strongly about the unnecessary discomfort we were subjected to at Fargo Camp. After all, we were volunteers and not pressgang recruits. I seldom drink spirits and I didn't then, but I felt annoyed that they were forbidden in the bare Nissen hut which passed for an Officers' Mess and bar, so I persuaded another officer to go with me to the Army Officers' Mess used by the senior instructors and administrative officers, which boasted a billiard table and a bar dispensing spirits. After my colleague and I had signed the visitors' book, we went to the billiards room which fortunately was empty. I set up the balls for a game of snooker and told my colleague to wait while I went to the bar and bought a whisky for myself (on principle) and a beer for him. I ignored the raised eyebrows of the 'brown jobs' who probably saw me for the first time in best blue, bought the drinks and without a word returned to the billiard room.

We had barely resumed our game when an army captain in a rather imperious manner enquired if we were on a course, and if so, would we leave at once. After asking his name, I pointed out that the many and various regulations posted in our quarters had no instruction forbidding visits to the Permanent Mess. In any case I felt such an instruction would be contrary to King's Regulations – that irrefutable Bible of the services. Moreover, I fancied a whisky which wasn't available to me elsewhere. As we were of equal rank, I suggested he go and find a senior officer to order us out. Should this occur, I would follow it up with a redress of grievance application to the CO. The captain no doubt went back and conferred with the others and we finished our game. We soon left, but not before I had made my point.

Much as I disliked my stay at Fargo Camp, I must grudgingly admit that when I left I was much fitter physically and much more competent to face an enemy at close quarters. However, I still consider that the same result, or better, could have been achieved in a less spartan and more friendly manner.

After being kitted out with khaki battle dress uniform and the famous red beret of the GPR, I spent about two weeks with J squadron at RAF station Keevil near Trowbridge for refresher lifts on a Horsa. I was sent on a senior officers' training course at Oxford University on 11 March. This was the first time I had been inside a university of any kind and I was most impressed. The magnificent buildings seemed to emit power and authority. The course itself was mainly an introduction to management of a military unit. Some of the problems were involved, owing to the unusual situation of the GPR being a mixed Army and RAF unit with procedures peculiar to each of those services, especially those concerned in dealing with miscreants. During the course we were taught the limitations of power of commanding officers, Army and RAF law and delegation of authority. In short, what to do and what not to do. We also had to handle hypothetical situations likely to occur. The aspect of the course which surprised me most was the giving of orders on the parade ground. I did wonder whether the course was designed to prepare you for command, or to check whether you might be suitable to take command.

It is said that if you have sufficient knowledge of King's Regulations it is possible to get away with almost any crime or misdeed in the armed forces. One lovely example of this is the story of the officer who was found stark naked in a bedroom in the women's quarters. When he was charged with 'Conduct prejudicial to good order and discipline', he obtained his acquittal by quoting KRs: 'An officer should at all times be dressed appropriately to the sport in which he is engaged.'

Operation Varsity (the Rhine crossing) was carried out while I was on the course. After all the sweat and bodily aggravation suffered to prepare me to take part in a glider operation, I had been left out. I experienced a sickening feeling of let down. I suppose from one point of view I was lucky to miss the operation. Although the losses were relatively slight, I might have been one of them. Perhaps I should have felt thankful rather than frustrated. It is, however, quite amazing that, in just ten weeks, the GPR had reorganized, trained and carried out Operation Varsity successfully.

After the course I was engaged in flying as 2nd pilot in Albemarles from Keevil to Netheravon and towed back in a Horsa, making eight flights each way over a four-day period.

Flight Lieutenant McGregor mentioned that he was to fly to Germany to pick up casualties. I requested permission to go with him as co-pilot and this was granted. On 7 April, with Warrant Officer Connolly as navigator, we took Dakota KN 278 to Gilze Rijen where we had lunch. We were served by attractive German girls, but noticed that there was a prominent sign 'No fraternization'. We flew on to Nijmegen to pick up the stretcher casualties and their nurses, and then to Redhill to discharge them. I could only spend a short time in the cabin, but the looks of pain and the moans at any involuntary buffeting of the aircraft made me return to the cockpit where I disconnected the autopilot in an effort to fly the aircraft as smoothly as the weather and my ability allowed. The dreadful effects of war are seldom experienced at close quarters, although often caused by operational pilots.

A famous wicket keeper and cricketer, Lieutenant Colonel S.C. Griffiths DFC, was the one to tell me that I had been promoted and appointed CO of M Squadron GPR with effect from 18 April, 1945, and allocated a Tiger Moth for personal use. The few weeks which followed at Great Dunmow were probably the biggest challenge of my RAF career. The responsibility of command, particularly of mixed Army/RAF personnel, was taxing to say the least. Without the help of a very worldly-wise and experienced old sweat of a Warrant Officer I might well have foundered. His insight concerning the miscreants taken to task was enlightening and I relied heavily on his pre-judgement and suggested punishment, before hearing the varied and sometimes tear-jerking excuses put forward.

I gave a demonstration spot landing to a group from the Air Ministry on 25 April, but an exercise, Alabaster, planned for later had to be abandoned owing to an explosion at the bomb dump. We then had to prepare for a Balbo (mass landing) exercise, Amber, on 3 May. The intention was that 280 crews should land 360 Horsas and forty Hamilcars on to five landing zones in two lifts. My squadron was to provide thirty-six crews, with spare crews to take the place of any who might not return from the first lift. I also had to detail and supervise the loading of the gliders to be flown by the Wing Headquarters crews, this to include Major General Urquhart's glider. Times at target were for the first lift 1055 hrs and the second 1825 hrs. My own load on this occasion included two jeeps with crews.

Only five days later all squadrons were given 48 hours off duty to celebrate VE day. I remember it well, going directly to Piccadilly Circus to join the huge crowds rejoicing and dancing in the streets. With tears of happiness mixed with laughter, it was a day and night of memories to be cherished. (Yes, Bette, you were wonderful).

It was sad that such an occasion should have caused the death of two of our officers. Flying Officer J. Bower was killed in a crash at Golders Green and Flying Officer Brabner in a road accident returning from Bournemouth. It was inevitable that quite a few over-stayed their 48-hour pass, but for the most part I was sympathetic and dismissed the charges.

Japan still had to be beaten. Lieutenant-Colonel Griffiths gave the squadron a talk and briefing at Earls Colne on the subject and told us that crews were needed to take conversion courses on to Hadrian gliders as these were more suitable for use in the Far East. The GPR then arranged summer camps at Gorleston-on-Sea. However, the initial cheers which greeted this announcement changed to groans when it was emphasized that the camp was not a holiday camp, but a field training exercise with mobile kitchens. The aim was to keep fit by PT, bathing, games and marching, and to practise small arms shooting. Troops were to take bare necessities and full field equip-ment for fourteen days during which no laundry facilities would be available. The order and instructions ended: 'Squadron Commanders are invited to visit the camp whenever possible. The camp commandant will arrange accommodation if given short notice!

My penance at the Armys' Fargo camp had been enough to last me a lifetime. Although, as CO, I would be looking at, rather than subjected to 'the mire', I am not of a sadistic nature, so I found that I was busy elsewhere.

On one of my rounds of inspection, I saw a Mosquito land and went to meet it. The pilot, who had about an hour's business to attend to at Station HQ, said he would have no objection to my flying it so long as it was not pranged. What a joy to fly a real aeroplane again. Joe and Mossie Mk 30 MT 481 were united for half an hour.

Tom McGeorge was a JP and greatly respected farmer in Milden Pound in the Lavenham neighbourhood of Suffolk. I forget how I became friends with him and his wife, Connie, but I remember introducing him to flying by landing in one of his fields in the Tiger Moth when staying there for the weekend. Another house guest at the time was Colonel H. Todt from the US Air Force base at Lavenham, who was interested in the fact that I had carried out sixteen sorties for the US. I had taken with me an article from *Illustrated* magazine on 24 March, 1945, showing two pictures of myself involved in briefing. The caption read, 'The cream of Britain's fighting forces.' Tom's remark, 'You know what cream is Joe? The scum off the milk.'

Colonel Todt expressed a wish to see the gliders, so I invited him to Great Dunmow. When he arrived with jeep and driver, I sent the driver back saying that I would take the Colonel back to Lavenham by air after he had looked round and had lunch. I gave him experience of the Tiger Moth on the way to Lavenham, ending up with a display of aerobatics over the airfield. After landing, he asked if he could make a circuit solo. I agreed so long as I could do the same on the B17 (Flying Fortress). He arranged this, naturally with a safety pilot in the other seat. I was astonished how docile and easy it was to fly. She seemed to handle just like an overgrown Anson, that wonderful, viceless old lady. Todt's flight in the Tiger Moth, however, caused me a number of anxious moments as a wind had developed and it was only after two overshoots that he managed to get it down. I had visions of a Court Martial if he had pranged it. I stayed the night and returned to Dunmow next day.

During my stay Tom mentioned his difficulties in harvesting, and I suggested that I would deploy a squad of the GPR to help if he was willing to feed and house them. Although there was no obligation for me to ask for volunteers, I did so, and the squadron responded to a man. I organized a rotation of men using a three-ton truck. McGeorge looked after them so well that I never heard one word of complaint. I explained the operation as an initiative scheme. I visited him frequently and gave him some dual in the Tiger Moth. The flying bug got into him and later when I returned from Palestine he had his own pilot's licence and, eventually, his own plane. On one of my visits, he seriously suggested nominating me to his local Conservative committee as a parliamentary candidate. 'Tom,' I replied with a chuckle, 'I know I'm a bit of a crook, but I am too honest and outspoken to be an MP.'

Shortly after taking over M Squadron, it was suggested to me that we should operate initiative schemes to keep our high-spirited glider pilots out of mischief. After consultation with my officers, we devised various problems for pairs, one Army and one RAF. The tasks were formidable and varied. The prizes were weekend passes for the best three results from NCOs, while for officers there was one prize of a week excused OO (Orderly Officer). I was paired with Lieutenant Maclain (the Maclain of Lochbuie) who amazed me with his bare-faced cheek. Our task was to obtain a print of a Horsa glider and then get it signed by King George VI. The conditions of the exercise were that it must be finished within three days and that no more than half a crown could be spent by each person. After a confab with the other officers, it was agreed that I could use my jeep, providing there was the same amount of petrol in the tanks when we returned.

The first move was easy. We went to De Havillands at Hatfield where I was known and managed to get a print with little trouble. I confessed that I was worried about the petrol situation, but Maclain said not to worry as he had a plan which he refused to divulge. I knew of a picture framer in St Albans. I told him how proud he would be to have a picture framed by him, signed by HM and shown in an officers' mess. It worked like a charm and the carefully framed Horsa picture was on its way to Buck House. We had to leave the jeep outside the palace, but were allowed through to the equerry's office where we were dismayed to learn that HM only signed pictures of himself for officers' messes.

What now? We conferred and agreed that the next best thing would be the Prime Minister's signature. We were astounded at the ease with which we entered the War Office in Whitehall without being challenged, and we actually got near the PM's office before being arrested. Had we been armed we could easily have assassinated a whole mass of high dignitaries. We were detained in a cell at Scotland Yard for a few hours while all sorts of rumours were circulating about two spies roaming round the offices in Whitehall. We were visited by a Colonel Intelligence Officer who had thoroughly checked our unlikely story and ordered us to discontinue our project and return to our unit. Fortunately, he omitted the word 'immediately'.

Maclain then took me to his club in Pall Mall for a meal and to my surprise added a third pip to his epaulettes. I have heard of immediate promotion in the field, but not in Pall Mall. We then went to an exclusive night club where he was greeted warmly by many young 'plum in mouth' socialites. The following month a society magazine printed a photograph (myself included) with the caption 'Captain the Maclain of Lochbuie and friends'.

On our return to Dunmow, Mac routed me to enter an American Motor Transport Depot and, with 'leave this to me', asked to see the officer in charge. When he arrived Mac informed him that I had been ordered up to Buckingham Palace for the investiture of my DFC. 'No problem, Buddy, congratulations, hey sergeant, fill this goddamned jeep up will yer. Have a nice day, guys.' I am sure that I was blushing at the sheer cheek of it, but at least we returned to base with more petrol than we had set out with, and I still had my half-crown.

The following days were spent with the various pairs recounting their adventures, and votes were taken to judge the winners. I was astounded by the versatility of these young men who for the most part would shortly be returning to their civilian jobs. I am convinced that there are certain sorts of genes which seem to make fliers a species apart from the rest of the human race. The future will, I am sure, be influenced by them.

While at Dunmow I was elected PMC (President of the Mess Committee). During my period of office I arranged a ball and managed to get quite a few celebrated guests to attend, including Douglas Bader. I collected Lucy (who wore my Irvin jacket to keep warm) in my jeep from St Albans, having arranged to stay the night (or what was left of it) at the Saracen's Head in Dunmow. The next morning we were much amused to see Rowly (a Flight Lieutenant) who had brought an obvious 'mutton dressed as lamb' lady to the party, walking a pekingese while she was having breakfast.

Demobilization was now in progress. I had become friendly with Squadron Leader Fisher, a flight commander with 620 Squadron (Halifax Airborne Support) who were our tugs at the time. He suggested that I should apply for a transfer back to powered aircraft with a conversion to heavies. As 620 Squadron was scheduled for Palestine, it would be necessary to sign on for an additional eighteen months in order to qualify. Not knowing what I would do in civvy street, I agreed to the further period of service in the hope of a permanent commission later. I was, however, a little dubious about the peacetime air force which even then had started to revert to unnecessary bull.

*　　*　　*

After release from my command of M Squadron GPR, I was sent to 1665 HCU Saltby (where I flew the Halifax four-engined bomber) on 17 July, 1945. There I was introduced to my crew. They were Warrant Officer Fisher (navigator), Flight Sergeants Mitchell (bomb aimer), Mutton (wireless operator), Hayden (flight engineer) and Griffin (air gunner) – 'with whom I was well pleased'. On 19 July I was given nearly three hours familiarization, circuits and bumps on the Halifax with Flight Lieutenant Maloney DFC and the next day sent solo for just over an hour. Another two and a quarter hours solo next day was followed by night flying dual with Flight Lieutenant Clapperton for seventy minutes, followed by an hour's solo.

The very next day I joined 620 Squadron and flew with my crew to Brussels with some army chaps plus loads of kit, then on to Copenhagen and back to base. Then we went to an airfield called Schleswig-land on 23 July to pick up twelve RCAF men with their kit and obvious booty. I now had two days to get to know the crews of 'A' flight which I had taken over.

While I was a Flight Commander with 620 Squadron at Great Dunmow a Flight Lieutenant attempted to take off in a Halifax and crashed at the end of the runway. The crew clambered out unhurt though shaken. I arrived at the crashed aircraft almost immediately and was the first to enter the cockpit. I checked 'switches off' and so forth and was about to leave the aircraft to question the crew when I had a double take. I could hardly believe it, but the ground locks were still on the controls. The cause of the accident was cut and dried, or so I thought. There are enough natural hazards in flying aeroplanes and I have always taken the view that a pilot who makes careless mistakes deserves to die. In this case I was very angry, as he could well have killed the other five members of his crew.

I was astounded when there was a whipround among the officers to help pay for a London Barrister, Mr Bernard Gillis KC, assisted by Mr C.S. Brown, to defend this officer at his trial, although I knew that I was to give evidence which would convict him. Or, so I thought. At the trial on 7 November, 1945, it was suggested that I had put the control locks on. Although I protested, I was told to answer nothing but 'yes' or 'no' to the next question. This was 'When you entered the crashed aircraft, would it have been possible for you to have put the locks on?' I was reminded that I must answer 'yes' or 'no'. Obviously it would have been possible and I had to answer 'yes'. I was then dismissed. The barrister received a fat fee, the pilot was acquitted and I had the most uncomfortable time, my faith in justice shattered.

Shortly after joining 620 Squadron, I was sent on an RAF/Army cooperation course at Old Sarum and arranged to live out at a guest house in Salisbury where Lucy joined me. We had a most enjoyable time, just like a second honeymoon. The course itself was not very demanding, and mostly concerned inter-service cooperation, signals, availability of back-up and discussions in depth about the lessons learned at Arnhem and from previous glider invasions. On Sunday we called a taxi to take us to the evening service and asked the driver to go to the cathedral. When we stopped, he opened the door, and we found that he had taken us to the Cathedral Arms. We all had a good laugh but he was quite embarrassed when he realized where we wanted to go. During the sermon, which was about gambling, I burst out laughing at one point, and enjoyed a chat with the preacher after the service.

The functions of 620 Squadron were many and varied. They included glider towing, parachute and container dropping, and bomb disposal in the Channel. As a flight commander, most of my flying was for the purpose of making periodical fight checks with my crews. On 2 August I was briefed to fly Wing Commander Slater AFC plus eight others who were all specialists (or supposed to be) in some aspects of proving and planning a route from Brussels to Athens in order to repatriate Greeks from the concentration and work camps in Germany. We night-stopped in Brussels, Naples, Athens and Istres (Marseilles) on the return. The problems of night stops with a load of repatriates were daunting and it was decided that this would be overcome by an early start from Brussels with a refuelling stop at Foggia and flight to Athens the same day. This I carried out with my own crew on 25 August. Mattresses were laid all along the floor for the pitiful shells of human beings we carried like cattle from Brussels to Athens. From the way they had staggered into the aircraft, I was surprised that they arrived alive. The stench was almost unbearable and I insisted on a two-night stay and fumigation of the aircraft before we returned to the UK. It was a depressing experience and I managed to avoid a repetition.

The exchange rate in Greece at that time was very good so I took my NCO crew into a decent restaurant for a good meal. A pompous army captain came over to our table and barked, 'Do you know this is an officers' only restaurant?' After the trauma of the flight, my mood was not conciliatory, so I stood up. 'Did the Army not teach you to address senior officers as Sir? Now bugger off and mind your own business.' The next day I almost expected some sort of reaction, but nothing transpired so we all went on a tour round the city. In the evening I was asked to take Wing Commander Papanagiotou (I couldn't pronounce it) of the Greek Air Force through to the UK, which I did next day, reversing the route.

On 5 September it was arranged for me to demonstrate to a large gathering of very senior brass at Old Sarum a jeep, gun and container drop by parachute at low level. These were slung under the belly of the Halifax. As we peeled away after the release, my crew informed me that one of the chutes had not opened. Wanting to have a good look, I made a steep turn. Meanwhile the crowd of brass had hurried towards the drop. When completing my turn I made a banked dive to low level to see the result for myself. As I neared, the crowd stopped, hesitated, then thinking perhaps that I was dropping some-thing more, scattered in all directions, much to our amusement. I then thought it expedient to vanish quickly from the scene of the crime and returned to base.

The remaining weeks of 1945 were involved in provision of trop-ical clothing, training and preparing for the roles we were to play when we transferred to Aqir, Palestine.

I left Dunmow with my crew on 30 December, landing at Aouina (Tunis) after a flight of five hours, forty minutes, and night-stopped. In the morning we picked up six passengers and arrived at Aqir on New Year's Eve after a flight of seven hours.

In the evening, although the normal festivities were in full swing, I could not help noticing a lack of welcome from the residents. Seeing in the New Year in the Holy Land did not quite live up to my expec-tations. Next morning Squadron Leader Brooks, our engineering officer, who was a regular and had served in the Middle East before, introduced a Sudanese 'boy' called Abdul and instructed him to look after me. What a great little chap he was, and so clean. Even the tribal scars on his face did not mar his almost permanent smile. He looked after my room, my clothes and laundry extremely well and there was always a bowl of fresh fruit in my room. I hardly ever had occasion to criticize his service. Several weeks later I berated him for the first time as there was no fruit. Poor Abdul burst into tears as he explained that he had no money for it. In my ignorance I had not realized that for weeks he had supplied me with fruit bought from his own meagre wages. It has to be said that the taste of Jaffa oranges bought at home cannot be compared with those virtually straight off the tree. I felt awful and ashamed. I had mistakenly thought that the fruit was provided through the mess funds. However, the situation was quickly remedied. In future I gave him a weekly sum as well as compensation for the previous weeks. It was generally agreed that Sudanese servants were much more reliable and trustworthy than the locals.

What most impressed me was how bonny, rosy-cheeked and care-free all the children looked. They played together amicably, just like their fathers. Although one side of a street in a village might be predominately Jewish, the other side Arab, from both sides they mixed and sat together, playing their interminable tric-trac (backgammon). What a contrast it was a few years later when I saw the results of dirty political work in the disgusting squalor of the refugee camps in the Jordan Valley.

6

Middle East

The heat, the flies and the sand, the dearth of supplies and all the other discomforts of desert life came as quite a shock. It was certainly very different from the conditions we had known in a permanent mess in England. Even so, as soon as I got out to Palestine, I determined to visit as much of the country as I possibly could. Many of my colleagues laughed at my eagerness and said that there was plenty of time for all that, but they were sorry when, less than three months later, we were transferred to Cairo West in Egypt at very short notice. Many of them never saw Jerusalem or Bethlehem, although they probably knew every nightspot and bar in Tel Aviv.

Shortly after settling down at Aqir, I borrowed a three-ton truck and took about a dozen of my Flight to Jerusalem with Flight Lieutenant Mike Garnett as my co-driver. I had never driven a lorry before and to a lesser extent was reminded of Norry's gear-grinding experience when he took his RAF test. However, I soon got used to the double-declutch and we arrived at the King David Hotel (officers only). As we were accompanied by some of our NCO crews, we went elsewhere. I regaled myself with a large steak adorned with three eggs (admittedly the local eggs were relatively small) while Mike ordered six on his. I thought that this was a bit off! A brief look round was not enough to explore the fascinating old city and I determined to come again at the first opportunity. Although I managed to return to Aqir without any visible damage, I was not above spending a part of the next morning with the MT sergeant from whom I obtained a few tips on driving heavy vehicles.

During the time I spent in the Mediterranean I was surprised at the antipathy and, in some cases, the outright hostility shown to those arriving from Europe, both Army and RAF. Whether being fresh from home and receiving the attention of the few women officers there caused the discord, I wouldn't like to say, but the feeling certainly existed. The frequent and sarcastic 'Get your knees brown' remarks once provoked a well-decorated friend of mine to retort, 'If the searchlights over Berlin had been ultra violet, I'd be a nigger by now.' Many times I wondered if we had been fighting the same war. Much resentment was caused through unfortunate mishaps between the services. Army lads had been strafed by RAF aircraft and, to believe some reports, trigger-happy RN personnel are credited with shooting down more RAF planes than the Luftwaffe in the Mediterranean.

I had an enjoyable break from Halifax flying all day when I air tested a Hurricane. Up to this time my experience of single-engined aircraft had been restricted to the elementary trainer Tiger Moth. I certainly did not expect any similarity between that and the sophisticated, ten times more powerful fighting machine known as the Hurricane. This particular aircraft had undergone an engine change and needed to be air tested before being returned to its parent unit. As there appeared to be no one with experience on the type, I offered to fly it. Nearly every pilot would jump at the chance to fly a Spitfire or Hurricane, those magical names associated with the Battle of Britain. Invariably those with experience had flown an intermediate powered aircraft like the Harvard, so the transition was not too great. Fortunately I had extensive experience of the surge of power inherent in the Merlin from my Mosquito days, so at least I knew the feeling of a push in the back that I would receive when I advanced the throttle. In the absence of pilot's notes, the ATA (Air Transport Auxiliary) note book which I had acquired gave me all the information needed to fly and test the Hurricane 11B KZ 397 on 10 January, 1946, for thirty minutes of sheer delight. The only discomfort was the lack of forward view on the approach and landing.

The Jews were trying desperately to increase the size of their population in Palestine and to provide homes for as many of the survivors of the Holocaust as possible. Under the terms of the United Nations Mandate for which Britain was responsible, the balance of races in the country had to be maintained and this meant that immigration was strictly controlled. Ships suspected of carrying illegal Jewish immigrants to Palestine had to be searched for and tracked down by the two Halifax squadrons at Aqir and Qastina. This was in addition to their routine glider towing and parachute dropping. We would shadow and report anything suspicious to the Royal Navy and thus became more than a nuisance. Jewish freedom fighters – the Stern Gang, Irgun Zvi Leumi, terrorists, call them what you will – got very upset at our efforts. Retaliation was swift in coming. On 28 January, 1946, the 160 Maintenance Unit armoury at Aqir was raided and robbed of 600 Sten guns and ammunition. It was a well planned and executed military operation which left many red faces in the security force at Aqir.

The outcome of this was the issue of weapons to all and sundry. Our young Flying Officer armaments officer was a little too enthusiastic in the execution of his duty and put several chaps on a charge for leaving their guns for a minute or two unattended. I remember aircraft maintenance crews trying to keep rifles or Sten guns to hand while crawling over the aircraft. Our hero's enthusiasm covered both on and off duty periods and he seemed to relish catching anyone out. He sported his own revolver, emulating the popular western film stars of the time. The final pay-off came during a drinking session in the crowded mess. The local forces' radio station was tuned in and a record request was announced for Flying Officer . . . from all the airmen at Aqir. He himself was in the bar and everyone looked up wondering what was to come. We nearly choked on our beer when the music of a popular song blared out 'Lay that pistol down babe, lay that pistol down, pistol packing momma, lay that pistol down'. He was certainly the only one there not to be amused.

I knew no one in the RAF who had any strong views on the rights and wrongs of the conflict between Jews and Arabs in which the

British were the meat in the sandwich, but we did get very upset when some poor bugger got his head cut off by a piano wire stretched across a road or put himself or his vehicle on a land mine. Most of us were pretty cheesed off, having willingly fought the Germans, Italians or whoever, but we were now involved in something none of us wanted or expected. The main dissidents were the ground staff who felt that by now they should have been repatriated or demobbed. Their low morale was not helped by the politicians (one of them Stafford Cripps) who came out for a day or two and prattled a load of unconvincing codswallop about the necessity for keeping them there.

An almost cloak and dagger incident was to follow. On 1 February, 1946, I was instructed to place myself and my crew under the orders of GOC 6th Airborne Division, Major General Eric Bols CB, DSO, for an important mission. I was surprised when he turned up at Aqir with Group Captain Wardman OBE, DFC, Lieutenant-Colonel Pike, Lieutenant-Colonel Wheeler, Lieutenant-Colonel Brewis, Lieutenant-Colonel Stanley Clark and Private B. Hills (a batman). With no further information as to what was involved, I was told to take this lot of august targets (from a terrorist point of view) in one basket to Habbaniya, near Baghdad, in Halifax V11 PP343. The next day I flew them on to Shaibah, possibly the most god-forsaken place on earth, then consisting of dust, sand and nothing. The reason for my being there became apparent when I was invited to a very interesting briefing and asked to volunteer to recce an area well inside Persia (Iran). Intelligence had been received that this might be a suitable place for a force to be landed and later possibly retrieved by aircraft, glider tow or snatch take off should trouble erupt. I was to report on the suitability of the area and, if possible, test the surface with a 'touch and go'. Selecting me was due to the fact that I was probably the only officer in the area who had extensive experience of both towing and flying heavy gliders, with a knowledge of their operational limitations. I was then told that if by any chance there should be some mishap which resulted in a forced landing, crash, or otherwise, our presence there would not be acknowledged.

I now began to realize the implications. We were not at war and therefore not covered by the Geneva Convention as POWs. The area was nomadic and some of the inhabitants had extremely nasty habits with prisoners. I certainly had no wish to become, at best, a eunuch.

I had gone to Palestine aware of the dangers involved, but this was a different ball game. However, they must have known their man, for I had no hesitation in accepting the task and volunteering for my crew. The extent of the penetration into Persia is evident by the six hours recorded in my log book as a local recce, with two hours shown as being in cloud. My protective saints were with me still. We found the area, carried out our instructions and returned without anything untoward happening. The information I gave at de-briefing seemed to be what they wanted, but whether any use was made of it later I was not to know.

We flew to Bahrain on 4 February with two passengers, returning with thirteen, carrying out another local recce of three and a half hours on the way. Returning to Habbaniya the next morning, with the rest of the day to relax, I borrowed a Proctor(111) and flew two of my crew to Baghdad. It was my first visit to that fascinating city of market places and we made the most of it. Never did I dream that I was destined to return later on many occasions.

On our return to Aqir we were thanked by the General and his staff. My cynicism has increased considerably since I made an extensive study of honours and awards at the Public Record Office and else-where. I wonder how much more ribbon and metal decorates the chests of my illustrious passengers as a result of my efforts and those of my NCO crew.

I feel very strongly about this question of Honours and Awards, especially in relation to Bomber Command whose pilots and crews often suffered great injustice. The refusal of successive British governments to issue a campaign medal for Bomber Command's offensive against Germany was on the petty grounds that aircrews were operating from Britain and Britain was not an official theatre of war. That, to those who spent five long years in Bomber Command, whose bases moreover were frequently under attack, is a cruel joke. How can that stand be justified when the Defence Medal was given to the Home Forces and the Battle of Britain rosette on the 1939–45 Medal was given deservedly to 'those few who were owed so much', but who also operated from Britain which was not an official theatre of war?

It is recognized that there have to be 'men for the moment' and that Winston Churchill was such a man. Another was Air Marshal 'Butch' Harris. However, as soon as the need for him ceased, the whingeing, weak-kneed bishops, politicians and so-called humanitarians conveniently forgot the discriminatory annihilation of millions of men, women and children whose only 'sin' was to follow the religion of their parents, and castigated that honourable gentleman for carrying out the job he was appointed to do, selecting with particular venom the bombing of Dresden.

It is well documented that Dresden as a target was not selected by Harris but by his superiors, who named Dresden and told him to get on with it. Harris was too much of a gentleman to reply to his critics. In view of the atrocities carried out in Germany during that period, it is the most blatant cheek on the part of those like the Mayor of Dresden who object to the erection of a memorial to the man who was prepared to sacrifice his own men, knowing that it would undoubtedly eventually save the lives of countless thousands of others (incidentally Germans too) by shortening the war.

The available and reliable statistics may not be well known. The total RAF losses, starting with the command least affected were Ferry 209, West Africa 461, WAAF 464, Balloon 499, Army Co-op 634, Maintenance 662, Transport 1,147, 2nd Tactical 2,828, Flying Training 3,863, SEAC 6,182, Technical Training 7,345, Fighter 7,436, Coastal 9,145, Middle East 13,225, Bomber 58,378. In short, the total of all other fourteen command losses were over 4000 less than those sustained by Bomber Command, whose existence, efforts and losses were deemed insufficient to warrant the issue of a commemorative medal.

I am frequently astounded at the misconception of the facts of the Battle of Britain. Knowledge is invariably restricted to Fighter Command and the Spitfire, certainly a superb fighting machine.

When one mentions the Hurricane, the normal response is, 'Oh yes, they were there', yet the 'Cinderella' Hurricanes were far more numerous during those epic air battles and much more successful.

A greater misconception is the thought that the Battle saved Britain from invasion. It most certainly saved a great number of lives and much devastation of our cities by preventing the German bombers from getting through. However, during that short dramatic period, Bomber Command, against horrific opposition from flak, had almost completely destroyed the huge concentrations of troop-carrying invasion barges, equipment and shipping which had been amassed by the Germans along the French coast. Thus Hitler was forced to abandon his invasion plan Sea Lion. Dramatic confirmation of this is evident from the Battle of Britain Roll of Honour in Westminster Abbey. This contains 280 names from Coastal Command and 448 from Bomber (the forgotten) Command.

* * *

The only long period of 'no flying' shown in my log book was between 9 February and 9 March, 1946. This must have been the time when I was struck down. I could hardly move without severe pain and I was diagnosed as having Bornholm's disease. A doctor friend later confessed that this was a common diagnosis for the unknown. Known or unknown, the slightest move or jolt as I was taken to hospital by ambulance (from which I swear the shock absorbers had been removed) extracted a yell of abuse at the driver from yours truly. I was accompanied by the Catholic padre. Although Church of England throughout the whole of my service career I found the RCs to be the most human of the Holy Joes. This particular friend played a good game of poker, as I found to my cost, and caused much surprise and amusement during one late night session when he casually remarked, 'That bastard the bishop is coming tomorrow.' With complete rest, I recovered, seemingly without any medication. I did have the thought that, had I died in the Holy Land, it might have improved my very slim chance of getting past St Peter.

* * *

The opposition struck again when the radar station on Mount

Carmel was put out of action. On the night of 25/26 February, using amatol explosive and defensive crossfire from the perimeters, (probably using the Sten guns stolen earlier) a simultaneous attack was made on dispersed aircraft at Qastina, Petah Tiqva and Lydda: eleven Halifaxes damaged, six beyond repair, seven Spitfires and two Ansons destroyed. It was an expensive night for the RAF. It is understandable that the guards kept a low profile. During the 'big' war they would no doubt have tackled the opposing forces with acts of heroism and courage. Probably because of our vulnerability to these sporadic attacks, on 24 March our squadron was detached to Cairo West, a desert airfield quite close to the pyramids.

Although now based in Eygpt, we continued with identical work. On one of our parachute drops we were unfortunate to suffer a 'Roman candle' – a man's parachute failing to open. This must be a terrifying way to die and is horrific to watch. We also carried out considerable photographic reconnaissance of possible DZs in Cyprus and the Persian Gulf.

I returned to the UK with a Halifax via Castel Benito, the last time that I flew with my original crew. This was followed by a most welcome leave, returning on 30 May from Lyneham in a York. This was my first experience of that square-bodied modification of the Lancaster and was flown by Flight Lieutenant Birch. On the leg between Libya and Egypt I was surprised that the pilot decided to return owing to bad weather, but the night stop in Tripoli was welcome and I rejoined my squadron the following day. We were relocated back to Aqir on 18 June. I think that this move was associated with an agreement with the Egyptian government for all the RAF elements in Egypt (including Headquarters MEDME) to be in the Canal Zone.

★　　★　　★

There are times when you instinctively dislike a person, and unfortunately my CO, Wing Commander Alexander, was one of these. At mealtimes in the Mess I would avoid being near him if possible. The way he ate would have resulted in a rap over the knuckles from my father had I behaved in the same way. I think the dislike was mutual and this was evidenced by a row I had with him over seniority. When a CO leaves his station, a notice is put in daily orders naming the officer to be put in charge during his absence. The other two flight commanders were Squadron Leader Fisher and Squadron Leader Brown with whom I got along very well, especially Johny Fisher who had stayed with my family. One of them had been a squadron leader longer than I had but had joined after me; the other had joined before me but had been promoted after me. When I first queried the appointment, I was given first one reason then another. I complained to the CO but he suggested it was too trivial to be important. However, I said that if it happened again, I would make an official complaint to a higher authority.

While we were in Cairo West the Jews were still harassing the troops in Palestine in every possible way. On 26 April seven soldiers were murdered in a car park. This led to a curfew from 8 pm to 5 am and all places of public entertainment were closed. At the barracks at Sarafand and elsewhere there was severe unrest as no retaliatory action was allowed. The anger was more towards the governing authority than against the perpetrators of the atrocities. Even after the blowing up of the King David Hotel in Jerusalem, only limited searches were allowed. The unrest spread to the RAF at Aqir where there was a virtual mutiny. It seemed that the only senior officer the men were prepared to talk to was me. I emphasized the seriousness of their actions, despite the justification, and advised them to parade. I would then hand them over to the CO. They agreed to this after some murmuring and I duly carried out the formal procedure. The exact details are now hazy, but I clearly remember being very angry when a friend told me later that he had overheard the CO suggest that I had been the ringleader in the first place.

In all the circumstances it is quite surprising that we were able to hold a successful dance a month or so later. Obviously we had to be very careful over the arrangements, but an agenda of the entertainments committee of 27 June showed what was involved. A list should be placed in the mess for members to name the guest they wished to bring (no local talent) and accommodation should be laid on for those

12. With 620 Squadron in Palestine, 1946 (see p.112). The author is second from left in the middle row.

13. 'I was introduced to the Contessa M. 'Dodi', a very attractive young lady' (p.121).

14. 'The lovely Simone from St Ruf, Avignon' (p.125).

15. A Sea Otter at Heliopolis in REAF colours (see Ch.7). In the foreground (L to R) are Pilot Officer Osama Sidki, ?, Senior Mechanic Ashri and my brother Jim.

16. 'It was suggested to me that I should buy some Horsa gliders which were on sale in Kabrit' (p.158).

17. 'The Chrislea Ace, a neat four-seater aircraft powered by the very reliable Gipsy Major 10 engine' (p.160). Seen here with brother Jim at Heliopolis.

18. The Consul at Amman in Arab Airways registration (see Ch.8).

19. 'Two of the children flew back with me in the Gemini' (p.193).

20. The author showing the Dornier 28 STOL to Prime Minister
    Foncha of the Cameroons in 1962 (see p.210). *(Cameroon
    Information Service)*

ladies who wished to stay the night. It was estimated that we could muster about sixty suitable ladies. The dance went off without a hitch. This was quite remarkable, considering that almost all the VIPs in Palestine, including many from HQ MEDME, were guests. Two days later I was sent back to England on detachment to RAF Pershore.

There had been several electrical fires in the new Halifax Mk 1Xs which were to replace the Mk V11s in use in Palestine. While at Pershore I flew and tested the new planes, one of the tests lasting six and a quarter hours. Many tests were made with modified wiring before they were eventually sent to Aqir. Between 2 August and 25 September I visited no fewer than fourteen different airfields in connection with these tests. When I arrived back at Aqir with a new Mk 1X, I found that 620 Squadron had been redesignated 113 Squadron. I was on their strength for only two days before being detached again to 47 Squadron, Fairford. There, I was occupied in organizing the return of the Mk V11s to the UK, testing for acceptance the Mk 1Xs at St Mawgan and sending them, or occasionally taking one myself, to Aqir. My old crew, with the exception of Ernie Coulson, had left the service. After leave Ernie arrived to return to Aqir and told me he had recently got married, so I sent him home again and arranged for a substitute wireless operator to return in his place.

During October, 1946, I was surprised to find myself assigned to HQ MEDME as Command Chief Test Pilot. I had reason to believe that Wing Commander Jimmy Hickey had something to do with what was a prestigious appointment. Meanwhile I was instructed to complete the re-arming programme.

Having delivered a MK IX to Aqir, I got a lift to Heliopolis to collect another MK VII to take back to the UK and was instructed to go via Rome to deliver diplomatic mail to the Embassy.

This was to be my first visit to the Eternal City. When I had delivered the mail I was invited to a party that evening where I was introduced to the Contessa M, a very attractive young lady. Hungarian by birth, she had married an Italian nobleman who had disappeared, like so many others, during the unholy alliance of Hitler and Mussolini. As we were both fond of dancing the result was inevitable. It was the beginning of a wonderful relationship with Dodi, as her friends called her. As she had a comfortable apartment, our relationship meant that I seldom slept in the room at the Hotel Royal which had been taken over for use by the RAF on the many other occasions that I visited Rome. I invented excuses for delaying my departure another two days (and nights) to enjoy some of the many historic wonders of the city and, finally, to enjoy the unbelieve-able splendor of the opera *Aida* accompanied by Dodi.

As most of my visits were unpredictable, Dodi always left a message telling me where she was to be found. On one occasion I met her at a night club and suggested we went somewhere else. To my surprise our way was barred by an obviously irate police officer who spoke to Dodi in Italian. His tone was objectionable so I pushed him out of the way, whereupon he drew his Beretta. He must have been dumb-founded when I took the gun from him, put it in my pocket and walked out with Dodi on my arm.

Late next morning I returned to the Hotel to find the police officer with a friend who spoke English. He apologized for his behaviour and begged me to return his gun. I invented a story that I was so furious at his stupid action that I had thrown it into the river. This was the gun which I later used in Egypt.

I was loath to leave Rome but another adventure was in store for me.

*   *   *

Arriving at Istres (France) we were told not to return to the UK on the Sunday, to avoid the need for customs clearance which would have called for overtime payments and inconvenience. As I am always keen to explore places when the opportunity occurs, I decided to go to Marseilles. After changing a few pounds into francs, I caught the train there and wandered round the harbour area with its numerous cafés and even more numerous smells. I was fascinated to see prickly-looking sea urchins being eaten raw. One old fisherman noticed me watching and offered me one. I declined, however, preferring to enjoy

122

a bowl of onion soup on the quayside such as only the French can make it.

I had asked about trains back and left it as late as I could. Meanwhile I was propositioned by ladies of various shapes and sizes with varying degrees of insistence. The delights on offer were described in a mixture of French and broken English. Fortunately I have never needed to resort to those employed in the oldest profession. I caught the train with a few minutes to spare and dozed off in the carriage, waking up just as it was about to leave a station. There was a young woman with a child in the carriage so I asked her if this was Istres. I was told no. At the next station I asked again, with the same reply. I conjured up the French words for 'How many stations to Istres?' and from her reply gathered it was two stops back. She must have thought I was mad because I grabbed my hat and jumped out of the train just as it was starting to move. I was at Tarascon.

It was a tiny platform and I walked across the track to an equally tiny platform on the other side. The station-master-cum-porter-cum-ticket-collector carried a dim hurricane lamp. I was in trouble. There was no train to Istres or anywhere else until early the following morning. I was wondering what to do when three young men who had been loitering at the gate asked if they could help. They claimed to have been members of the French Resistance. I explained my dilemma as best I could, including the fact that I had no French money left. They conferred among themselves and managed to scrape up enough to pay for a night's lodging at the nearby Terminus Hotel. I was really impressed by this gesture of hospitality and offered them my gold signet ring as compensation for their kindness. This was emphatically refused. They then led me to the bar of this quite small hotel and confronted the Madam behind the bar, requesting a room for me. Just as they were collecting their few francs together, it occurred to me that I might be able to pay in English pounds. This was illegal, but I felt justified by the circumstances. The lady was large and jovial with a smattering of English. When asked if she would except sterling, her face lit up and she positively beamed. The prospect of a miserable and hungry night was instantly dispelled. Almost giving a cheer, I insisted on buying a couple of rounds of drinks for the three young men, plus the lady behind the bar who turned out to be the proprietress.

It happened to be a Feast Day in the little town and the lads had been waiting for the festivities to begin. They invited me to join them but I was tired and hungry. I made for the dining room where I had an excellent meal washed down by an equally good bottle of local wine. There were only a few tables, of which only one was occupied by a young man with two attractive young ladies with whom I exchanged smiles. Towards the end of the meal one of the ladies came over and suggested that we had met in Avignon. Having never been to Avignon, I went along with the game to see what would happen. I then inivited the three of them to join me for a glass of wine. The two girls had come for the Feast Day and weekend. Being now warm, mellow and in good company, we returned to the bar from where, after a final drink, the others went off to join the local merrymaking, leaving me alone with Madam.

I was surprised when the one I was supposed to have known returned and joined me in the bar. It is amazing what fun can arise from an imperfect knowledge of a foreign language. I was tickled pink when, despite my meagre grasp of French, during a rather fast exchange of words between the girl and madam, I caught the request for the number of my room. As I was about to say goodnight the other two returned. The two girls had booked to share a room and the fellow could now see a golden opportunity of dividing the girls up. Who was I to frustrate a fellow human when everyone had shown so much kindness? Bidding them all goodnight I remarked, 'I shall leave the door of my room open,' not apprehensive of what I thought might follow.

It seemed that they had decided to play a joke on me, because I heard all three of them giggling along the passage. There was a timid knock on my door and I called, 'Come in'. To my astonishment both the girls in flimsy nighties came in and sat on the bed on either side of me. This was a situation I had not been prepared for. They began by each stroking a leg, leaning over me smiling and revealing a glimpse of their tempting young breasts. The result of this was predictable. With an 'Oo La La', one left rather hurriedly and I enjoyed the company of my 'acquaintance' from Avignon.

We were awakened at five o'clock, not by the concierge, but by the other girl, who got into bed with us. I started to giggle as, in my halting French, I tried to explain that I had experienced many things, but never before had I woken up with two girls in my bed. As I was reaching for my clothes, both girls jumped out of bed and removed them to the far side of the room. I expostulated but to no avail, so I pulled the bedcover round me, jumped out and bundled the (now laughing) girls out of the room and dropped the latch while I dressed.

Both walked with me to the train. As I emerged with a pretty girl on each arm, a Nun appeared leading a crocodile file of young girls. At once she stopped and turned them round to examine some architectural figure until we were out of sight. We arrived early at the station where coffee and croissants were available, but to my dismay I realized that I had relinquished the last of my francs to the concierge. The problem was solved by the lovely Simone from St Ruf, Avignon, paying for them. I occasionally look at the photo she gave me and remember when I was expecting to spend a miserable night on a cold railway station. Instead it turned out to be one of the most enjoyable and memorable occasions in a life full of them.

*   *   *

I often visited places where I had a virtually free passage through customs formalities. In areas where there was a considerable difference in the value of certain commodities and currency, I soon found out the easiest and most profitable black market activities. I participated in these in a relatively small way both for myself and as a courier. I have had offers of large rewards for drugs but I have never considered involvement with this diabolical trade even in its mildest form. I only wish that it carried the death penalty all over the world instead of in just a few eastern countries.

Gold sovereigns were then readily available and easy to dispose of. No agents or contacts were needed. Paper money was mistrusted because of frequent devaluations. Gold was a safeguard. Although the risk for me was slight, it was always just as well to have a reasonable excuse if caught, particularly if one was a senior Air Force officer. I did not relish the dishonour of being cashiered. As the cost of entertainment in Rome, Athens and such places was beyond the reach of service pay, nearly everyone did a little fiddling. Soap, coffee, an old battledress or overcoat, a sovereign or two, all enabled servicemen to enjoy the opera, first class restaurants, sight-seeing or, last but not least, the fleshpots available for all tastes.

My first minor escapade was to buy two sovereigns at £5 each in Cairo and sell them without difficulty for £14 each in Rome. I then went to a casino and won the equivalent of another £50. I used part of this to purchase silk scarves which I sold easily in Egypt. My £10 finished up about £110. Meanwhile I had also enjoyed myself. I realized that the gambling win had helped but could hardly be relied on. With enough capital now to buy twenty-two sovereigns, I could realize £308 plus any profit from purchases in the opposite direction. Two more trips and my original £10 could be £1,000.

These prospects proved too much of a temptation to ignore. However, such activities would no longer be just a fiddle to pay for entertainment. A blind eye could be turned to that, but this was smuggling. I had to be quite certain that whatever commandments I had already broken, I must never break the eleventh: 'Thou shalt not be found out'.

There was always the risk that someone suspicious or jealous might inform the authorities. I therefore devised a method which would enable me to get away with it should I be stopped and searched at customs. When I bought the sovereigns, I would search through hundreds at different dealers (the prices were nearly always the same) to ensure that each one had a different year date. Some years were easier to obtain than others and I built up duplicate sets at home, taking note of those dates of which I only had one example. For safety's sake I carried my gold coin collection on me. I was afraid to leave it in Egypt in case 'cliffty wallahs' robbed me. Normally I had between seventy-five and eighty, all different, of which I would dispose of sixty, replacing them later with comparative ease. The mathematically minded reader will at once realize that, after a very few trips, my initial tentative exploit resulted in a more than comfortable MIP (money in pocket) position, in view of the considerable difference in the value of the pound in 1946–48.

*   *   *

My first encounter with a Spitfire was not a very happy one. In fact it resulted in a rather red-faced Joe. I started to run up the engine without the tailwheel anchored or groundstaff lying on the tailplane. When the tail surprised me by saying goodbye to the ground, I throttled back too quickly causing a loud clonk as the tailwheel kissed the ground and collapsed. The fitters were not amused.

A very late mark of Spitfire, the 18, was to be test-flown in Rome and then flown to Fayid. A test on 23 January was plagued with faults including an electrical fire. Compared with the Mk 1X, which was a joy to fly, the 18 was a bastard. It had been developed for long-range photographic reconnaissance but the fore and aft stability left much to be desired. I did not relish the flight back, but my compensation was to spend six nights in Rome waiting for the faults to be rectified. During this period I made useful contacts which were beneficial to me for many years. I made frequent ferry flights returning via Athens.

On the retest of the Mk 18 I informed control that if the aircraft was OK I would carry on to Athens without landing again and this duly occurred. I found enough faults on this leg to warrant two nights in Athens. The last leg from Athens to Fayid was interrupted by a blinding sandstorm which forced me to divert to El Adem and spend the night there. After delivery to Fayid I got a lift back to Abu Sueir with Flight Lieutenant Michailov who had taken me through to Rome thirteen days before. When I later came across the pilot's notes for the Spitfire Mk 18 I was surprised to read, 'This aircraft should only be flown by very experienced pilots'. These are the only pilot's notes I have ever met with this annotation.

Organizing the transfer of ninety Mk 1X Spitfires to Greece was my next task. The rumour that they had been sold for £100 each caused much resentment among the maintenance crews. They had to prepare them in batches of ten, which I considered a convenient number to control in transit. I could thus avoid stragglers and not overload the refuelling facilities at Nicosia in Cyprus and Calato in Rhodes. Calato was only used when the winds were strongly adverse. The decision to refuel was mine when I considered it necessary. I suggested flying direct and refuelling at Rhodes if required, but this was overruled as it would mean overflying Egypt with military aircraft as against transport aircraft. The political situation was somewhat sensitive at the time.

Taking off on 11 February, 1947, with the first batch, I flew a Spitfire to Nicosia and then went to Athens in the escorting Warwick. Although the weather was reasonable, I wanted to test the facilities at Calato, so I instructed the flight to land and decided to nightstop, completing my first delivery the following day. I had been besieged by offers to fly the Spitfires from many pilots who had never flown them. I insisted on examining log books before putting my neck on the block by losing an aircraft, or perhaps the life of an enthusiastic opportunist. In order to liaise with the Greek Air Force unit receiving the Spitfires, I decided to stay an extra day in Athens. At least that was my official explanation. I had always enjoyed Athens and as a few of my pilots on this trip had not had that pleasure, it would have been heartless to return immediately. In any case, I had some trading to do.

With the second batch we spent the night in Cyprus for some reason. I then flew a Spitfire from Nicosia to Hassani, overflying Rhodes with ample reserves as we were carrying 90 gallon (slipper) overload drop tanks. We arrived on 22 February. Having been told that there had been a fin change on Warwick 844, I decided to wait and test fly it, which I did on 24 February. The fin was OK but the Air Speed Indicator (ASI) was not. Hassani was not the best airfield to land on when in difficulties, and my experience with Warwicks had not been extensive. I asked a Spitfire which was in radio contact to make a wide circuit and approach at 90 knots whereupon I would fly formation with him until the threshold of the runway. This we did and I thanked him as I landed, while he followed overshoot procedures. Slight modification was needed to the rudder trimming and of course the ASI had to be changed and lines checked. I retested on 26 February and all went well until the escape hatch flew open. This produced an excellent 'hoovering' (albeit a noisy one) as every small loose object and the dust in the near area were sucked out of the aircraft. This meant landing again to examine the hatch and fasten it securely before proceeding without further incident back to base.

While in Athens the GAF commandant had asked me to use a few of their pilots to ferry some of the Spitfires in the next batch. I was happy to arrange this for 4 March. The normal procedure was to fly from Kasfareet to Nicosia on main tanks then fill up both mains and overload tank for the flight from Cyprus to Greece. From Nicosia I was flying a Spitfire and, as the winds were favourable, just before Rhodes I gave the go-ahead to overfly. Immediately the air was full of protest from the GAF pilots. 'No, must land. No fuel,' was the chorus from all the Greeks. Under the circumstances I had to change my mind, but I was a little puzzled to understand why. While the refuelling was being carried out, I tried to question the Greeks, but all of a sudden they had lost their previous command of the English language and shrugged their shoulders. I was not prepared at this late stage in my service life to create an international incident by perhaps provoking these volatile and excitable gentlemen. I therefore thought it best to leave it until I got to Athens and was able to speak to their senior officer. I got very little change from him either, although there was back-slapping and thanks all round. By pure chance I later found out that the real cause of their being short of fuel was that they had filled their overload tanks with Cyprus brandy. Although I admired their opportunism, I refrained from using our Hellenic friends for any further ferrying.

A signal was received from Bahrain that a Hornet Mk 1 which had been to the Far East for tropicalization tests had to be flown back for examination. A pilot had flown the aircraft as far as Bahrain but refused to fly it further. I was detailed to collect it. Flight Lieutenant Packenham-Walsh flew me to Bahrain via Lydda, Habbaniya and Shaibah, arriving on 28 March. No one knew anything about the

Hornet, so I hoped to find pilot's notes with the aircraft. There were no such notes. All I could gather was that it was a scaled-down Mosquito with virtually the same power units but with contra-rotating propellers which I had never experienced.

I made a ground run and, as nothing seemed amiss, I signalled chocks away and decided to give it an air test, intending to treat it as a hotted-up Mosquito. The take off was straightforward as, owing to the contra-props, the throttles could be advanced together. There was no tendency to swing, as in the Mosquito, which required a lead of one throttle. I let her fly off rather than lift, which she did about 20 knots faster than the Mossie, so I decided to approach with the same differential. Temperatures, pressures, turns and trim were normal and I began to wonder what the fuss was about.

Making a powered approach as I rounded out, I closed the throttles and received my first shock. The aircraft fell out of my hands with one hell of a bounce. I opened up to hold it off and it bounced again. The port engine did not respond as quickly as the starboard, with the result that I was screaming towards the control tower. Fortunately it came in just in time for me to avoid crashing. The overshoot at last accomplished, I stooged around for a few minutes to recover my composure and then made a landing, keeping the power on until I touched the runway. This emphasized to me the neccessity of obtaining pilot's notes before flying a strange aircraft. I asked the engineers to make a good examination of the undercarriage in view of the two heavy landings on my first circuit. If nothing was broken I intended to take it away the following day. Later, in the bar, the flying control chaps admitted diving for the floor, as it seemed certain that I would crash.

Bahrain, or anywhere else in the Persian Gulf for that matter, was then without air conditioning and a place to get out of as soon as possible. In the morning, with a favourable report from the engineers and weather man, I set off for Shaibah. Just before arrival, while still with plenty of height, I decided to test the stalling characteristics. On closing the throttles, I found that the port would only partially close, giving the feeling that there was an obstruction. This could prove awkward, so I feathered the port and made a single-engine landing. At the end of the run the obstruction to closing the throttle seemed to vanish, so I unfeathered, restarted the engine and taxied in for re-fuelling. The engineering facilities at Shaibah were minimal so I decided to carry on to Habbaniya where they were better equipped. The same thing happened again and I took the same action.

Deciding to nightstop to see if the engineers could come up with some answers to the Hornet problem, I scrounged a lift into Baghdad. There I saw a 14 carat Omega wristwatch with a leather strap the colour of a suit I'd had made for me in Cairo. I paid fifty pounds for it and as I left the shop, a twinge of conscience prompted me to return and buy a similar Omega for Lucy. Habbaniya was one of the largest RAF stations outside the UK with a separate mess for senior officers. It was the practice of the Baghdad carpet dealers to loan Persian carpets for use in the mess. While there I took a liking to a matched pair of very fine Ispahan carpets, bought them, and barely managed to cram them into the limited space available in the Hornet.

The engineering officer had no answers to the Hornet's unusual behaviour and wanted to ground it for further investigation. However, as chief test pilot, I was able to override his wishes and, after refuelling, took off for Lydda. Making a check before landing, I found to my dismay that I was unable to close either throttle. Whatever the fault had been in the port was now evident in both. Although experienced in gliding, no way was I going to try a dead stick with both props feathered. Warning the control to have a fire tender ready and traffic clear, I made a long, low approach from way out, undercarriage and flaps down, with throttles as far back as they would go. Even then, I was still well above normal approach speed and as I crossed the boundary I cut both switches and wheeled her on. It seemed a long time before I could get the tail down to apply the brakes and I thought I might have to ground loop to come to a stop. In the event I managed it with no damage other than burnt-out brake sacs. Spares would have to be sent from the UK, so I got a lift back to my old station, Aqir, where I stayed the night. In the morning I borrowed an Anson X1X to get back to Abu Sueir and make my report.

I was asked to test Mosquito Mk 111 299 and one of my pilots, Flying Officer Slusarov, asked to fly with me for experience. I was always pleased to fly the Mosquito which I considered the finest piston-engined aircraft ever built. I refer to this mundane flight of one hour because a few years ago at an Air Show, my eldest son pointed out to me that the Mosquito which had just flown past was the only one in flying condition in England. It was the very same aircraft I had flown in Egypt in 1947.

A points system calculated on length of service overseas, children and so forth, qualified you to have your family with you at certain overseas stations. A governing factor was the availability of quarters suitable to the rank held. I had been looking forward to my family joining me and, when the opportunity arrived, Lucy had only a very short time in which to get the necessary inoculations and make all the many other arrangements for herself and four children. The train journey from Port Said would have been long and uncomfortable, but my Greek friend, Siffi Colocotronis, insisted that I should have his car and chauffeur to take me there and pick up the family. Looking along the mass of faces lining the onshore deck rails of the SS *Dunnottar Castle* at Port Said, I was disappointed not to see my family. However, I was told by the ship's officer at the bottom of the gangway that the officers' families were congregated in the lounge. There I found them, anxiously awaiting me. It was a memorable reunion.

My one clear memory of that day was the scene shortly after arrival at our bungalow in Abu Sueir. At the sight of the flowers, our smartly dressed servant and my presents, which included a radiogram, sewing machine, clothing, toys and games, Lucy was overcome. She sat on the bed and wept.

As soon as we had settled in we had to throw a party and, as I did not have to rely solely on my RAF pay, it was one to be remembered. Lucy with her easy manner, lack of pretension and ability to mix was soon a firm favourite and we would often be invited to join the 'top brass' when visiting the mess.

The most admired 'passion wagon' on the camp was owned by

Flight Lieutenant Palmer of the Huntley and Palmer biscuit family. He was going back to the UK shortly after Lucy arrived and his Packard straight eight was for sale. I became its proud owner. The Packard held six in comfort but was often full to overflowing. There were frequent parties at weekends but often several of our closer friends, Rene and Jimmy Hickey, Wing Commander Scrivenor, Paddy Waugh and others would go further afield to the popular French club at Ismailia. Champagne, a good meal and dancing into the small hours was the norm with probably a sing-song on the way back. When we got within a hundred yards of the perimeter of Abu Sueir, we would all join in singing loudly 'Land of Hope and Glory' whereupon the guards who must have thought 'that mad crowd again', would open the gates and present arms as we passed.

We had several ex-Africa Korps prisoners of war working at the base, the most memorable being the band and the swimming pool attendants. Without exception they were a credit to their nation. Despite being prisoners, they showed many of our chaps to disadvantage in both deportment and behaviour.

It was, of course, inevitable that my frequent purchases among the gold and currency vendors would attract the attention of the professionals – or the Egyptian mafia to give them a more descriptive name. An almost Mata Hari situation resulted. I was introduced to a very good looking young woman at the Helmia Palace. After I had met and entertained her a couple of times, she asked if I would take five hundred sovereigns to her family in Rome as they needed assistance. My reply was immediate 'No, but I will take 1000 and deliver 750 if your friends are interested.' The charade was dropped and she admitted that she worked for and had protection from a group of high officials to whom she would convey my message. My proposal was accepted and I was given the first consignment at her apartment. I couldn't help smiling at the additional 100 sovereigns she coyly asked me to deliver to another address, just for her. How could I refuse such a charming woman?

This was now big business and the excuse of my 'collection' was no longer valid should I be caught. As an insurance against losing everything, I decided to leave my 250 sovereigns share with Lucy, (£1,250 was enough then to buy a fine house). She prepared a waistcoat from an old bush jacket by removing the arms, collar, lapels, belt and pockets and shortening it to above battledress waist line. We invariably flew in battledress and took our best blue, toiletry and other clothing in a folding canvas carryall. Pockets about 4 inches deep and just wide enough to slot in a roll of sovereigns were double-sewn in various places where the battledress was not close-fitting. These balanced the weight but avoided the back except for just above the waistline in the small of the back. I could not risk a slap on the back and anything further up would be most uncomfortable in the pilot's seat. I had seen cursory examinations of officers' luggage at customs in Rome and Athens, but never a body search. In any case, the RAF were dealt with separately when flying through. There was in fact very little risk, but inevitably the adrenalin flowed while I carried such huge sums of money. I did not have the problem of transporting cash back to Egypt other than what I received for my own sovereigns. This I usually managed to get exchanged for US dollars with part of which I would buy silk scarves etc, dependent on whether I was flying directly back to base or via Athens.

At every RAF mess, parties are given for various reasons. At squadron and station level they are less frequent than at HQ where entertainment is generally provided for local bigwigs on a more lavish scale than at the lower echelons. In order to do this a levy is imposed on all the officers with an occasional grant from the mess funds to augment the amount available for the goodies. The elected purchasing officer then had to get the best value for the cash available. On these occasions an aircraft is usually provided to collect food and drink from wherever it is least expensive. Other aircraft and motor transport are also used to collect VIPs, a band, WAAF officers from other stations, and nurses, to increase the feminine company essential to a good party where there are many single or unaccompanied married officers. To ensure that I would be selected to assist in future purchasing, on the first occasion I used a portion of my ill-gotten gains to obtain all the food and drink well within the money allocated. My stratagem paid off. For the next buying trip to Rome I was given cash for private purchases as well as for the mess. I took sovereigns instead, enabling me to uphold my reputation and still make a handsome profit for myself.

Squadron Leader Gordon Packe and I were briefed to go to Udine (about sixty miles north-east of Venice) to collect a sum of money large enough to warrant sending two senior officers to do the job and return with it in an Anson Mk X11 to Abu Sueir. We went in a Lancaster to Malta, by Dakota to Rome and by train to Udine, arriving on 25 May, 1947. It was obvious that Gordon knew nothing about my propensity for indulging in the import/export trade. In the train he actually suggested that we should buy a number of piano accordions in Italy and sell them in Egypt. I could hardly suppress a laugh at the thought of lugging such heavy and bulky items from the aircraft without drawing attention to ourselves. I pointed out the obvious snags and suggested that he could buy 6,000 silk scarves instead, which would be less than one piano accordion in bulk weight. He could even buy a piano accordion case in which to hide the scarves. But he would keep on about the piano accordions.

I was told to liaise with Wing Commander Chamberlain who turned out to be most helpful and sociable. As the money and aircraft were not yet ready, he asked if I would like a trip to Venice the following day. He took me in an Argus and allowed me to fly it back. We only had a limited time at our disposal so I went to see the famous Venetian glass blowing.

I had changed a few sovereigns in Rome and now bought a magnificent set of six dozen glasses and four decanters of which only a few have survived the attentions of children, grandchildren and frequent moves.

On 28 May I flew Anson X11 PN 707 to Athens via Bari with Gordon and Flight Sergeant Russell. Further signals had been received cancelling the money transfer. As there was no great hurry, we spent the night in Athens and another at El Adem. The aircraft (without piano accordions) was delivered to Abu Sueir where it was maintained as a communications aircraft for HQ staff.

On 12 June I took Halifax 1X (853) through to the UK via Malta and Udine, off-loading nine passengers and night stopping. On 13 June we lost brake pressure during the flight and were diverted to Wittering. Our unexpected arrival there from foreign parts demanded the services of HM customs. After waiting a considerable time, I contacted a customs officer by phone who authorized me as captain to make out a list and declaration of the imports of my crew with their names and addresses and to leave it with flying control. Naturally, none of us declared everything we had brought in, but when the flight engineer said he had nothing to declare, I thought that was a bit dodgy, so put him down for a carton of cigarettes. After a short leave, the crew reported to Lyneham and was flown back to Egypt on a York. We all had a good laugh at the flight engineer's expense when it turned out that he was the only person to have been charged import duty by the customs.

The Hornet at Lydda had by now been refitted with new brake sacs. On 30 June I flew in a Proctor to Aqir but arrived there with the aircraft unserviceable, so took a Magister on to Lydda and then completed the business of getting the Hornet to Fayid, landing with the port engine idling. The fault had been located in the throttle housing and bearings on the engine. These were made of two metals with different expansion rates so that when hot (after prolonged flight), the elongation of one bearing when throttled back resulted in a geometric lock. This would explain the normal response when a run up of the engine was made when cold. This information was sent to Rolls Royce and De Havillands and modifications were made which rectified the fault.

The last batch of the ninety Spitfires for Greece was despatched on 8 July. One of my pilots on this occasion was Warrant Officer Brown. I decided to fly one of the Spitfires (Mk 753) and as usual took off last. On arrival at Nicosia, Brown mentioned that his oil pressure warning light kept flickering and that he was worried about it. As the temperature had remained normal, I felt sure that it was nothing more serious than an instrument malfunction. I suggested that he should take my aircraft Mk 753 and I would take his. An idiosyncrasy of the use of overload tanks on Spitfire 1Xs was the need to shut off one set of tanks before selecting the other. Failure to follow this drill often caused an air lock in the system with dramatic results. Even when the correct drill was carried out, it was customary to have a little more height, as often the delay in engine response resulted in anxious moments. This was particularly the case over water or inhospitable terrain as you waited for the engine to pick up/respond during the glide and loss of height. Following the others and confirming the ground speed and weather at Athens, I ordered the flight and escorting aircraft to overfly Rhodes and proceed direct. I then observed those in front losing height during their fuel change-over.

One aircraft seemed to be losing much more height than usual. As I had already changed tanks, I throttled back and followed him down. It was Warrant Officer Brown in Mk 753 who transmitted that his engine was not responding to the tank change. He was getting dangerously low. I warned him not to leave it too late and to jump rather than ditch. I then saw the canopy open and for the first time actually saw a pilot exit from an aircraft by parachute. There was an almighty splash as the Spitfire hit the water. Once Brown had waved to me from the safety of his dingy, I instructed the escort to circle, plot the position and send a WT message to base. I caught up with the rest of the flight and went on to Athens to make my report. Meanwhile, the escort found a nearby fishing boat which was directed to and picked up our unfortunate airman. He was taken to the small island of Cos where he spent a few uncomfortable days without a change of clothes or toilet gear.

Unfortunately, as it was recorded that I had left in Mk 753, Lucy was told that her ever-loving husband was in the drink. This caused her no little anxiety and my officer friends much amusement until a further message was received giving the true story.

Ever an opportunist, it instantly occurred to me that I could now benefit considerably at the expense of my mafia friends. I told the contact in Athens that the consignment they were expecting was in the Spitfire at the bottom of the sea. As I had already made several successful deliveries from which they had made about £50,000, they were much more concerned about my safety and the future profits I might bring them. Naturally I did not try to dispose of the contraband on that trip but took it back to Egypt for disposal later.

Lighter flints showed a very good return in Greece. A government monopoly of both matches and flints made the differential enormous, but they were bulky and difficult to get. They were sold in one kilo tins, rather like the old circular tins for fifty cigarettes. I made many friends in Athens customs and air traffic control by casually leaving a tin where it could be seen for them to collect and share out later.

Problems of a different nature arose from the collection of a Tempest V1 from Elmas in Sardinia. The hydraulic system had failed so I had to pump the undercarriage down for each landing. A leak developed while I was flying in cloud half way across the sea between Malta and Benghazi. This added to my troubles by spattering the windscreen with oil. All in all, it took me eight days to complete that trip. This was especially tiresome now that my family was with me. It should have been a straightforward ferry flight on which I could have sent one of my pilots.

The period of extended service for which I had contracted was now about to elapse and the decision had to be taken whether or not I should seek a permanent commission. The six years of my service had given me a variety of experience that nothing else could rival but I knew that all good things must come to an end and that life in the peacetime RAF was not for me. I must take my hard-won skills and experience of life with me and make a new way in the world, one that would enable me to give Lucy and the children the advantages I wanted for them.

As a family we went home together on the SS *Samaria*, leaving Port Said on 27 October, 1947. It was a fretful journey for me as I was anxious to get on with my plans for the future. I had little to do but play bridge. My usual partner was a naval lieutenant commander who would look at me while bidding. At first I thought that he was trying to communicate by some sort of facial expression until I realized that he had a pronounced tic which became more pronounced with each drink consumed. There was a Brigadier who had invited me to join his group and, owing to my army days with the GPR, we found much criticism to bandy about between us. Some of the others at times seemed edgy at my frankness with their 'top brass'.

At Hallowe'en, which happens to be our wedding anniversary, I threw a party and invited the Brigadier and his group to join us. Champagne was the order of the day, although I consumed brandy sours, a drink I had been introduced to in Tel Aviv. After we had disposed of a few drinks together I asked if he was familiar with 'Cardinal Puff'. He had heard of it but refused my offer to initiate him, suggesting instead that his aide, a major, should be a guinea pig. The game is a series of simple words and actions during which a pint of beer or the equivalent is consumed. If a mistake is made, the remaining drink has to be downed and the glass refilled before starting again. A demonstration has to be given at the start and also after each three failures. If cold sober it is not difficult, so no one suggests playing it until the intended novitiate has had a few. Alas, the poor major did not complete the course, but under the influence created a disturbance later that night by trying to force his way into the women's quarters in what can best be described as deshabillé.

In the morning I was told to report to the Colonel OC Troops who, without being specific, ranted on about senior officers taking advantage of their rank and consuming more than their fair share of the drinks available, making it necessary to ration it for the rest of the voyage. I corrected him about the amount I had downed, but he attributed the night's unfortunate outcome to my suggestion of Cardinal Puff. A meeting was called just before lunch for all officers. The Brigadier then said a few words (tongue in cheek I imagine) about behaviour on board and the importance of still maintaining standards of decorum irrespective of the fact that most of us were returning for demobilization. The major was confined to quarters for the rest of the voyage and I was never again invited to the Brigadier's table.

We disembarked at Liverpool on a miserable, grey, misty morning on 10 November. Upon arrival I was given a rail warrant to present myself on 14 November, 1947, to 101 PDC Warton. There I was to receive my final separation from the RAF. Despite the frustrations of service life, one emerges from its coils more efficient to grapple with the outside world. The final checking of health and other particulars ended with the issue of civilian clothes, the look, cut and style of which simply yelled 'Demob'. Even so the spivs were outside offering £3 for the suit and there were plenty of takers.

A few weeks later I was reminded of how small our world is. While staying with my in-laws in West Hampstead, we all went round to the local one evening. To my astonishment, the first person we met was the naval bridge partner complete with an even more pronounced tic.

I had no idea that while I was in the RAF a gratuity was mounting up. How it was worked out I have no idea, but shortly afterwards I received the magnificent sum of £114 5s 0d. This was a source of great amusement to my bookmaker friend, Wally King, at Park Royal dog track a few days later. There was a race which was an obvious match between two dogs. I spun a coin to decide which one to back. I have to admit that the accumulated wealth from my two thousand, three hundred and forty-three days of RAF service disappeared in a little over twenty-nine seconds. Wally thought I was crazy, but the bonus of being still alive was quite enough for me.

7

Sea Otters

A golden opportunity presented itself shortly before I was demobbed. I knew that there were eight complete Sea Otters (sturdy, single-engined amphibious aircraft) which had only been test flown before being crated and sent out to the Canal Zone. There they had stayed in their boxes and were to be disposed of by the BSDM (British Stores Disposal Mission). If I could buy them, erect and fly them to East Africa, they would be ideal for carrying freight for the Ground Nut Scheme and other enterprises. Their ability to land on lakes and in remote areas would be invaluable. It was certainly a risk worth taking. After life as a senior officer in the RAF I could not contemplate the daily grind of the fitters' bench at De Havillands.

With some of the money accumulated from my nefarious escapades and a little inside information, I became the owner of eight aeroplanes. I formed a limited company 'Enterprise Aviation Services' with myself as managing director, and managed to persuade Air Commodore Cunningham to become a director. He was the brother of Sir John Cunningham, the First Sea Lord. Through his good offices and introductions, I was able to achieve much more than Squadron Leader Joe Patient could have done. Even so, there were formidable difficulties to be overcome. I never thought it would be easy, but I certainly did not expect to have to cope with so many bureaucratic, hidebound, toffee-nosed civil servants and others. They seemed to resent anyone who was trying to do something enterprising or unusual.

It was relatively easy to get the aircraft put on the civilian register, but every aircraft has to have a certificate of air-worthiness, renewable yearly after examination by the ARB (Air Registration Board) inspector. Although I knew that certain fire safety modifications would be needed and that fuel and oil cut-off valves and pipes would have to be fitted to meet civilian standards, I was not prepared for the shocks that were in store for me. I was able to get drawings and specifications for the modifications, but was flabbergasted when every manufacturer gave three to six months for delivery. Even standard items like tyres, batteries, aircraft fabric and dope were difficult to obtain. I had not visualized such delays and was afraid I might run short of money. As a precaution, I borrowed as much as I could from the meagre resources of my family and friends. I placed orders for the modifications and, with the help of Air Commodore Cunningham, I obtained the tyres and batteries from RAF sources.

A Sea Otter had been 'typed' by the Shell Company of Venezuela. The ARB now told me that, as it had been fitted out as an executive aircraft, with a heater and upholstered seats, I would have to fit these too. I began to have a nasty feeling in the pit of my stomach. I argued that in East Africa the last thing needed was a heater and that carrying freight hardly called for plush seats. I was informed that having fitted the seats I could always remove them. I was then shown a huge book of rules and told, 'This is our bible and this is what you have to do if you want to fly those aircraft'. I rejoined with, 'If they had fitted gold-plated bloody handles, would I have to fit gold-plated bloody handles?' and he replied, 'Yes'. I felt trapped and had visions of going broke and losing the money lent by family and friends. Cunningham could not help so I went to seek aid from D.C.T. Bennett, 'the greatest complete airman that I knew' (Bomber Harris's words not mine). He was then involved with BSAA (British South American Airways). He remembered me from my Pathfinder days and, after hearing my problems, was quite straight with me. 'Patient, if I cannot get anywhere with the idiots, what chance have you got?' I felt

142

stymied, snookered, frustrated and bitter, but no way was I going to allow the money I had taken so many risks for, plus my relative's savings, be lost through hidebound bureaucratic bullshit.

One solution might be to get the aircraft to a country outside the ARB sphere of control. In any case I needed an export licence. So off I went to the Board of Trade thinking that this would be a mere formality. I must be a simple soul to think that a government department can act in a rational manner. I explained that I owned the aircraft which were British registered but located in Egypt. I wished to take them elsewhere so please could I have export licences for them? 'No problem, sir.' I thought this can't be true. The next moment my hopes were duly dashed. 'Just bring them to the UK and we will give you the export licence.' What madness was this? Bring them to the UK only to take them back again? I began to wonder what sort of country I had risked my life for and which was now about to bankrupt me.

I had skirted legality before of my own free will, but now I was forced into dishonesty. During my time as chief test pilot in Egypt I had been sent to Cairo several times to test aircraft for the REAF with whom I had developed a good relationship. In fact, when it was known that I was leaving the RAF, they had offered me a job. The Egyptians were short of many items which they were unable to get through normal channels because of embargoes. Many of these, including the batteries used on Spitfires, were common to the Sea Otter. By arranging a loan, I was able to buy a most generous back-up of spares ostensibly for the Sea Otters, as well as the modification sets. I could count on Squadron Leader Demerdashe, an REAF public relations officer, as a friend and we had made a tentative agreement in order to help out if things went wrong.

When I had gathered all the bits and pieces together from various suppliers I was faced with the possibility of problems in getting an export licence for certain restricted items. Luckily, the aircraft were now on the British register so I could prove that the spares were required to service British planes. To my surprise, I obtained the export licences without hassle. To get all this to Egypt was the next problem, but that turned out to be the easiest part of it all and involved me in a very pleasant interlude. Minos Colocotronis, the brother of my good friend Siffi, had recently married the daughter of Hadjepateras, a Greek shipowner, who had given her a converted US Liberty ship and named it *Katingo*. I made contact with the family through their agents in London and discovered that the newlyweds were going to Alexandria shortly on the *Katingo*. As a friend of the family, I was made most welcome and given a date to deliver the spares at the docks. As it was a freighter with limited passenger accommodation, I jokingly told them that I still had my NUS card, so I was signed on as crew at a shilling a day. I got a message to Cairo through the Egyptian Embassy in London.

When we arrived at Alexandria, the customs officers and Squadron Leader Demerdashe came on board with an escort as soon as the gang-plank had been positioned. They asked to see the ship's manifest and produced a requisition order from the Egyptian Government confiscating all my spares. They told me that I must make an official claim to recover them or get compensation. I made a great show of protest and indignation, but heaved a sigh of relief that Patient's fortunes had been saved. Demerdashe, or Dommie as we called him, was always full of fun, but, in spite of his slaphappy attitude, he seemed to get things done. His calling card was to sing a little ditty in the style and wail of the muezzin calling the faithful to prayer from the minaret. 'If you're ever in a ja-a-am, here I a-a-am, here I a-a-a-am-m.' He introduced me to a friend of his, Major Moh'Taher Nimr, who was the complete opposite. He was a reserved, scholarly man, strictly correct at all times, fond of classical music and a good conversationalist. We got along very well and later, when my family arrived, we entertained and were entertained at each other's homes, though we never established any real intimacy.

One day I was asked to go and see Brigadier General Missiri Bey who was then the Minister of War. Fortunately his English was good. I am ashamed to say that, despite many years spent among the Arabs, my Arabic is extremely poor. He immediately cleared his office when I entered.

'Squadron Leader Patient, I have heard a lot about your efforts to help us and I would like you to help me further.'

I was a little puzzled at the change from us to me. He had a file on his desk which was obviously a dossier on yours truly. Even more obvious was the fact that there were more than mundane details about me in it. As he fingered the pages, he remarked that I had already assisted the REAF on occasions and was obviously on good terms with them, though he was well aware of their shortcomings. Would I be willing to work for him as Aviation Adviser, reporting directly to him and not to the Air Force. To make this easy, he would requisition my Sea Otters, compensate me generously and give any help I needed to transport or erect and fly them to Heliopolis, and then instruct the REAF on their use. 'Please think about it and report to me as soon as possible, outlining your requirements for establishing a flying school with the Sea Otters.' He left me a lot to think about. My reaction was 'in for a penny, in for a pound' and the adrenalin started to flow as I began to make plans to submit to Missiri Bey.

I knew that I could rely on help (for a small consideration) from trained RAF personnel and could get equipment to build the Sea Otters in the Canal Zone. The test flying I would do myself. Their maintenance at Heliopolis by Egyptian fitters and riggers had me worried. Although many of them were British trained, I would not entrust my life to them without adequate expatriate supervision. Although a fair mechanic myself, apart from not having the time, I should have lost face if I got my hands dirty. I needed an engineer who had first-hand knowledge of Sea Otters and the only place where I was likely to find one was in the place where they were built. It would only be for a short time, long enough to erect six of the aircraft. I intended to cannibalize the other two as one hundred per cent spares backing.

My main concern was for the condition of the fabric on the wings and of the expanding brake sacs after so long in the heat of Egypt. Although I had examined one of the wings before I put in my tender and found it in good condition, the remainder were crated and I was unable to examine them. I had in any case purchased plenty of fabric which had been taken from me at Alexandria and there would be no difficulty in repossessing it. For the long term I would need an airframe rigger and an engine man as supervisors, and another pilot as an additional flying instructor. I put this proposal to Missiri Bey who agreed to pay me, tax free, £E40 per week for each of my expatriate staff, plus £E60 per week for myself. I was told that this was the highest payment allowed to anybody. In 1948 £E60 would be the equivalent of a superstar's pay. Before I returned to the UK to organize this not entirely unsatisfactory diversion from my original plans, I obtained authorization to draw money from the Egyptian Embassy in London.

Lucy's brother John Graves, who had served in the Mediterranean and the Persian Gulf in the RAF as an airframe mechanic, being unattached agreed to join me. I located an aircraft which would suit my future needs and arranged for John to accompany me to the Egyptian Embassy as a bodyguard. There I picked up £5000 in five pound notes, crammed them into a briefcase and hotfooted it to White Waltham where I examined and air-tested Airspeed Consul G-AJLK (the civil version of the RAF Oxford). I liked it, paid for it on the spot and flew it to Elstree. My brother Jim, who had served in the Army as a sergeant and had been in a motor transport unit in India and later in Japan, was my next target. I knew he would be ideal and trustworthy. He had doubts at first, as he had never worked on aero engines. I persuaded him that an aero engine was very little different from any other engine only a little larger, with some ancillaries duplicated for extra safety and eventually overcame his reluctance by saying that I could probably maintain them myself but that he was a far better engine man than I. I gladly accepted his condition that he would only come if his family could join him.

I now had to find a good pilot who could make himself available. Mike Garnett had been one of the flight lieutenants in my flight in Palestine. I eventually discovered that he had taken a job in a supermarket in the US but was now home again in Low Moor, Clitheroe, in Lancashire. On spec, I went off to Low Moor, where I was amazed to find the name of Garnett everywhere. Even the pub was the

Garnett Arms. When he had got over his surprise at seeing me, he took me on a tour of the huge dilapidated mill which had been operated by his ancestors. They had built the chapel, school and many houses and were the local squires. Although Mike had been given a good education, the family fortunes had vanished. We went to a local football match together and afterwards, over a drink, I asked him if he would come to Egypt as a flying instructor for me. He pointed out that he had not flown for some time and was quite open about having had a bad experience in severe weather conditions which had caused him to lose his nerve and give up flying. I said I would give him some dual and practice on my Consul in the UK and he could then make up his mind whether or not he wanted to join me. He had been such a good pilot that I was sure he could cope and I explained that the job we had to do would not involve any bad-weather flying. I arranged for him to meet me at Elstree.

After half an hour or so flying with me and a few landings, I patted him on the shoulder and told him, 'OK, its all yours. I'm getting out. Make a couple of landings and bring her into the hangar.' I was taking one hell of a chance. I would not have been covered by insurance and I did not ask Mike to sign an indemnity chit, so I sweated it out during the next few minutes. All was well. I asked him to go home and be ready to leave at a moment's notice. As he had already served in Egypt he knew what sort of clothes to bring.

Three arranged, one to go. Taking advantage of my prestige director Air Commodore Cunningham's influence, I was invited to A.V. Roe at Southampton. I was fortunate to be shown round by Wilf Shephard, the very engineer who had been directly involved in the conversion of the Sea Otter for Shell. Although a bit of a stick-in-the-mud, he showed great interest in the boldness of my plans but felt that it would be foolhardy for any of the well-qualified chaps to leave their jobs, even for the excellent pay, just for the short time it was going to take to erect the aircraft. I therefore tried to persuade him that he was senior enough to get leave for a few weeks, and to come when we had already prepared the trestles, jacks and tools for the final erection. Before I left, Wilf said that he would make tentative enquiries and let me know. I felt he was hooked. A few days later he phoned to say that he had arranged to take indefinite leave once he knew that everything had been prepared. He insisted that I should send him a formal contract and advance payment to cover fares and other expenses. Now I could relax a little. Things seemed to be working in my favour at last.

While I was at St. Albans, waiting for the Sea Otter spares before returning to Egypt, I was visited by a bowler-hatted, dark-suited gentleman who wanted to talk to me about PAYE regulations. It had been reported to him that I was employing Messrs Garnett, Patient and Graves. He explained the various intricacies of the system which he claimed were simple but time-consuming. I adopted a confused air and confessed with a straight face that I had difficulty in reading and certainly could not manage anything so complicated.

'It's the law,' said our bowler-hatted friend. 'It has to be done, otherwise you will be in serious trouble. If you cannot make the returns you must employ somebody else to do it.'

'Do you seriously suggest,' I asked, 'that I should employ a fourth person to make the returns on three employees?'

'If you cannot do it yourself, you have no option,' gloated the visitor.

'Oh yes I have,' said I, picking up all the papers and handing them back to him. 'The solution is simple. Messrs Garnett, Patient and Graves are now unemployed. Good day, sir.' And I showed him the door.

My journey back to Egypt with Lucy, Jim, John and Mike was not without incident. Our first night in Cannes was spent in the Hotel Montana which had been a favourite with the RAF and they proudly showed us the squadron plaques, famous signatures and other mementos which they had collected. Our next stop was at Ajaccio in Corsica, then Cagliari in Sardinia. Here we had trouble. Although I had sent signals of my flight plan well in advance, the authorities claimed that they had not recieved them and refused to let me go on to Malta. I sent an urgent signal to Rome but had no choice but to stay the night, paying exorbitant prices for unpalatable food and dingy rooms. I was awakened by a scream from Lucy as she found cockroaches crawling over her in bed. It was only after bribing an official that I was allowed to continue. Meanwhile the amount of fuel they claimed to have put in my tanks could only have been accommodated had they been almost empty before refuelling, which they most certainly were not.

Luckily, the rest of the journey went smoothly though we had to make a very early start from Malta in order to make up for lost time. We landed at Mersa Matruh. There, owing to the special endorsement in my passport, we were treated royally and quickly provided with a feast of omelette and quail while refuelling was taking place. Then on to Cairo where the irrepressible Dommie met us.

After brief introductions all round, we were rushed through formalities and taken to the National Hotel where we stayed until I managed to find a flat large enough for us all at Heliopolis. The first thing Dommie arranged for me through Missiri Bey was to have my passport re-endorsed, as visas were then needed for both entry and exit. This privilege was held by very few and ensured preferential treatment at airports and checkpoints, with only cursory examination of my luggage. Invariably, when I made a trip outside Egypt I returned with goods unobtainable there which had been asked for by senior officers or government officials with whom I had dealings. I was paid for these, but at prices less than I had paid. This was an acceptable form of bribery for the higher echelon. On these occasions, I was met at the aircraft by an official with a car and driven, complete with my purchases, through the gates without customs or passport control.

The flat I had found was near Heliopolis airfield, but we had only been there a few days when brother Jim complained to me that our servants' room had no bedding or suitable furniture. I explained that this was the norm, but he was so disgusted that he said he would not stay there unless I rectified the matter. It was useless to argue so I gave him the money to buy what he thought fit. About three weeks later I suggested that he should take a look at the servants' quarters and of course the additions had been sold. We live and learn.

149

Esmet Gammal was a very good friend to me the whole time I was in Cairo. His father owned a large and fashionable bar. We got to know each other at Almaza airport as he also had a Consul and pilot's licence and was hoping to fly lobsters (crayfish) from the Red Sea to Cairo commercially. He was much younger than I, but became a firm friend of the family and was a great help when I was away on business. His father was worried about his son's flying and made me all sorts of offers, hoping that I would discourage it.

*　*　*

Preparation for the erection of the Sea Otters now began. I sent Jim and John to the Canal Zone to get as much done as they could, but in the meanwhile, with the imminent arrival of Jim's family and my own children, I had to find two more apartments, preferably near the English School in Heliopolis. This was not too difficult. When I was told at last that everything was now ready at Kasfareet, I cabled Wilf Shephard to come as soon as possible. The RAF were allowing him to stay in the Officers' Mess while he was supervising the erection of the Sea Otters. Dommie and I met him from the BOAC flight and drove him straight to Kasfareet, explaining on the way how his supervision of the work was to be carried out. Engine runs and taxiing tests for brakes and so on were carried out by Mike Garnett but on no account were the planes to be flown. I intended to do all the test flying myself before ferrying to Heliopolis. I had arranged with the Warrant Officer in charge for a small supply of fabric and dope taughtener which might be needed for repairs but was in any case essential for inspection patches to be opened up, as a search needed to be made for erosion or foreign bodies. Should a large amount be needed, my brother would go to Cairo and arrange a supply through Dommie. I impressed on them all that as far as the RAF was concerned these were British civil-registered aircraft belonging to me and on no account were they to divulge the REAF's interest. It was of course accepted without question that I was Jim's older brother as it would be inconceivable to an Arab that an older brother could work for a younger.

It was time for me to return to England. Lucy had been back there

150

for medical treatment and the children had now finished school. All had to be collected. I also had some business matters to attend to. My old friend Sid Plumb had located two spare engines in Blackpool suitable for the Consul so we drove to Southend and hired an Auster for the day. On the engine run-up, I queried the petrol situation, as the fuel gauge showed only three-quarters full. I was informed that the gauge was misreading and when it showed empty there was still forty minutes cruising left. It is just as well that I was experienced as a glider pilot and in flying single-engined aircraft. Contrary to my information, the engine stopped immediately the fuel gauge touched zero. I have forgotten on which aerodome I made a 'dead stick' landing, just managing to clear the runway and roll onto the perimeter track. From there Sid and I had to push the bloody thing to the reception area for refuelling. The air was full of obscenities directed at the aircraft's owner. When it was refilled the gauge showed full, confirming the outrageous lie which could have resulted in a serious accident. We carried on to Blackpool, completed our business and returned to Southend. Unfortunately I had paid for the hire prior to leaving and the owner was conveniently absent.

Lucy feeling better with the children now with her and after a shopping spree for clothes, we were ready to return to Egypt. Paris was our first overnight stop on the way back. Unfortunately there was a large convention in progress and it soon became obvious that we would have to find a hotel in the suburbs. By an extraordinary coincidence, however, we met Yousef Khorrasani, a very good friend who had a small jewellers' shop in the Khan-el-Khalili in Cairo and was an official jewel evaluator for the Egyptian customs. Yousef used to say with a smile that the only difference between us was that he had been born at night and I by day. He insisted that we should go back to his hotel. That too was full, but, after much cajoling, the proprietress put a couple of mattresses on the floor of the linen room which was of course considered a great lark by the children. After a substantial meal we all had a good night and Yousef saw us off at Tousous-le-Noble with a large basket of fruit.

Jim, John and Dommie were waiting for us and we were swiftly installed in our new flat. Dommie was a frequent visitor and had an easy way which made him popular with the children. He often brought a companion with him, usually somebody who might be useful to me in business. Shortly after we had settled in, he came with a true gentleman of the desert. The bearing and carriage of such desert chiefs has to be experienced to appreciate the Arab fully. Most Europeans only see the dockside or town Arab, who bears little resemblance to his noble brother. This chief had a turquoise mine in Sinai, but his visit to me was simply a courtesy call. While we were having coffee I stupidly admired a fine turquoise ring he was wearing. As soon as I had spoken I realized my mistake. He immediately removed the ring and gave it to me. I felt awful but knew better than to refuse a gift. Later I managed to get it returned with a gift from me.

News travels quickly, for, within a week of Lucy returning, Ebraheim, our cook at Abu Sueir, who had been drafted into the Egyptian Army, visited us. The children were all for getting him back, so making a note of his unit and number, I had a few words in the right quarter and, three days later, he was working for us again.

To gain or retain one's place in society, it was necessary to be seen at functions attended by King Farouk. These occurred almost weekly during the Cairo season (winter) and then of course the Alexandria season (summer). If they valued their virginity or honour, good looking young women, or even the not so young, stayed away from the soirées, otherwise the notoriously amorous successor to the Egyptian throne might take a fancy to one of them. She would then be approached by an equerry and told to invite the King to dance. Protocol forbade the reverse procedure. To refuse would be to court disaster. If an expatriate employee, she would be sent home for some trumped-up reason. In other cases, it might lead to the loss of their family's residents' visas. One young lady got away with it by whispering to the equerry, 'I would very much like to, but it is the wrong period of the month', and quietly left.

On our frequent drives along the desert road between Cairo and the Canal Zone we would often stop for a rest at a café/bar. Not knowing when or where I might have the chance of doing business, I usually carried cash in my briefcase. Returning with Jim once, I left my briefcase containing papers, my Beretta pistol and £E 2,000 in cash in the café. When I got home I realized where I had left it and sent Jim back to collect it. I was lucky. He returned with the briefcase and money intact. I often use quotations and one that I used more than others was one of my father's. 'The only difference between a wise man and a fool is that a fool will make the same mistake twice.' A few weeks later I did the same stupid thing, although this time there was no money involved. Again, Jim was sent to retrieve it. When I next used the car there was a notice stuck to the window. 'A fool will make the same mistake three times.'

Some of the Sea Otters were now ready to be collected and arrangements were made for offices and a hangar to be at our disposal at Heliopolis, while six pilots had already been selected for the conversion. I rushed off to Kasfareet with Jim who told me that Wilf Shephard had been very thorough in his inspection and had helped in every possible way. I had never flown a Sea Otter but I found the testing straightforward. I did, however, spend considerably more time than was necessary on the test as I wanted to have a few hours' experience on the type before instructing pilots who might be less well trained than RAF graduates. I flew Wilf back to Heliopolis with me, showing him a few of the sights on the way, including the Abdin (Farouk's) Palace. Wilf stayed a short while with us for sightseeing before returning to his 'nine to five' existence. He admitted that he envied us, but it was not the life for him.

Missiri Bey was pleased with the start we had made and, after inspecting the aircraft, he told me that it had been reported to him that I had flown near the palace and was lucky not to have been fired at. I was then instructed to liaise closely with Air Commodore McCarthy Bey, the senior Egyptian Air Force officer. He was a charming man of the old school whose son became very friendly with my own. We had met before and we had got on extremely well. He realized some of the difficulties ahead of me. It was the group captains and wing commanders who resented the fact that, as I was working for the Minister of War, they had no jurisdiction over me. The other aircraft were tested and then given to Mike Garnett to fly to Heliopolis, with a warning to avoid the palace. This gave him plenty of time to get to know the plane thoroughly before embarking on the training programme we had worked out between us.

By this time Jim was much more confident about handling the engine side of things. The senior Egyptian mechanic in charge of the ground crew allocated to us, Ashri, was extremely efficient and he and Jim became firm friends.

One night, when I was returning from Ismailia, a light was flashed at me just outside the town. As I slowed I could see a chain stretched across the road. I knew that this was no police block. It was a very hot night and my side window was partly down. A ragged individual jumped onto the running board and held on as I accelerated and broke the chain, the end of which whipped round and shattered the side window. Meanwhile I had removed my pistol from the side pocket and fired a shot through the window. There was a yell, and whoever it was departed from his perch rather smartly. I certainly didn't stop to find out if he was hurt. When I got home I found that there was only a small dent in the upright pillar of the windscreen apart from the window damage.

The most promising pupil we had at Heliopolis was undoubtedly Osama Sidki, whose father held the very first Egyptian commercial pilot's licence. Sidki was a natural flier. There is, however, more to being a good pilot than the ability to make good landings, and in the areas of navigation, meteorology and other allied subjects many of our pupils were sadly lacking. The main reason for this was the simple fact that no Egyptian officer could be allowed to lose face and therefore no officer was allowed to fail an exam. This was arranged by the simple expedient of reducing the pass mark so that everybody got through. Despite the protests of British instructors, the Egyptians were paying the piper and so called the tune.

One glaring example of this was a pupil named Bogdadi who was one of the six originally selected for us to convert to Sea Otters. The lad was just not up to standard. He would repeatedly forget to lower the undercarriage on the final approach. Even when he was reminded to go through the final checks again, he would continue, oblivious of the red warning lights. After several attempts without any apparent improvement, I passed him to Mike Garnett as a change of instructor and a slightly different approach often makes all the difference. Mike later gave him a negative report but I thought I would give him one last check. Again, on final approach, no wheels were down. I asked him to look outside to see if everything was ready for landing. He looked, but failed to notice the lack of wheels. We are getting quite close to the ground now. 'We are not landing on water,' I said sarcastically, but it still didn't sink in. 'Put the bloody wheels down,' I yelled at him, but his only reply was to look round and say, 'Don't be nervous.' I took over, dived for the ground, pulled up sharply and just missed the hangar roof. After making a circuit I landed and immediately drafted a letter asking for him to be grounded. A week or two later I was told that he had been given an instructor's job at the elementary flying school run by his brother, Wing Commander Bogdadi, with whom I later had many a contretemps.

Sidki was a pleasure to teach. Good-looking and good company, he spent many a social evening with Jim and me. One evening at the Auberge de Turf we were drinking in the upstairs bar. Jim and Sidki were sitting on either side of Farouk's current girl friend who happened to be a Greek singer. She was wearing Sidki's peaked cap. By a lucky chance I glanced down the staircase and recognized one of Farouk's bodyguards. In a few seconds I grabbed the hat off the girl and pulled Jim and Sidki to the bar just as Farouk walked in. He gave a slight acknowledgement to my bow and passed through to the games room. It was a lucky escape. He could be very vindictive towards anyone who encroached on his private preserves.

On another memorable occasion at the Auberge de Turf I shared the bank at baccarat with my friend Siffi Colocotronis. We opened at £200 (£100 each) and built the bank to £800. Then Siffi withdrew, leaving me with £400 in the bank. I continued and, by a run of good luck, built it up to £1,600. I was willing to continue as the whole was not being covered. Just as I was about to draw the cards, King Farouk walked in and called 'Banco', covering the remainder. I had two choices, either to take the £1,600 (which would have resulted in loss of face) or draw the cards for £3,200 or nothing. I have made some big bets in my life but that was the biggest. I drew the cards and lost, but received a nod of appreciation from the King.

Stories of debauchery and worse were continually circulating about Farouk, many encouraged and exaggerated by his enemies. There was more to one of them than merely rumour. He was said to have taken a fancy to the wife of a lieutenant who was then promoted to Captain and sent to the Sudan without his wife. Returning unexpectedly to his home, he met the bodyguards who always accompanied the King. Warned not to go into the bedroom, he did so and was shot. This apparently did happen and the concensus of opinion was that the enraged cuckold was not killed by the bodyguard.

It is easy to condemn, but one wonders how one might have developed in similar circumstances. I remember Farouk's visit to the UK as a young prince. He was a handsome lad, fawned upon, and his every whim and fancy acceded to. His hangers-on were only mindful of their own gain when procuring beautiful women and objects to please him. Idolized by his people in the early part of his reign, his later excesses and the divorce of a much loved queen, his youthful figure having been transformed through debauchery to ugly obesity, completely lost him the respect and affection of his nation and the outside world.

While gambling at the Auberge de Turf, I became friendly with Hamed, a young Egyptian aristocrat. We spent many a night together, often with a Turkish bath to speed our recovery. I knew that he was never short of money because the casinos never hesitated to replenish his chips. Although they required a signature from me, they never bothered him. He used to run a Rolls Royce 20/25 which he changed every two years. I noticed once that Hamed had lost over £2,000 two evenings running. I told him that if he carried on at that rate he would soon be broke. 'Very difficult' was his quiet reply. I discovered later that among his other possessions he owned almost the whole of one side of a fashionable shopping street in Cairo, roughly the length of Bond Street.

*　　*　　*

People brought up in humble circumstances, when faced with the sudden and unexpected accumulation of considerable wealth, frequently indulge in rash and extravagant behaviour. In this regard I was no exception.

My previous trip to UK had been brought forward a few days by receiving a phone call from a friend, telling me that his secretary, Joan, had received news of her father's serious illness. She could not afford the BOAC fare to the UK, so I offered to take her with me. Shortly after her return, my gesture was repaid when I was told of the coming disposal of approximately 100 tons of new aircraft spares which were to be sold virtually as scrap. With this information and by making a quick trip to the Canal Zone, I was able to make a fair appraisal of the contents through my RAF friends. I felt I would need a partner for this deal. I discussed it with Hamed who, unusual for an Arab, had not the slightest interest in making money. He offered to lend me any cash I might need but insisted that he must not get involved with anything even slightly connected with military, political or government matters. With this backing I was prepared to go it alone and on the appointed day became the owner of a huge mish-mash of spares.

I now had problems of security, transportation and storage until I could find time to sort and catalogue them. Security was easy. A few pounds given to hard-up RAF lads, with the promise of more to come later if nothing was missing, ensured a fair degree of safety. The storage problem was solved by renting an old, derelict palace of King Fouad nearby, where fortunately the roof was in good condition. Most of the spares were stacked in various rooms. Dommie helped me to get all this moved on low-loaders from the REAF and I borrowed a couple from the RAF. This was enough to transport the lot to Heliopolis. In the following weeks every minute of our spare time was used in sifting, sorting and listing. I also rented a small lock-up garage where I stored small but valuable items such as bearings.

157

It was suggested to me that I should buy some Horsa gliders which were on sale at Kabrit. This done, I sent Jim and John to liaise with the RAF and erect three of them for me to test and fly to Cairo. No Egyptian pilot had ever done glider towing, but, of course, Mike Garnett had. It was all rather difficult because although the REAF had Dakotas, none had the towing attachment and release gear. I eventually found a cannibalized Dakota and, through the old pal's act and a case of Scotch to the Sergeants' Mess, the necessary piece of equipment was 'found' in the boot of my car after I left on my next visit to the Canal Zone. Fortunately the crates containing the Horsas also contained tow ropes. I saw no point in making a test flight. Once the towing gear had been fitted to a REAF Dakota, I arranged for Mike to tow me to Heliopolis.

I decided to take my brother on the first flight. He sat in the cockpit with me as I gave the all clear sign to go. Being light, the Horsa lifted off quickly, but, as the speed built up, the pressure, even with full forward trim, was as much as I could hold. Fearful of the control column breaking, I knew that I would have to pull off before levelling as then the speed would increase further. At this stage we were still too low over the water to pull off and make a safe return. I shouted to Jim to go and sit in the rear seat for safety. Even as he was doing this, I realized that perhaps being so tail heavy the trim might have been reversed. It was a big gamble. If I was wrong, I would have to pull off or endanger the towing aircraft. Mike was completely oblivious of the drama being enacted behind him. But, what a relief! The trim wires had been crossed so I was able to carry on. I let Jim come back to the cockpit and we were eventually dropped at Heliopolis. I blamed myself for the whole thing, not having made a thorough inspection before taking off.

A few days later the second Horsa was delivered without a hitch. For the third, arrangements were made for the delivery to be witnessed by government and military officials. Shortage of space meant that this was the last to be erected; the rest, still crated, were brought up by low loaders. I decided to take John with me. Shortly after take off there was an almighty thump. I sent him back to

158

investigate and he reported that we had lost our starboard undercarriage. The Horsa is designed to enable the pilot to jettison the undercarriage when landing in rough terrain or restricted space, a skid under the fuselage usually resulting in a smooth, short landing. But with one wheel gone, I was left with no alternative but to drop the other. I had arranged with Mike to tow me a little higher than before so that I could better demonstrate the amazing manoeuvrability of the glider. As the assembled VIPs were standing near the control tower, I made a very steep approach towards them and stopped barely ten yards from the scared onlookers.

Apart from training, and running the flying school, I was also responsible for the exercises of other units. Frequently there was considerable frustration for me over the endless and ridiculous excuses for badly executed tasks and some not done at all. I had no disciplinary powers. Even the complaints put through various senior officers were for the most part ignored. As I was getting very edgy and nervy, Lucy asked me to see the doctor who looked after BOAC crews when they needed help. He gave me a very thorough examination, all the time asking me about myself and my work. He then went to his typewriter and proceeded to type what I thought must be a letter to a specialist. When he had finished he said, 'Captain, you haven't followed your inappropriate name. However, here is a complete cure for what ails you. Learn it and follow it. That will be five pounds.' When I looked at what he had typed, I recognized a piece of Kipling. I learnt it by heart.

'Now it is not good for the Christian's health to hustle the Aryan
    brown,
For the Christian riles, and the Aryan smiles, and he weareth the
    Christian down;
And the end of the fight is a tombstone white with the name of the
    late deceased,
And the epitaph drear: "A fool lies here who tried to hustle the
    East."'

Soon afterwards, I laid on a night exercise only to find in the morning that it had not been carried out. On investigation I was told that it had been the Group Captain's birthday, so they had a party. I think I surprised them when I asked why they hadn't invited me and walked off without another word.

On one of my visits to England I was invited to a demonstration of the Chrislea Ace, a neat four-seater aircraft powered by the very reliable Gipsy Major 10 engine. This aircraft had some novel and unorthodox controls and was quite viceless. By coincidence, the sales manager had been an officer in my squadron at Great Dunmow and in Palestine. I was willing to purchase one of these planes which I thought had great potential provided I was given an agency agreement for the Middle East. A demonstration flight was proposed before I was allowed to fly solo, but I insisted that, as it was claimed that the differences in control were so easily learned, from a sales point of view it would be much better to be able to say that I had flown it with only a briefing on the differences. They agreed, and after signing a waiver of claim I took off. I was quite impressed by the performance, stability, simplicity of handling and lack of any vicious characteristics. They did not have another Ace available, so I bought the demonstration aircraft I had flown. The only snag was that it only had six months left out of the twelve-month C of A (Certificate of Airworthiness). This led to many difficulties later. I got a 'carnet de passage' to export the aircraft and, after obtaining a small spares backup, flew it by easy stages to Cairo. Although I dislike flying single-engined aircraft over wide stretches of water, particularly without parachute or dinghy, I flew the long water crossing via Malta and Benghazi, thus saving both money and time.

Before I left England I took my friend Sid Plumb for a flip and while he wasn't looking I loosened a hidden thumbscrew holding the control column. Later I pulled it back with a cry of, 'Oh my God,' as it became loose in my hand, together with a feigned look of horror. This stunt gave me some laughs on many occasions and an insight into the nervous make-up of my various friends.

I gave quite a few demonstrations with the Ace, including one for invited prospective customers at Almaza. They were impressed with a short landing when I managed to stop in just a width of the perimeter track, but no sales resulted. I had a lot of fun with it and it was far more economical to run around in than my Consul.

The Air Attaché in Cairo asked my help to get a couple of pilots back to England, who, for some reason, were stranded in Cairo without means of support. I made a point of keeping a good relationship with the Embassy and, as I intended to take the Ace back for its C of A renewal, I offered to let them take it for me. To this end I picked them up and drove them to my flat. My brother thought they were a pair of shysters but I foolishly ignored his warning. They had their shoes repaired and laundry attended to while I housed, fed and entertained them. I also got Jim to do a 'top overhaul' on the Ace although it had only flown for about forty hours. Then I loaded it up with a considerable cargo of goodies unobtainable in the UK for my mother and family. With the carnet for petrol and plenty of food, money and sovereigns for emergency use, I sent the pair off with route maps and instructions for the delivery of the aircraft.

A sorry trail of sheer inefficiency and outright skulduggery followed. At Benghazi (Benina) they complained of rough running of the nearly new engine and asked for a new carburettor. I cabled London and Sid Plumb obtained one and air-freighted it to Benghazi. The RAF, who knew me well, fitted it and sent them off. During this time they stayed at the Sergeants' Mess and ran up a bill which they said I would settle. From the flying time logged they must have flown all round the coast and they eventually left the aircraft at Tunis, having disposed of all the contents. They then conned an airline to fly them to Paris and send the bill to me. The final ingratitude was to go to the Royal Aero Club and state that I had sent them off in an unairworthy aircraft.

By the time I was free to fly to Tunis and collect the Ace, the C of A had expired. An American engineer who had looked after the plane thought that the two pilots had been scared of the short water crossing to Malta. I gave the engine a test run and found nothing wrong, but when I worked the carburettor hot air intake there was no reaction. On investigation I found that the cable had slipped and, being spring-loaded to return to hot air, had remained in that position. The trouble was obvious. In the cool of the morning the engine would run well, but, after flying for a while with the sun well up, with hot air intake rough running would occur. I am not an engineer, but the simple normal test on a pilot's run-up revealed all. A new costly carburettor plus the aggro, loss of gifts for my family and eventually a costly row with the Board of Trade was the result. I returned to Cairo in less than half the flying hours they had taken to Tunis. At Benina I was given the bill they had left for me to settle.

The sequel to all this occurred later when, on my next visit to England, I was informed that a certain gentleman from the Board of Trade wanted to get in touch with me. I duly phoned him and he demanded to know why the Ace had not been returned to Britain. I patiently explained that I had gone to great lengths to get it back and that it had cost me at least £600 and a lot of disillusionment and inconvenience. Despite this there was a curt 'That's nothing to do with us', which was like having salt rubbed into the wound. I was furious. 'If you want the bloody aircraft come and get it,' I replied, and slammed the receiver down.

End of story? Not quite. I had bought a new Rover car in Cairo in 1948 for which I paid £1,000. In 1951 Padre Johnson, our local vicar and our friend, was returning to the UK with his family, so I offered to let him drive the car home. He was glad to do this and duly delivered it to Sid Plumb. At that time there was sixty per cent purchase tax on car imports which was payable on disposal of the vehicle within three years. I lent it to Sid, not knowing that in the small print it was forbidden for anyone other than the owner to drive it. On a later visit, Sid gave me the sad news that I no longer had a car to drive. A Board of Trade official had turned up at St Albans just as he was driving into his nursery and had asked him how he liked the left hand drive. 'OK when you get used to it,' replied Sid in all innocence. He thought the chap was interested in buying it. He was then astounded to be told to have the car ready for collection the following morning as it was now confiscated owing to contravention of the terms of import without payment of purchase tax. 'Furthermore,' said our not so civil servant, 'you can tell Mr Patient that if he wants his bloody car, he can come and get it.'

By rare coincidence this so-and-so had come across my name which is perhaps not too common and had put two and two together. I went to the AA and asked their advice. There was nothing I could do. They advised me to go and see the relevant department and explain the situation, so I made an appointment to do this at an office near Chancery Lane. I appeared before a panel of three haughty-looking officials, having explained that I had not knowingly contravened the regulations and had sent the car to England on humanitarian grounds. Having presented my case, I was asked to put it in writing and send it (in quadruplicate) to them and they would reply. I asked what the normal outcome might be and they told me there would probably be a small fine, then, after paying the purchase tax (£600), I could have the car back. Otherwise it would be put into an auction, but they would let me know so that I could buy it back if I wished. I pointed out that the car was only worth about £400 so if that was all it would fetch, would I be responsible for any differential? When told that my only liability was the confiscation, I could see that there was no more to be gained. I thought that I would shake up these petty bureaucrats so I simply said, 'Gentlemen you can stick the car up your arses,' and walked out. It was an expensive joke but the memory of their shocked faces has given me much amusement over the years.

Joan (see page 157) showed me the plans of a 34-foot motor launch named *Marina*, which was for disposal by the BSDM. The one-upmanship in owning a boat appealed to me, particularly as I had friends at Kasfareet and Kabrit who would look after it. Having purchased it, I sent brother Jim to Port Said to collect it. He ran into difficulties, but being 'Patient' overcame them. The first hiccup was the battery – dead as a Dodo. He commented on this to the sergeant in charge, and an exchange of views followed something like this: 'Sorry mate, but bought as is'. 'Would it be possible to get another?'

'Might be. Depends.' 'As one ex-sergeant to another, would a fiver find one?' 'Expect so; will go look.' Within half an hour both battery and fiver were exchanged.

The sergeant returned with a squaddie who had a few days' leave and asked Jim to give him a lift to Ismailia, which he was pleased to grant. Owing to the delay a night stop was made at El Kantara check post, where they were offered a hut to sleep in. After the accustomed baksheesh to the superintendent they left early in the morning. I admonished my brother for not checking, but with hindsight, he had spent only a short time in the Middle East, with the result that they had only gone a few miles before the engine spluttered and stopped, having run out of fuel. The tanks had been 'milked' during the night. Fortunately they drifted to the west bank of the canal and Jim went to look for petrol. He was lucky to find a small village nearby where he bought petrol, engaging local boys to carry it. On their way once more, the fan belt broke, a problem solved with the use of the squaddie's leather boot laces. Taking it gently, they arrived at Ismailia where Jim treated his companion to the best meal the NAAFI could rustle up and proceeded alone to Kabrit. With *Marina* at last in safe keeping, brother James returned to Cairo and poured out his tale of woe to the merriment of us all.

While in Cairo with friends I often visited Madame Badia's floor shows. These were well established and Madame knew everyone of importance. Her protégés were famous international names in the world of Arabic entertainment. When I was approached by an Egyptian friend, who knew I had an aircraft in Cairo, asking if I could get somebody out of Egypt unofficially, I naturally wanted to know who and why. He was not prepared to tell me unless I was willing to help, but did reveal that the person concerned owed a great deal of money to the government in taxes, was not a criminal of any sort, but was in fact somebody I knew. 'Let me know how much it's worth and I'll think about it,' was my reply. The following day 2,000 Egyptian pounds (worth a little more than English pounds) was handed to me in cash. I could keep this if I would do the job quickly. It was then revealed that the person was Madame Badia.

I discussed the matter with Jim who agreed to go along with it if I would arrange the details. I had two aeroplanes in Cairo at the time and, knowing the area between Cairo and the Canal Zone well, both from the air and by land, I thought it could be done without too much risk. But I needed another pilot for a safe operation as I could not afford to be linked directly to the event. As luck would have it, I had met a pilot called Monty Muir a few days before who seemed a possibility. I contacted him and asked if he would like to earn £200 for just one flight. At that time £200 was two months' salary for a pilot, so he knew there must be something dodgy about it. I reassured him that it was nothing to do with drugs, so he asked to know more about it. We went back to my flat where I told him my plans. He would take my own Consul which was stationed at Almaza, clear customs with manifests showing nil passengers and freight, with destination Amman, Jordan. He would take another manifest with him showing a passenger. This he would produce at Amman.

Jim and I had already reconnoitred the place where the pick-up would be made both by air and by car. At the same time we measured the distance and tested the firmness of the sand. We clocked exactly, keeping a uniform speed, the time needed to reach the police check point on the Suez road which we used regularly on business trips to RAF stations in the Canal Zone. We stayed for a few minutes to exchange courtesies with the guards and disbursed a few cigarettes and other goodies in the usual way to ensure speedy clearance. A few miles further on (measured exactly) there was a winding gap through sandhills. These obscured the view of the intended landing strip from the road. We drove up to the strip a few times looking for soft spots but all was well. Our only worry was the possibility of a sandstorm blowing up which would obstruct the passage through the dunes.

I told Monty Muir all about this, instructed him to stay low after take off and showed him the precise landing place. I gave him an exact take-off time and told him to waste any surplus time at the aircraft which had already been refuelled and checked. I drove him to the airport myself as I had arranged to take the Chrislea Ace, ostensibly for an air test but in reality to act as master of ceremonies. I intended to fly on the same path as Monty was to take, hoping to confuse the radar watch. I would also be listening out on a prearranged frequency with an agreed code word to abort if I saw anything going amiss, in which case he would return to Almaza claiming some engine fault.

Meanwhile Jim and my brother-in-law John went by car to the rendezvous with a folding table, a well-filled picnic basket and a large white tablecloth to spread over the top of the car when he heard engines and if everything was in order. The passenger was to travel by chauffeur-driven car to about two miles past the police check point, stop, open the bonnet and pretend to have broken down. A minute or two later Jim would drive up, offer assistance and, if all clear, transfer the passenger, laying her down on the back seat. He would then proceed to the pick-up area. I watched the switch from my aircraft and saw the car drive off the road through the sand dunes. The tablecloth was put on top of the car with seconds to spare. With very little wind Monty was able to go straight in, load the passenger, turn round and take off in the opposite direction. I did not see the end of this as I thought it expedient to fly the other side of the road, near the checkpoint, turning and deliberately cutting and gunning my engine as if I was in trouble, thinking that this might keep inquisitive eyes away from the dust raised by the plane's take off. Eventually I returned to Almaza on Monty's backtrack. Jim takes up the story from the time when Badia was transferred to the plane:

'As she was getting in, Badia was half-crying as she kissed John and me and slipped me a fifty pound note. She never knew if she could really trust us and could hardly believe it was happening. So far, so good. After a while we packed up the picnic and headed out to the desert road. Before we got there I was stopped by an Egyptian policeman on a motorbike. My heart stopped too. I gathered from his broken English that he wanted to know what the hell we were doing there. I explained as best I could and showed him the half-eaten picnic. He tapped his head – more or less indicating that we were mad (I can't blame him) and then said that he had heard a plane and saw it circle round this area and land. What did we know about it? I just shrugged my shoulders so he told me to follow him to the checkpoint where four or five police searched the car thoroughly. They thought the plane had landed with drugs on board. I knew the sergeant and one or two of the others as I often used that road on business and always gave them cigarettes. I did this again as well as some food from the picnic basket and everybody seemed happy. Although I don't smoke, it always paid to carry cigarettes and the odd bottle out there. The sergeant said, "You English are mad." I was grateful. At one point I saw a terrible prison cell confronting me.'

I gave Jim and John fifty pounds each for their part in the operation. It was not until forty years later that I heard about the fifty pounds each that Badia had given them. I was also surprised to find out later that although Monty Muir flew my aircraft to Amman, he did not go direct but via Beirut, where he dropped off Madame Badia first, having been bribed by her with another two hundred pounds. Badia confirmed all this when I met her in Beirut some years later. I had planned the exercise with military precision and could not help feeling gratified by the efficiency with which it was carried out.

* * *

I had earlier bought sixteen Pratt and Whitney twin Wasp engines (ex-RAF) which were sold as 'time expired'. This meant that they would have to be completely overhauled before being used again. It was the policy of the RAF not to release the log books of the engines, but having only recently left the RAF, where my job kept me in close touch with the maintenance units, I was able to cash in on my good relationship with those in charge. I was therefore able to find out the contents of the various lots which were being put up for tender. The log books of the sixteen engines showed that three of them had in fact been overhauled and were not time-expired, knowledge which would have been useless without the supporting documents. Should I have lost the tender the only interested buyers were scrap dealers and Mike Day for EAE (Egyptian Aircraft Engineering).

I had met Wing Commander Day socially, but now various business deals were to prove advantageous to me while he was with EAE. I managed to get the sixteen engines brought to Cairo and deposited on the veranda of King Fouad's derelict palace in Heliopolis, which

I had rented from Prince Abbas Halim. A week or two later Mike Day visited me and asked to buy the engines. We haggled over the price, but I stuck out for £50 each and told him that, what was more, they would cost £100 each in a fortnight's time. He left in high dudgeon. About a month later he was back. 'Joe you are a robber, but I have persuaded my directors to give you £50 each for the engines.' 'Sorry Mike,' I replied. 'They are now £100 each and in two weeks time will be £200 each.' He departed in even higher dudgeon. Six weeks later I was given a cheque for £3,200 but he saved face by sending it by one of his minions.

Mike Day was probably a good engineer but he could have benefited by learning to play poker or by taking a commercial course. He claimed to have a free hand but I rather doubt it in view of subsequent transactions.

There was an embargo on the supply of arms and aircraft spares to Egypt, but the REAF was in urgent need of Pratt and Whitney main shell bearings. I was asked to obtain these but did not hold out much hope. However, I made a note of the part number for future reference. On my next visit to an auction in the Canal Zone, I happened to glance at a pile of three or four hundred assorted unlabelled boxes and just caught sight of the corner of a box with the last three numerals showing, which I thought I recognized. The lot had already been bought for £40 by an Egyptian scrap dealer whom I knew. Strolling back to the dealer, I told him that I was only interested in three or four boxes but would give him the £40 he had paid for the lot. He quibbled, and wanted to know which were the boxes. I assured him that the items were of no use to him and were not the platinum-pointed spark plugs all the dealers were looking for. As he hesitated, I took out a bundle of notes and prepared to walk away. This seldom failed and he accepted my offer. Scattering the pile, I found two boxes with the identical numbers and because of the size of the box felt sure that they were shell bearings. I confirmed this as soon as I was in my car. A week later my brother sold them for £900. I must explain why.

All my invoices were signed J. Patient and by my brother Jim. Much of what I had done was (marginally?) outside the law. If, therefore, someone had to go to prison it was good sense that Jim should be that person. We had a private agreement about this. Jim was a very good plumber but nevertheless could not earn enough to keep his family and mine, whereas I as a pilot could. In the unlikely event of him being incarcerated, I would pay him £1,000 for every year spent inside – far more than he could earn as a plumber outside.

We all took a moonlight trip on the Nile in a felucca. I recall the lapping of the water, distant snatches of music, myriads of stars as the boat, with creaks and flapping of sails, makes its almost majestic, lumbering way along, pausing for a picnic on one of the small islands dotted along the Nile. It is difficult to imagine a more relaxing or romantic setting. Space prohibits my describing the beauty, degradation, opulence, poverty, despotism, tourist wonders, climate, bugs, smells, music and all sorts of manners, habits, political and religious persecutions, which in any case have been written about by writers more qualified than I.

I was sent to see Prince Abbas Halim (Farouk's uncle and he from whom I had rented the palace). He was most affable and proceeded to pump me on the possibility of obtaining four-engined bombers for the REAF. I went to the UK to explore availability. I had previously met Freddy Laker, so I went to see him at Aviation Traders to discuss the purchase of Halifaxes and spares. We agreed what I thought was a very modest figure for eight or ten aircraft and I returned to Cairo to report. I was thanked and told that was the end of the affair as far as I was concerned, which surprised me somewhat. However, I had quite enough on my plate. A few weeks later Halifaxes began to arrive and I was asked to convert selected Egyptian pilots to the aircraft. A bigger surprise was that they were the very aircraft for which I had negotiated except that they had been bought for a price many times greater than the one I had discussed. To add insult to injury, I was then asked by the Prince to sign a declaration that the aircraft were equipped to war standard, despite the fact that turrets and ammunition racks were not operable. It was an embarrassment but, having tested the aircraft, I eventually signed a statement that the aircraft were eminently suited for the training of four-engined bomber pilots and for limited operations.

Wing Commander Bogdadi and I were destined to cross swords on several occasions. He obviously bore me a grudge over my grounding of his younger brother so far as Sea Otters were concerned. The situation was not improved when he was to take a Halifax to Alexandria and I among others was to be given a lift. I was the last to go on board and noticed heavy freight towards the tail which, apart from not being lashed down, was stowed too far aft. I had a quiet word with Bogdadi, suggesting a relocation of the freight. He took umbrage and said that he was the Captain of the aircraft. I simply replied that I would make my own way to Alexandria and left the aircraft.

A further cause of discord with Bogdadi was my being accused of teaching the wrong approach speed when involved with the Halifax conversions. The way it was put to me was that as an experienced pilot it would be safe for me to approach with a minimum of safety speed but that with less experienced pilots it would be suicidal. Bogdadi maintained that I had been teaching 20 knots slower than the recommended speed in the pilot's notes. This was a serious accusation and I was puzzled. I asked to see the notes and quickly realized his error. With hindsight it might have been better to let him off lightly, but I was fed up with his antagonistic attitude. I cross-examined him.

'You have flown the Halifax, Wing Commander?'

'You know I have,' was the reply.

'Can you tell me what mark of Halifax you have flown?'

'Yes, of course.'

'Then why is it that the pilot's notes you have referred to are for a different mark of Halifax? For your information, owing to a re-positioning of the pitot head, the other notes recommend the approach to be made exactly as I have been teaching. If you have been approaching at the speed you thought to be right, you must have made excessive use of the brakes with severe tyre wear. I suggest you should take more care with your facts before wasting these gentlemen's valuable time.'

I left the room in what I believe is called a pregnant silence, but I can imagine the dressing down he must have received after I had gone. Later, when Nasser took over from Neguib, Bogdadi became a senior minister so I was undoubtedly *persona non grata*.

The training of Sea Otter crews had continued apace and I was now asked to conclude it with water landings at Alexandria. This was something I had hoped to put off until after I had made a quick trip to the UK where I wanted to organize a couple of take offs and landings on water. Mike Garnett and I had never tried them, but we kept this to ourselves. Mike made it quite clear to me that he would have no part in it. By sheer chance I met a pilot who was in transit through Cairo and who at one time had flown amphibious aircraft, though not the Sea Otter. He considered that the technique was the same and explained the salient points to me with great emphasis on what to do if the aircraft began 'porpoising' when landing on water. The method to use when landing at night or on dead calm water was equally important. If I had not had that advice I could have had a serious accident.

Choosing Sidki and another of the brighter pupils, I arranged for the three of us to fly in formation to Dekhelia airfield just outside Alexandria. On the pretext of wanting to test whether the hulls were watertight, I arranged to land in the normal way at Maryut and run down the slipway into the lake rather than risk making my water landing without knowing how to manoeuvre once it was done. I soon got the hang of taxiing on water. It was no good putting it off any longer, so I opened up, full throttle, hard over with the wheel to get the wing float out of the water, centralize, ease up onto the step and bingo – lift off. The thing which surprised me was the clatter of the water on the hull. I decided against a water landing and flew back to Dekhelia, ostensibly to examine the hull for leaks or strained rivets. The next day I repeated the operation with the second aircraft, then followed with the third. But on this occasion, after taking off I decided to make my first water landing. It turned out to be the smoothest landing on water I have ever made.

My first experience of porpoising scared me rigid. A bouncy

171

landing will generally diminish and get you down if allowed to continue, but when porpoising the bounce on water increases with each hit until you stall and the nose dives in. You must be quick enough to slap on full power, hold off and go round again. Another difficulty was landing on dead calm water as it is virtually impossible to judge your height above the water. For this reason when the old Imperial Airways routes with flying boats were operating, they used to maintain two high-powered motor launches to criss-cross the lake disturbing the calm water so as to make it safe to land. The other method is to use the night landing technique of a powered approach at a low speed, with a minimum rate of descent, completely on instruments until striking the water and immediately cutting the throttle. Although I managed this successfully, I never persuaded a student to complete a landing on water at night.

While I was in Dekhelia for the water landings, I was stabbed in the back by Mike Garnett. I don't know who made the initial move, but he negotiated a separate contract with the REAF. Jim and John were both furious with him, knowing the risks I had taken to get him back in the air. However, he only had a short time to enjoy whatever gain he made from the switch. If he had stayed with me I would almost certainly have given him a job with Arab Airways. (See Chapter 8)

While we were in Alexandria Johnny married an attractive Italian girl named Nanda. I arranged a party for our close friends at a Cabaret. There were Algerian identical twins who danced superbly in unison and after an excellent dinner and floor show, I gave my brother money to cover the bill and told them to stay. Having to pass the Auberge Bleu on the way back, I suggested to Lucy that the day had cost me about £200, so it might as well be £400. Lucy didn't like to watch me gamble so went and sat away from the baccarat table, from where I collected her about 20 minutes later. We spoke little on the return but as we entered the room my eldest daughter, Patricia, greeted us and we all sat on the bed and counted up a little more than £2,000. With the Sea Otters and Horsas erected, John's importance to us had diminished, so, with his new bride, it was mutually agreed that they returned to the UK.

My admiration for Osama Sidki's natural flying ability and easy manner prompted me to pay for him to obtain a British Commercial Pilot's Licence, on the understanding that he would return to work for me in Arab Airways, enabling him eventually to repay my expenditure. Once again my trust was misplaced when Sidki obtained his licence but went to work for others and conveniently forgot me.

* * *

Cairo was now becoming a dangerous place for expatriates. There were several unpleasant incidents and the renewal of residents' visas was becoming difficult. There was revolution in the air. Farouk had seen the writing on the wall and had fled the country. I received a letter saying that we would be welcome to keep on running the flying school, but we would have to move into Abbasia barracks if our safety was to be guaranteed. Unfortunately there were no facilities for families so they would have to leave. My brother and his family sailed from Port Said on 5 May, 1951 but Lucy stayed on with me in Egypt.

8

Arab Airways and Beirut Charters

The political scene in Egypt had been suggesting for some months that life for expatriates was likely to become difficult and I had come to realize that, if another job outside the country looked possible, I should apply for it. By good fortune, the management of Arab Airways, based in Amman, fell open. I was offered the post and accepted as soon as I was satisfied that it looked reasonably stable. We began to settle our affairs in Egypt and I flew to Amman in the Chrislea Ace to finalize the details of my contract.

I had been negotiating the sale of the bulk of the spares remaining in the old palace and had left instructions with Lucy not to accept less than £E20,000 for them. While I was away my friend Yousef Khorassany went with a Greek businessman to see Lucy, who offered her £E10,000 for the spares, eventually raising the offer to £E15,000 which Yousef strongly recommended she accept, but Lucy (unfortunately, as it transpired) correctly refused in accordance with my instructions.

All sorts of disturbing rumours started to filter through to Amman, bringing me rushing back to Cairo. I loaded the Consul with as many of our personal belongings as I could, boarded Lucy and the children, and no doubt well overloaded, I took off for Amman. By the time I could manage to get back to Cairo again, my garage had been stripped of all the spares and valuable bearings and the rented palace had been ransacked. I was called to see Missiri Bey who told me in private and as delicately as he could that there were likely to be radical changes in Egypt. Immediately, any expatriate who had a close association with Farouk or the Egyptian hierarchy was *persona non grata*. Not waiting for the ignominy of being deported or possibly something worse, I decided to make a run for it. In the very early hours of the morning, dressed as an Arab, with a Sten gun on my knee, which I was quite prepared to use, I was driven in a military jeep to the place where I had left my Consul. I vanished into the darkness without lights or clearance, taking off along the perimeter track regardless of the wind direction.

★　★　★

When I joined Arab Airways, Reg Ledger, whose job as general manager I was taking over, warned me that the two most important directors were Tewfick Pasha Kattan, who had the ear of King Abdullah, and Mohammed Ali Bdia, a very astute and successful businessman. When I met these two men I remember telling them of my enthusiasm for opening up aviation prospects for Jordan and my wish that I would eventually be able to converse with them in their own language. This turned out to be a forlorn hope.

I soon realized that the financial picture which had been presented to me was far from true. The monetary assets were on paper only and never collectable, owing to the fact that government departments and the palace were in the habit of chartering aircraft without the company making any effort to obtain payment. When questioned about this, they answered that it was no good asking for money they didn't have, but to refuse them aircraft would cause insurmountable problems. This meant a serious cash flow problem as we were not given unlimited credit. One ministry had the cheek to demand payment from us with dire threats of action if we didn't pay, yet at the same time they owed us more than we owed them. I tried to get the help of various directors but they never did anything, believing it to be a lost cause.

The situation was aggravated by a Captain Sanders, with whom I had encountered earlier difficulties. He was setting up a company in Jordan to compete with Arab Airways, backed by Pasha Bilbeisi. With

Ledger as interpreter, I went to see Bilbeisi to suggest a merger but it soon became obvious that there was enmity between him and some of our directors.

*   *   *

I had gained some insight into the infighting between King Abdullah's close associates and advisers when I was invited to meet Glubb Pasha, the British Commander of the Arab Legion. He introduced me to the King but I quickly realized how closely and jealously the latter was guarded from outside influences by his cronies.

Glubb was beloved by his men and known to them as Abu Farris (father of Farris), a name bestowed by the King himself on Glubb's son. Due to the heavy scar he had from a wound to his face, which he had suffered in the First World War, he was also known as 'The Chinless One'. Glubb's contribution to Jordan was immense and he had considerable influence with the King, a source of discontent among the King's circle, particularly those who sought to get rid of the expatriate elements in Jordan. So it was that later, after the murder of Abdullah and the accession of his grandson, the young King Hussein, who, perhaps naturally, felt the need to dominate the Army himself, that great man was unceremoniously driven out of Jordan and into retirement in England. There he received a knighthood in recognition of his remarkable contribution to the stability of a country in which Britain had much interest.

Since any approaches to the King were likely to be frustrated, I decided that I must seek to gain the friendship of his son, the Emir Talal. Reg Ledger took me to Jericho to lunch with him. Most of the conversation was in Arabic but the remarks made in English gave me the impression that the Emir understood most of it, but was hesitant to speak it. Mention was made of his younger son's health, which was fine while in Jericho but deteriorated when in Amman. I remarked of the possibility of mild anoxia owing to the height differential. Reg told me I had impressed the Emir. Shortly before we left, I was introduced to his elder son, Hussein, who would soon become King and who I would often meet again.

I got Dave Albrecht, my licensed engineer, and David Jabber, a radio and electronics expert, to build a radio-controlled model aircraft which I had bought in kit form as a present for the Emir's younger son. When all was ready and tested, the Emir and his son were invited to witness the first flight and receive the model. When I was duly instructed as to time and place, I was dismayed to find that the aerodrome at Amman was to be closed to all traffic for the period chosen. David Jabber explained, in Arabic, the various controls and technicalities of flying the machine and the demonstration was successful. The Emir was pleased with it but the boy, who was I think under the weather, was quietly polite in his thanks.

Emir Talal was often to be seen riding alone through the market on his magnificent horse. This was in striking contrast to the motor cavalcades with outriders and blaring horns which usually accompanied Farouk through the streets of Cairo. Similarly, it was quite a novelty to go to the primitive little cinema and have Prince Hussein come and sit two seats away with complete disregard for any formality. Cairo and Amman, both capitals and only a few hundred miles apart, were different worlds.

Compared with Egypt and Lebanon at that time, Jordan was an undeveloped country with entertainment facilities at village level. It was quite difficult to adjust to this new way of life, but the transition from being a relatively small frog in a large pond to a large one in a small puddle had its compensations. Even so, the loss of so many of my assets in my brisk departure from Egypt meant a drastic readjustment of my budget.

Finding a bungalow suitable for a manager was an expensive business, I bought a car from a consular official who was leaving and also inherited his servant Delli, who was a wonderful addition to the family. She worked hard to support her invalid husband who had been injured when the King David Hotel in Jerusalem had been blown up. Education was another problem as there were no suitable schools in Amman. In the end, the girls were sent to St Joseph's in Bethlehem, while my son went to the *Collège des Frères* in Jerusalem, all close enough for us to see them frequently.

Through my children I got to know Father Eugène whose main

duty was looking after the Garden of Gethsemane beside the Church of All Nations. He came to see me in Amman in a rather anxious state and begged me to raise £4,000 to buy some Dead Sea scrolls which had been uncovered in a cave. The first of these had been found in 1947 at Qumran but the Ta'amireh tribesmen had uncovered important ones early in 1952. The Father had asked the Jordan Government to buy them to prevent their crossing into Israel where he feared they might be destroyed or suppressed. He was sure that they were genuine and of great historical and financial value. The government had refused or was unable to raise the money, so I set about doing it myself. I had made a plan to get them to a place from where I could negotiate the best return for the investment – having visions of retiring to the Bahamas, lolling on golden sands and relaxing to the ministrations of dusky maidens for the rest of my days. I managed to raise the cash, only to be told that, after all, the government had changed its mind. The adrenalin had been in full flow for a couple of days, but you can't win'em all.

One of my biggest problems was getting and keeping pilots with any sense of loyalty to the company. Two such pilots, John McOmie and Eric Ireland, were easy to get on with but frequently found all sorts of excuses for not returning from the Beirut schedule at weekends. It became so blatant, particularly John, who had a very attractive Palestinian girl friend there, that they would go to the aircraft with their night-stop bags. If we had a charter or some other use for the aircraft, I had to take the flight myself to be sure of getting the plane back. John eventually solved his and my problem by leaving for a job with Middle East Airlines in Beirut.

In England I found and employed a young pilot called Tim. I was collecting a Rapide and as he had never flown one I intended to give him experience during our flight back to Jordan via Paris-Lyon-Cannes-Rome-Bari-Athens-Rhodes-Cyprus-Beirut. Had I been alone, I would have overflown a few of the stops, but this gave Tim a good introduction to the aircraft. While in Paris, I took him to the Folies Bergères. Whether the galaxy of beautiful bodies had affected his young and (I suspect) inexperienced frame, I do not know, but he asked me to translate for him when he was propositioned outside. That done, I said to rendezvous at a nearby café. I had not finished my coffee when he reappeared and he never quite lived it down. I timed his return at thirteen minutes, including travelling time.

My senior local assistant, Wadia Salami, who managed the office and accounts very efficiently, was another victim of the Palestine débâcle. Imagine a well-educated man of good family, having achieved high office as a judge, suddenly deprived of his home, orange groves and other possessions and being forced to work as a clerk. No wonder there was a great bitterness among the Palestinians. The better educated were generally more able to cope with their misfortune but the peasants, reduced to living amid slime and filth in (at best) dilapidated tents, lost hope and became apathetic in their rags and misery.

I remember how during one particularly wet and cold period the camps in the Jericho Valley became quagmires and a family known to our cook Delli had walked to Amman. I was so ashamed of my own luxury that I took my car out of my garage and allowed the family to shelter there. I felt even worse when they knelt on the wet floor and kissed my feet in gratitude.

It was one of those sad examples of colonial misjudgement and mismanagement which will forever leave a scar with those families affected. I have personal experience of the American Peace Corps and Aid projects. It is a shame that, among those who are sincere, there are so many who join these charitable efforts for their own selfish ends. The degradation and hopelessness of so many in the refugee camps had to be seen to be believed. It was not helped by the arrival of the so-called inspectors in their brand new cars. It was too much to expect that they would double up to save petrol. The effect of their extravagance could hardly be expected to raise morale. Added to this, with all their expenses paid for, all the good servants had been enticed away within a few weeks for inflated wages. The servants could hardly be blamed in view of the economic situation. Among residents it was considered bad taste to employ another's servant without permission, bearing in mind the time and trouble spent training them.

179

Our storeman Basil Hermandes, was another Palestinian who had lost everything in the enforced exodus. He was now living in one small room with his family. It so happened that he had managed to bring away a good but very large Persian carpet which he could not use in his tiny room. At one of the social evenings I held for the staff he mentioned that his carpet would fit admirably in my lounge and asked me to buy it. This I did and had the pleasure of it for thirty years before selling it (still in excellent condition) to my friend and mentor John Diamond.

Our public relations officer and supervisor at Amman airport was a genial man of the world called Emile Farkour. The essential formalities of Arab greetings, '*keef el hal*' (how are you), '*mabsoot*' (very well), '*el hum d'l Allah*' (thanks to Allah), was reduced to '*keef, mab, hum*' as we shook hands, much to the amusement of bystanders. He was a fountain of information about what was going on in the country and seemed to be one of the few who was accepted by the many factions in the land.

Seeing is believing and I wanted to confirm the 'sitting in the water with a cigarette in one hand and a beer in the other' reports of the buoyancy of the Dead Sea by doing it myself. A dozen of us, armed with ample food and cold boxes with plenty of ice stacked with drink, set out one warm evening under a full moon to Jericho to satisfy our curiosity. It was true. It was difficult to keep the legs in the water, so movement was easier on your back. We were advised to take fresh water for washing down afterwards. After an enjoyable evening and preparing to leave, one decided to have another dip. The rest of us were dressed and as he was washing down we collected the contents of the melted ice buckets and, with a full frontal attack, threw it at his midriff. The yell which followed could have been heard in Jerusalem.

One particularly unpleasant charter which none of my pilots wanted to undertake was to Kuwait to pick up a coffin complete with its usual contents. The hysterical crowd seemed intent on pushing the coffin through the door and out again through the other side of the fuselage, despite there being no opening there. The Rapide is only a small, canvas-skinned aircraft, and, although the seats had been removed, it still needed care in handling the coffin round the corner. This was made difficult by the reluctance of the countless bearers to let go. I almost gave up hope of getting the aircraft away undamaged, even when the coffin was in and lashed down. It was some time before I could start the engines for fear of injuring the many mourners who were too close for comfort. Needless to say, I was anxious to get airborne as there was already a distinctly unpleasant smell emanating from the close confines of the aircraft.

I stopped for fuel in Baghdad where I was surprised that an ambulance came out to the aircraft and the driver wanted to know where the patient was. The confusion had been caused by the signal sent from Kuwait which, as usual, included the pilot's name. It took quite a lot of explaining and the situation was not improved when some official wanted to open the coffin. Patient was getting very impatient, which doesn't help with our Arab friends. Fortunately the senior air traffic controller arrived and was able to sort out the confusion and I was at last able to refuel and get away. My arrival in Amman was now well behind schedule. The crowds waiting at the airport for hours in the heat of the day were understandably a little tetchy, but fortunately there were enough police to keep the crowd at bay until we got the coffin clear of the aircraft. After all that I had endured, I almost expected someone to ask me if I had an import licence for my freight.

*   *   *

On 20 July, 1951, there was a strange aura of silence in Amman which I failed to understand until the rumour spread that the King had been assassinated. Confirmation was not long in coming. King Abdullah had been shot and killed by a young Arab as he was entering the Agusa mosque in Jerusalem for prayers. The assassin was killed immediately by the King's bodyguards and was later identified as Mustafa Shuksi Ashou, who was a member of the Holy War organization. Abdullah had made many enemies through his friendship and close ties with Britain and particularly by working for peace with Israel. There was turmoil and unrest everywhere. The Emir Talal was in Switzerland for health reasons, so the cabinet elected his younger brother, the Emir Naif, as Regent. Strict curfew for several weeks made life difficult, especially for the women, who had to be escorted when shopping. Many notable Arab heads of state flew in for the funeral. The cortège was led by Glubb Pasha and consisted of a ninety-minute procession. The chiming of church bells mingled with the thunder of gun salutes along the route.

*　*　*

A desert sheikh in full riding dress, with a jewel-hilted dagger and ammunition bandolier across his flowing robes, is a most impressive sight. When he is also tall and fair-skinned with blue eyes, I could be forgiven for being a little startled when introduced to such a man, especially when he said in excellent English, 'Do not be surprised. There are many descendants of crusader bastards such as I in the desert.' Lucy and I entertained the sheikh and his brother at the Philadelphia Hotel in Amman, and learned from them a great deal about the double-dealings in the Holy Land. Later, when I was out walking with my eldest daughter, we met the sheikh also accompanied by his daughter. A delighted cry of surprise was followed by the two girls embracing. They had been firm friends at the English school in Heliopolis.

*　*　*

I was always on the lookout for new ways of saving money. When Arab Airways was set up, the 'new' Rapides were bought and insured for £5000 each. By the time I took over, there were no new Rapides and replacements could be bought for £1,000. I considered that our insurance premiums were excessive and cancelled the coverage with the exception, of course, of the third party liability. This move resulted in a saving of £1,000 per annum which meant that we could lose an aircraft each year without being out of pocket. It was two years later that an aircraft was written off. Fortunately nobody was hurt, yet I received severe criticism for having cancelled the insurance. Their argument was that we would have received an equivalent replacement aircraft!

The IPC (Iraq Petroleum Company), who had operated their own Rapides in the Lebanon for the maintenance and supervision of their oil pipeline from Iraq, decided to discontinue their opera-

182

tion and asked for tenders from several companies to cover their work. This was just the shot in the arm necessary to give us the additional utilization for our aircraft needed to make a profit. I submitted a tender for the work which, surprisingly, I lost. Many months later I found out that those who had received the contract had tendered a price considerably above the one which I had offered. Knowing the aviation manager of IPC quite well, I went to see him and asked the reason. 'Joe', he said, 'I couldn't possibly accept your tender, it was so much less than what it had cost us to operate for the last ten years. It would have subjected me to criticism, so I had to accept the higher bid.' I asked him why the hell he hadn't talked to me about it first. We could both have made a packet out of it.

I discussed the possibility of setting up a training school for aircraft mechanics and possibly licensed engineers with Dave Albrecht and David Jabber. With this in mind, we put in a request for a loan or grant from the US Aid Contingent in Jordan in order to enable us to carry out this worthwhile project. I was disgusted by the shortsighted attitude of the officials concerned. They refused the application on the grounds that for the same amount of money they had put fifty people to work with the local cement company, carrying baskets of raw materials to and fro on their heads, and earning a pittance. It was typical shortsightedness, but no doubt the higher ups in the USA could gloat at the statistics, regardless of the actual lack of long-term benefits.

It was thought by some that Nevil Shute's unusual book *Round the Bend* had me as the central character. This was not so, the honour belonging to Freddie Bosworth, a contemporary but a more adventurous chap than myself. Trained in the RAF as an engineer, he later obtained a pilot's licence and with a minimum of funds purchased war surplus aircraft spares. These, when listed on paper, amounted to an impressive sum of money regardless of the fact that the wings shown were all one-sided. However, with this and an outstanding personality he obtained from the Ruler of Bahrain (against the wishes of the British Resident Adviser) a loan of several lakhs of rupees. With this he set up Gulf Aviation. The aviation situation in the Persian Gulf at that time was primitive, with just a few strips where he could deposit the odd engine against a possible failure. His method of operation is best described as flying unsophisticated aircraft in an unsophisticated manner – a method entirely suited to an area where the passenger was just as likely to get on an aircraft with a goat or kitchen stove.

Freddie Bosworth went down well with the locals, including the sheikh, but was barely tolerated by many of the long-established colonial expatriates. At Amman we were forced to operate strictly within the regulations of the ARB and Freddie would buy from us any time-expired components which were in any way serviceable. By this and other economies, as well as a virtual monopoly, he made a success of his operation. He had managed to buy the last existing DH 86, more or less a blown-up version of the Rapide, but with four engines. The engines as well as many of the components and instruments were identical to those used by him in Rapides. When he knew I was going to the UK he asked me to test the aircraft and ferry it for him to Bahrain. I carried out the fuel consumption and other tests at Gatwick to help in planning my route. It was easy to fly although a little tricky in a cross wind. Being such an unusual aircraft it aroused a great deal of interest from aviation buffs at all the stops between Gatwick and Bahrain.

The promise of a seismic survey contract in the Gulf waters for the Superior Oil Company gave Freddie Bosworth the chance to go a bit up-market, using a Dove aircraft. He asked me for the loan of my licensed engineer, Dave Albrecht, to maintain his aircraft while he went to England to get a Dove endorsement on his pilot's licence. A short time later Dave cabled me to go immediately to Bahrain, as Freddie had been killed while taking his endorsement in the Aly Khan's Dove. Once there, I held the fort for Marjorie Bosworth until the position became clear. I then suggested a form of liaison between our two companies. This would allow a rotation system for both pilots and aircraft which would benefit them owing to the much more pleasant weather, working conditions and maintenance facilities in

Amman. It would also mean substantial economies for both companies.

I bandied this idea about among the meagre staff who seemed enthusiastic. An amalgamation was also discussed, BOAC and KLM being the most likely participants. While I was in Bahrain, a senior BOAC official was discussing the situation with me as he examined the aircraft and maintenance equipment. I pointed out that if the old RAF RT sets were replaced by a miniaturized and moderately priced version, the weight saving would be the equivalent of half a passenger per flight. A day or two later it amused me to hear this same official expounding this information in great detail to a senior embassy man as if he were the fount of all knowledge.

I went to London to discuss the seismic survey contract. Marjorie Bosworth requested me while there to find out how Freddie had been killed. I was told that when the aircraft crashed, Freddie was alone in the cockpit while the check pilot was in the cabin with a lady. However, I informed Marjorie that the information she wanted was not available to me.

While in London I had a meeting with Charles Belgrave, the British Resident Adviser in Bahrain, with whom I talked over the merits of my proposals. As a diplomat, he was non-commital, but I felt he had no wish for another Freddie Bosworth type such as myself to be involved in Bahrain. Sure enough, when I returned Gulf Aviation was firmly in the hands of BOAC. I was at first much amused at the procedures for the short round trip Bahrain-Dahran-Bahrain, logged at thirty minutes total with the Rapide or Anson. The norm was to look at the passengers and what they were carrying and simply tell each where to sit according to their size, weight and what luggage they were carrying. No longer was this the case. Each passenger was weighed along with his goat, cooking stove or whatever, and a load and balance sheet was made out BOAC-fashion. Suffice it to say that Freddie Bosworth had made a reasonable profit on this small operation which BOAC turned into a loss of some £20,000 in its first year.

*   *   *

I arrived back in Amman just in time to take another party of tourists to Petra. While no one could deny that the magnificent antiquities of Rome, Leptis Magna, Palmyra, Baalbek and Jerash are each wonderful in their way, they are, save for size and the varying extent of what remains, decidedly similar, whereas Petra is entirely unique, with so much more to offer.

For many centuries Petra lay hidden to the Western world until rediscovered in the early part of the 19th century, when the Swiss traveller Johann Burckhardt explored the area.

The American writer, the Reverend John William Burgon, describes it aptly in his poem: 'Match me such marvel save in Eastern clime, a rose red city – half as old as time.' Most wonders and tourists' sights are easy to get to but getting to Petra in the 1950s needed a considerable amount of effort. Many hours on bumpy roads were succeeded by a long arduous walk or horse ride. Nowadays I presume a helicopter would be used, but the norm while I was there was a charter flight to Ma'an, a car ride to Wadi Musa (Valley of Moses), then the ensuing equestrian trek through a long dark winding crevice in the mountainside until, on entering a valley, you were stopped in your tracks by the breathtaking sight of the Khazne (treasury building) bathed in early sunlight.

Having made a study of the area and its monuments, it was natural for me both to fly the chartered aircraft and to act as guide. The sheer monumental magnificence of the valley, with its houses, tombs and temples carved out of the living rock, does more than hint at Petra's historic significance. A Nabatean city which flourished from around 150 BC (until conquered by Rome in AD 106), Petra had no super-structured buildings. It became a principal city because of its virtual impregnability. The only entrance through the narrow defile, never more than a few feet wide but rising hundreds of feet, could be defended by a few against an army.

There are several references to the area in the Holy Bible prophesying its fall. For example *Obadiah 3*, 'Thou that dwellest in the clefts of the rock, whose habitation is high'. One of the interesting features, (not for the aged or infirm) is the climb up winding stairs cut into the mountainside, where remaining traces of the original marble are still visible. Upon arrival at the 'high place' one has a view of the entire valley and beyond to the Dead Sea: an indescribable scene for all but the poor beast or person who, many centuries earlier, was led trembling through two large purifying baths, to the edge of the man-made plateau and made to kneel at a sacrificial altar, where a bowl to collect the blood is still apparent.

As most of the tourists were Americans, it amused me to tell them that they were not the originators of the protection racket. The Nabataeans beat them to it by a good few centuries. Many of the camel trains bearing rich eastern produce bound for the markets of Jerusalem and Damascus paid their dues to the mafiosi of Petra for safe conduct through the area. It is not certain whether the rooms cut into the rock face were habitations or tombs, so, as a tour guide, I made sure that tents were provided for the faint-hearted. All basic equipment had to be taken with you but occasionally I arranged for a typical Bedu Arab meal to be served at which a young goat would be butchered and cooked. Mind you, there were occasions when I could have cheerfully handed out the same treatment to one or two of the more awkward tour members.

One evening I was astounded at the misinformed rubbish that was being uttered about the Palestinian/Jewish problem. I was so incensed that I rudely interrupted them and refuted their statements. One of the party (a senior Rotarian) invited me to visit the USA to give talks at Rotary meetings, because much of what I told them, and based on my personal experience, had never been voiced or published in the USA. Unfortunately my commitments were such that I had to refuse his generous offer.

*　　*　　*

While with Arab Airways, Reg Ledger had rekindled my childhood interest in philately. Reg, who had one of the finest collections of Jordan stamps, was in the process of writing a book on the subject and I was able to assist in the purely statistical work at the Post Offices, etc. The book when published was and still is considered the authoritative work on the early stamps of Jordan. By pure luck I was able to obtain a few unusual items which were illustrated in the book.

187

When King Abdullah was assassinated the Emir Talal was to succeed his father and special stamps were prepared to commemmorate the occasion, but when Talal abdicated in favour of his son, Hussein, the stamps were ordered to be burnt. In a bizarre way I obtained a few stamps from the ashes and one from the minister in charge of the destruction, which is thought to be the only perfect copy known to the philatelic world.

★   ★   ★

When Sanders, through Air Jordan, solicited the help of an American aviation company who were going to bring in larger aircraft, it became obvious that we could not survive unless we did the same. At that time both BOAC and KLM were interested, but I rather stupidly (as it turned out) thought that we would get a square deal from the British company who had spare aircraft through their interest in Aden Airways. A well-known character by the name of De Graf Hunter visited me to discuss the matter. He suggested that with my experience of the Arabs I would be an asset to Aden Airways in connection with the Mecca pilgrimage trade. He offered me a job and also agreed to purchase my Arab Airways shares for £4,000. He then asked me to go to London to discuss details with the BOAC executive in charge of the necessary negotiations. I made an appointment to do this, but when I turned up I was told that he had been called to America unexpectedly on urgent business but would contact me on his return. I phoned several times after that but was fobbed off each time. I then received a telegram from De Graf Hunter: 'Offer you £1,000 for your shares, regret no post available Aden Airways.' During my absence a meeting had been called and the assets of Arab Airways voted over to some sort of holding company. The exact details are vague after so many years, but the double-cross and loss of my job was very clear. Everyone expressed their sympathy but that was poor compensation for having put my faith in a British company and being so badly let down.

★   ★   ★

After the trauma of those last few weeks with Arab Airways I was thankful to be offered the post of aviation manager of CAT

(Contracting and Trading Company) by Emile Bustani. He was a colourful Lebanese entrepreneur and business man, the volatile front man of the Lebanese 'three musketeers', Bustani, Shammas and Abdullah Khoury (the book keeper). Shukri Shammas was one of the most considerate men I have ever worked for. He was the engineering brain of the trio; after discussing a complex problem with him I left with a calm feeling of being enlightened. Sheer magic! As luck would have it, their aircraft engineer was a friend of mine, Ken Allen, who had often helped service Arab Airways with a reciprocal loan agreement on spares when we were in difficulties.

Having exchanged my Consul for a Rapide, I was able to get hangar space for it and my Chrislea Ace when I transferred them to Beirut. CAT operated Rapides for transporting engineers and small tools to various building sites, mainly in Jordan, Iraq and the Persian Gulf. They also operated Aerovans to carry bulky items of machinery. Import regulations and customs duties made it uneconomical to transfer my car from Amman to Beirut and I was advised by Ken Allen to buy an American car, as spares for British cars were difficult to get and very expensive. I bought a Studebaker with an electrically controlled hood which the children loved to operate. Whether this led a flat battery I can only surmise, but it almost led to a very serious accident. One morning I pushed the car from the side road outside the house onto the very steep road running down to the beach. I was not quick enough getting into the driving seat and was dragged along at an ever increasing speed. Had I let go, people might have been killed, so I pulled the steering wheel round and deliberately ran into a wall. The shock threw me off but I got away with a few grazes and bruises. A crumpled wing and a broken yoke was the only major damage. The biggest surprise was the speed with which I was able to get replacement parts at low prices, thanks to Ken Allen.

Quite a different kind of 'accident' happened when I was called out to help one of our pilots, Boshoff, a South African and a disciple of that particularly nasty disease, apartheid. I went to his rescue as his small Talbot's nose and radiator were embedded in the doors of a garage at the blunt end of a T-junction. His passenger told me what had happened. Apparently Boshoff came to the T-junction and hesitated before making a turn. A chauffeured Cadillac pulled up behind him and tooted its horn, at which our sensitive pilot switched off, got out of his car and stood with arms akimbo glaring at the driver. The passenger in the Cadillac which had Kuwait number plates said a few words to the driver who promptly moved up behind Boshoff's car, pushed it across the road and through the wooden garage doors. He then backed up and drove off without a word. I am afraid I laughed out loud at this which did not endear me to that particular pilot. I gave him a tow back to the airport where repairs were eventually carried out.

When John McOmie left Arab Airways he had been compelled to obtain the American ATR licence for his job with Middle East Airlines. He lent me the ATR books to study because, although I already held the American commercial, I thought the higher licence might come in handy. I did most of my work for this licence during my frequent flights between Beirut and Baghdad and managed to qualify for it before I left the Lebanon. By this time I had to wear corrected lenses for reading and I was most surprised to find that above 5,000 feet I could read small print comfortably without glasses. The reduction in air pressure caused this adjustment to normal sight.

One of the local cafés, called the Empty Glass, was run by a Mr and Mrs Smith. We became quite friendly though I never knew his first name. Smithy had been in the Palestine Police before moving to Beirut and was a keen but poor bridge player. I felt sorry for his wife who was a better player but was always blamed when a contract went wrong. Despite being well paid, I found the expense of keeping a family of six (shortly to become seven) left me very little to spare. Whenever I claimed to be hard up, the children would encourage me to go and play bridge, knowing that I invariably won and gave them additional pocket money. My children were given 'picture' money once a week. If they wanted more they earned it by soaking off and drying used postage stamps. These I would examine carefully for any varieties and errors. I was amazed when I found a Jordan 'Aid' overprint which I did not know existed. Taking it with me to Amman, I showed it to Reg Ledger who was excited at the find. He theorized that sheets of stamps must have been made up of broken odd remnants from outlying Post Offices and then overprinted. He discounted the possibility of it being a forgery as it was such a low face value stamp. I went through many thousands of similar stamps hoping to find another to give Reg as it seemed wrong that I as a comparative beginner should have something he as an expert had not.

★   ★   ★

The inspection of pipe lines running through Kirkuk was one of CAT's contractual jobs. We often flew engines, materials and tools there, on one occasion taking a full aircraft load of pickaxe handles. I can hardly imagine fiercer looking warriors than the Kurds appeared to be.

Instructed to pick up a party of MPs touring the area as guests of Emile Bustani, I brought them from Bahrain to Beirut where a cocktail party had been arranged for them to meet the local dignitaries. I have often attended similar functions and have invariably been disgusted by the snide innuendos made by such visitors, even at social gatherings. The worst offender in this particular group was undoubtedly Patrick Gordon Walker. When I got home that evening I told Lucy about it, but she said we were just as bad. 'Whenever you aviation chaps get together, you cannot close the hangar doors,' she said. She made her point, but at least I think we refrain from a continual flow of vitriolic remarks. A few years later I gloated unashamedly when Walker lost his seat.

One day, returning from Baghdad and about half-way home, I was confronted by a squall line which, although teeming, had no depth, as I could see the sun shining on the other side. It stretched as far as I could see in breadth so there was no way round. It was too dangerous to fly through it, so I warned the passengers that we would get wet and that once we had landed they would have to hold the aircraft down while the squall line passed over us. The quagmire which surrounded us as the storm passed through was amazing, but within minutes it was firm sand again. I had chosen what looked like a less active area of the line, but even so the hammering of the rain

191

was deafening as the squall passed over. The change from darkness to brilliant sunshine was startling and beautiful, reminding me of the times when I had emerged from the dark, winding crevice into the valley at Petra. We were, however, able to complete our journey with no more damage than a soaking.

One of the most important flights I made for CAT was a trip to Turkey with several engineers and one specialist from the Minneapolis Honeywell Company of the USA. He was quite an elderly man, obviously the VIP of the party and reputed to carry life insurance of over a million dollars. I was never told the reason for the routes I was asked to fly but at various places I was asked to make a circuit or two, so I imagine it was to evaluate the building of a road or pipeline. The most memorable occasion on the trip was on the evening before our planned return from Ankara. I was in the bar with the genial old boy discussing the consumption of alcohol in the armed forces. I cannot remember what led up to the challenge, but he offered to drink three bloody Mary's to my one. By the time the party was ready to go out to dine at a well known restaurant, I was a little unsteady, if not tipsy, but my companion was unaffected. While studying the menu I happened to glance round at the band only to see two lady saxophonists. Looking further along I found that the whole of the band was duplicated. I had only been drunk twice before in my life, so thought the best idea was to find a toilet and put my fingers down my throat, during which I passed out, striking my head on the 'Thomas Crapper' as I fell.

I remember nothing more until the next morning waking up in bed at the hotel with a bandage on my head which had a percussion group performing hysterically inside it. Through blurred eyes I made out an American army doctor who advised me not to fly that day. Although I was still very shaky, I managed to return to Beirut on schedule. There seemed to be a twinkle in the eye of the old boy as he thanked a rather crestfallen Joe for the trip and departed.

★   ★   ★

We all went to the local evening school to learn French. As a result, I introduced a French day once a week when the use of English meant penalties. This often produced a great deal of fun. The arbiter when called upon was my son Jimmy, who had become very proficient during his time at the *Collège des Frères* in Jerusalem. I was grateful for his linguistic ability later when he accompanied me to the airport. As we were leaving in the car I was unexpectedly signalled to stop by a guard. This was unusual but he was obviously new to the job. He wanted to look into the boot of the car, which would have been embarrassing. Unexpectedly, Jimmy spoke to him in fluent Arabic, explaining that I was a VIP and the manager of CAT. After a long conversation between them, the guard saluted me and congratulated me on having such a fine boy.

★   ★   ★

On 26 February, 1955, Lucy had a lovely baby girl. When she later ruptured her back lifting the baby, I was advised by specialists that she needed treatment which was not available in Beirut. It was imperative to return to England, so it was decided that I should resign and that the whole family should go back. I intended to offer my services to the racing fraternity and to this end I negotiated an exchange of aircraft with Emile Bustani – my Rapide for his Gemini. Everybody was most sympathetic and Shukri Shammas told me that there would be a job for me if I returned. Air France turned up trumps and gave us complimentary passages in acknowledgement of my relationship with them when I was with Arab Airways. Two of the children flew back with me in the Gemini, which I left at Southend Airport for the time being. I had to leave the Chrislea Ace in Beirut in the care of Ken Allen to be collected as soon as I could arrange it. This was not to be. I received news that riots in Beirut had apparently damaged the aircraft beyond repair – another problem and a blow to my decreasing fortunes.

Soon after my return home I visited various agencies and told them that my Gemini was for hire. The first charter I had (and the last) was when Mike Keegan of Aerocharter at Southend airport asked me to take my aircraft to Cannes as there was an Austrian industrialist who wished to rent it for a couple of weeks. He was said to be a qualified pilot but I was told to check this out until I was satisfied enough to leave the aircraft with him. I would be told when to go and collect it. The Austrian met me at Cannes airport in a custom-built two-seater Mercedes and drove me to my favourite hotel, the Montana, later picking me up to have dinner with him that evening. Naturally, our main topic of conversation was aviation and it was obvious that he was no beginner. He was a man of about my own age and I wouldn't mind betting that he had been a Luftwaffe pilot. This impression was confirmed the next day on the flying check by his competent handling of the Gemini. Satisfied that it was in safe hands, I went back to London to await a call from Keegan about collecting it. As I had heard nothing after a fortnight, I assumed that the Austrian wanted to keep it a little longer. However, the following Sunday my eye caught a short paragraph in the paper about a twin-engined aircraft which had run into the water at Nice. I knew it must be mine. For the next two or three days my calls to Southend were met with 'Mr Keegan is not available'. I went to Southend and eventually saw Keegan, who claimed that he had tried to contact me. This was a weak excuse as I had been at the address I had given him the whole time. It eventually transpired that he had an aircraft going to France and, to save the cost of my time and air fare, had sent a young pilot who unfortunately had only a couple of hundred flying hours, of which only twenty were on twin-engined aircraft. I knew immediately what had happened. The Gemini had the limitation of being almost unable to take off with more than a 5 mph starboard cross wind. In this situation, a downwind take off was necessary. Inevitably, as the pilot was not qualified, the insurers disclaimed any liability. Keegan offered me £1500 which was not enough to replace the aircraft. My solicitors advised me that a claim against Keegan could be delayed by as much as two or three years before settlement and that in view of my financial situation it might be better to accept the offer.

Perhaps I was being punished for past sins, for the next few years were plagued with misfortunes. I had gone to the labour exchange when I got home but as my last post was listed as aviation manager, the chap behind the grille said he could not help me. I explained that, regardless of what I might have been or done, I and my family still needed to eat so I was willing to do anything. They came up with a night job with Walls Ice Cream Co, loading lorries.

The first three days nearly crippled me. I ached in every part of my body. Fortunately I was paired with a much older and quite short Irishman who 'carried' me when working inside the lorries for the first couple of nights. After that I could hold my own. The work was simple and the foreman didn't care what we did so long as when there was a vehicle to be loaded and the ice cream was ready we got on with it. We had to take the tins (similar in size to the old biscuit tins) off the conveyor belt rollers and, in the case of the large lorries, put them onto their internal rollers and give them a push towards the front end. The smaller vans without rollers had a steel-lined floor on which ice would be crushed just before loading. Meanwhile, the chaps inside had to watch out for their ankles. My Irish friend would lift and stack five tins at a time by sandwiching the fifth tin between the two held in each hand. I could barely manage this on the low levels of the stack. I usually managed to partner Paddy, grateful for his help in the beginning. As I went to work in my car I always gave him a lift after work, dropping him off at Hammersmith. Despite asking him to call me Joe, he always got out of the car with a broad 'Thank you, Sorr'.

I enjoyed the purely physical factor and complete lack of stress with the job at Walls. Apart from the concern for Lucy, my life was great. When returning from work I would sleep for a few hours, have lunch, visit the hospital (often with a block of ice cream for the nurses) then go off to Acton via the Hammersmith Palais afternoon tea dancing and on to work. I considered then that the modest money I received from that job was the easiest money I have ever earned, despite the considerable difference to the huge sums that I received before and since.

Most of the casual labour was put off at the end of the season. The foreman thanked me and offered me a job on the delivery lorries but I declined. Lucy was by now convalescing after a successful operation on her back and I had some serious thinking to do. My plans for flying had been scotched by the loss of my aircraft, and for the next couple of years I had to support my family in other ways. I will pass over the details of most of the schemes in which I became involved. There was a chicken farming period. I had read many books on the subject and decided that simply buying chicks and rearing them for the table would not give me a job satisfaction I needed. So I plunged right in, raising my breeding stock by incubation using Mendel's sex-linked established theory and experimenting with free range, deep litter and battery methods including chemical caponising. I had some success, but, alas, some disasters. On one occasion the birds were attacked by dogs and many had to be killed; on another I rushed a growing clutch of pullets into their house one night only to find them in a pile in one corner the next morning. Only the top few birds were still alive. Final disaster struck when I was robbed of birds a few days before Christmas and lost about four hundred. Once again, the greed of others altered the shape of my life.

My old friend Sid Plumb came to the rescue. He had recently obtained a sub-contract with De Havillands for fettling drop hammer tools, mostly for the revolutionary Comet aircraft. Knowing that I could do the job, he invited me to lodge with him and work in the workshop he had built, complete with all the necessary hoists and tools. Because of the speed and quality of our work we were often given urgent jobs which meant we had to work all night. We had to take on two more men and for a time the work kept coming. Then it reduced to a trickle, but even this dried up after a while, thanks to union protests.

A return to flying seemed to be the easiest solution but required a British licence. I asked the Board of Trade for a senior commercial validation on the strength of my American ATR (top licence) qual-ification. They refused. I argued that they were implying that the top US licence was not as high a qualification as the junior British one when they even refused a commercial. It reminded me once again of the biblical 'kicking against the pricks'. I had to get down to swot-ting again and have no hesitation in saying that as I studied I made several cribs which I was quite prepared to use. In April, 1958, I sat and passed the exams for my British commercial pilot's licence, no cribs being necessary. In the same month I obtained the instrument rating. It was ironic that after five months of hard study, the first job I got was with World Wide Helicopters in Libya on the strength of my American licence. This only covered me for multi-engined aircraft, so I had to get a single-engined endorsement from the Air Attaché at the US Embassy in London. I had been told to get an endorsement for the EP9, an aircraft I had never heard of. I arranged to take both tests at Stapleford where one of these planes was available.

★   ★   ★

By July, 1959, I was once again flying in Libya. Lucy, Cathleen, Eleanor and Stewart joined me on Boxing Day, in a three-bedroomed flat, where we had American neighbours. After learning the ropes I joined the roster of three weeks in the desert with various drilling sites followed by three weeks in Tripoli. One of my first jobs was to fly a Mr Tucker, plus the Tripoli manager, Mr Nelson, and land in the desert to mark the spot where an oil rig would locate. There was a lot of soft sand in the area which compelled the three of us to manhandle the Cessna 170 onto firmer ground. Even then it was only possible for me to take off alone, so we searched the area and found a firmer place where I could land and pick up my passengers. The reason for mentioning this rather mundane incident is that the drilling at the seismic shotpoint marked by my passengers resulted in Zeltan, the biggest oil field discovered in Libya.

The main gathering place for expatriates in Tripoli was the Elizabethan Club. One associate, who had just returned from the Casino having won £10, stated that he always played red, using a six-point system. I glanced at his card and declared that, using his own system, he could have bet on both red and black, laying out less to win his £10 and moreover would have won almost twice as much. He gave a look of derision, so I offered to bet him £5 that I could prove it to him. He accepted and half an hour later gave me £5 and looked at me as if I were some sort of Houdini or Einstein.

An aircraft was based with the rigs for emergencies such as accidents or for speedily obtaining spares. The cost of losing drilling time was huge. Flights would also be made to Tripoli or Benghazi to exchange crews. I have never been content to sit around doing nothing, so I frequently helped the roughnecks and made friends with Bill Fearnow, a Halliburton operator. He was a bluff, softly spoken American who had nothing to do except to stand by with his pumping equipment and tons and tons of cement mixture ready to pour down the drill hole in the event of drilling into an underground cavern. Once filled, the drain stopped, the cement hardened and they would drill through it.

Before a camp could be established in the desert, mines had to be cleared from the surrounding area. The work was highly specialized and I enjoyed taking part in some of their searches. I was amazed at the ingenious methods used to disguise the small but lethal objects. The excitement of finding and then immobilizing or blowing up a mine reminded me of the feeling one had when taking off on a Berlin op, or when passing through customs with contraband. On one occasion I spent the night in the desert and awoke in the morning to find myself surrounded by pretty little flowers of all colours. Reading about such things is quite different from the actual experience. The same applies to mirages.

*　*　*

George Turner was one of the nicest men I have known. He was an engineer working for World Wide Helicopters. He often had a meal with us and used to take my children out for trips in his car when I was doing my stint in the desert. While working in the fuselage of a Catalina at Idris airport and, as is usual in the Libyan heat wearing only shorts, he suffered severe burns. Someone had washed the inside with petrol and a flash fire was the result. Although in great pain, he seemed to be rallying, but shortly afterwards appeared to lose the will to live. I went to England to see his father and did my best to lighten his sorrow. We all missed him greatly.

Bill Fearnow was another visitor to our flat and if I was away would take the children out and at the same time give Cathy driving lessons. I remember that he enjoyed mashed buttered swedes – a vegetable only fed to animals in the US.

During my first three spells at the Zeltan site I lost my spare cash when playing 'dealer's choice' poker. I learned the hard way how our transatlantic cousins played what seemed to me a purely mathematical game. I subsequently spent many tours there and left with the reputation (which I encouraged) of being the luckiest limey ever to have played poker.

Although warned about what might happen, I dared, one day, to go onto the rig floor to watch the tool pusher and riggers at work. When the next pipe was joined and rotating, they suddenly looked at me, then up to the platform with the inevitable comment, 'The limey's chicken'. Believe me, I was. As a flier it is strange that I dislike heights, and with the wind blowing I could see the top of the rig moving. At that moment I understood why people have died rather than be shamed. So with an air of bravado, which I certainly didn't feel, I put my foot on the bottom rung and then strangely, just as when I pushed the starter and booster buttons for a sortie, my apprehension left me and I climbed that long swaying ladder without a qualm. After watching the drilling procedures of the ants below, I was spared the climb down by descending standing on the hoist to receive a round of applause on stepping to the floor.

It is not generally known that in remote areas before drilling for oil it is essential to drill for water. This is to supply the cooling and lubrication of the much larger drill and depth needed for oil. An elderly American tool pusher had a wonderful fund of stories about the early days of wildcat drilling and I was especially amused by the ones about 'whip-stocking'. Apparently it is possible to drill a well near someone else's oil find and, by exerting certain pressures when drilling, you can force the drill to bend off at an angle and into the neighbouring oil field.

They had a German Doctor with whom I played chess. He was not popular and was particularly critical of the American tool pusher. During one game Herr Doctor was deriding the drill workers and the tool pusher as a buffoon and a fool. I intervened with, 'Doctor, if you as a professional earn X pounds, and the roughnecks 4X and the tool pusher on your own admission gets 6X, who is the fool?'

Once, when I was inactive for a day or two, I decided to do an air test and flew south, deep into the desert. After a while I suddenly saw a large number of oil drums, a vehicle and a hut, but no sign of life. Making a mental note of the position, on my return I discussed the find with my bomb disposal friend who said it was probably a Second World War Long Range Desert Group refuelling and rearming depot. It would be well worth salvaging but would most certainly be well booby-trapped. My intention to return never materialized.

Although I held an international driving licence, I was forced to take a test in Libya. I was told that I had failed for turning corners without giving hand signals. I protested that the car was fitted with trafficators which I had used but the reply was, 'Suppose they were not working?' The Arab mind is such that I knew it would be no good arguing with him, but he told me that if I cared to pay for another test and used hand signals he would pass me.

Our popular and easy-going manager was replaced by a brash Australian, Bruce. At the first meeting of the staff he introduced himself by saying, 'I have come with the power to hire or fire.' At the time we were using Cessna 170, EP9 and Beaver aircraft. Possibly because I was the most experienced twin pilot, I was the first to be converted to the new addition, an American twin Bonanza (E 50).

I ran short of fuel once when out on a search and, rather than risk running out altogether, landed in the desert and spent the night there. I had radioed my approximate position but was not sure that the message had been received owing to interference and static. I was found the next morning by a plane from the French rig nearby who were able to supply me with enough fuel to get back to Tripoli. As soon as I had enough height, I managed to make radio contact and thus avoided the embarrassment of a rescue party.

I was involved in two major searches. One was very strange and involved finding a whole rig en route to a new site. There had been very strong winds which had obliterated the tracks of even the large, heavy transporters. Apparently they had been forced to change their known route because they had met an escarpment which they couldn't descend and went miles before they could negotiate it. To add to their problems, their HF radio had failed. Delayed from reaching the advance base camp, the indigenous employees had run out of food when found two days later. I flew in cases of sardines as a stopgap, but there was difficulty in eventually getting paid for them. It seemed that even in emergencies the proper channels had to be used, even if this meant additional hardship and suffering.

The biggest manhunt costing hundreds of thousands of dollars was my other major search. A geologist and partner with a jeep were lost for several days. Individual aircraft searches were unfruitful and a base was set up deep in the desert from which a coordinated search with several aircraft was carried out. I eventually found them after a square search of the area allotted to me and, although unable to land, I was able to direct a vehicle to them. They were still in good shape but another couple of days would have been serious. The geologist was surely the most expensive man ever to have been employed in the oil business.

During my time in Libya I managed to visit most of the places of interest, although sometimes the distances necessitated a nightstop in areas with very few, if any, facilities for the tourist. The jerrican of water and roll of toilet paper were essential parts of the luggage.

My most profitable night in Libya was spent at the Sabha Oasis in the Fezzan region. Deep in the Sahara, it is an extraordinary place with a small hotel run by an Italian couple. One of my three passengers was being flown there to take charge of a convoy and I had been warned that he was a known gambler. After dinner we started to play poker with modest stakes at first. Although I had wine with my meal, I stayed relatively sober while the others got progressively more tipsy. By midnight one of the foursome called it a day and by two o'clock another said that he had lost enough. The boss wanted to carry on with a two handed game but I refused. I had won £600 and he wanted to play one hand for the lot. Just to keep up a good relationship I offered to play one hand for half of it, but on second thoughts he changed his mind.

The desert is full of surprises. Most of it is completely dry, but at Sabha there is water if you dig down for about three feet. In many places petrified wood shows that forest once existed there, and elsewhere the presence of sea shells shows that the Sahara was once under water.

Almost the last charter I carried out was to Ghat near the Algerian border, an old military outpost with dungeons and instruments of torture still very much in evidence. From there we went on a recce near the Tibesti mountains into Chad, followed by the long haul back to Benghazi. I estimated that this last leg passed close to the spot where I had found the abandoned compound but I was unable to spot it.

Zeltan had developed into a large camp, with comfortable, air-conditioned caravans. As a result I caught a bad cold. A relief aircraft was requested and against doctor's orders I flew back to Tripoli on 13 May. Despite going to bed immediately I developed pneumonia. I was slow to recover and although not yet completely well I helped out for a few hours in the office. On 23 May an emergency arose with an injured man at Mahagon, a flight of a little more than an hour each way. As no other pilot was available, I went myself. On my return I was totally exhausted. As my contract was due to be completed in July, it was agreed that we should return home immediately so that I could recuperate.

* * *

I spent the next four months studying the results of the roulette tables at Monte Carlo, which are published. I was convinced that I could make a living playing the tables. Earlier I had taken endorsements on my pilot's licence to enable me to fly on a freelance basis for Silver City Airlines. I planned to go to Monte Carlo and try out my system, telling Lucy that if it worked I would send for her. If not, I would return and fly for Silver City.

After four days at the casino I was devastated. One reads about situations which make your hair stand on end. This was one of them. It was uncanny and I had an awful premonition. Not daring to believe what I thought, I decided to place my stake on a different table each time. On my first bet a zero turned up (a loss). OK, just a simple 36–1 chance. At the next table again the zero. When the zero came up at the third table, a 46,656 to one coincidence, it was as if some higher authority was showing to me that this is not for you Joe. Although I had only lost a third of my finances, I returned home a much shaken man.

I realized that my employment with Silver City would only last the summer, so I looked around for a more permanent job. I found one with Air Safari, but having to obtain both Viking and Hermes endorsements. Unfortunately this only lasted a few months before the company went into liquidation. Once again I was unemployed. Almost the last flight I had with them was to Perpignan with passengers en route for Lourdes. The first pilot on that occasion was the estimable Captain Thomson, later to be head of British Caledonian.

I had earlier been in touch with Desmond Norman of the Britten Norman Company in the Isle of Wight, who were experimenting with a model hovercraft. I could visualize the tremendous potential of this invention and was told that they intended to enlarge their crop-spraying activities in Africa and also enter the chartering market there. When this was done there would be a job for me as a pilot-manager. My association with Britten Norman then moved a step closer when I was asked to go on a temporary basis to work for Aero Contractors in Nigeria.

9

Nigeria and West Cameroon

After a short time in Lagos, I moved to Kano. The Kano Club was a veritable haven for expatriates and I made many friends there. It was a relic of the old colonial days, still maintaining its orderly and efficient function with strictly enforced rules. Much of my time was spent in the billiards room and the card room, where I was able to indulge my next most favourite pastime, bridge. There was also an occasional late night session of poker. Charter work is sporadic and as I was often at a loose end during the normal working hours of other expatriates, I had plenty of snooker practice.

The contrasts in Nigeria are enormous, particularly noticeable when flying from the sandy drabness of Kano to the lush greenery of an oasis like Jos. There the first class club and hotel, together with the wonderful scenery, made it a favourite place for holidays. There are also marked differences between the inhabitants. Their customs, dress, looks and even stature betray their origins. Lagos, Benin, Sokoto, Kano, Ibadan, Nguru and Maiduguri are almost different countries with language and religious differences as far apart as Islamic, Christian, Animist and Heathen.

The extremes were probably most vividly displayed in Yola, tucked away near the eastern border adjoining what was then the West Cameroon, and very difficult to reach. In the market place there the local people, stark naked with painted bodies and faces yet so obviously clean, bartered their modest local produce alongside the Arabs in their flowing robes and others with tables displaying Omega and similar gold watches. Jewellery ranged from the crudest to the richest anywhere in the world, with currencies from the four corners of the earth. I was amazed at the astonishing display of wealth without any apparent security guards. I was told that shortly before my visit the government had sent two officials to collect taxes from the area. All they received in return were the heads of the two officials.

Hostility between the tribes became obvious to me when the Chiefs had to be flown to central government conferences. Each had to be flown separately and protocol difficulties were enormous due to their sensitivity.

There was a regular charter to Nguru, which lay at the extreme end of the northern railway line and was the collecting point for market cattle. The scene reminded me of John Wayne movies without the cowboys. However, this was no loss as the beasts were sometimes accompanied by possibly the most beautiful women in Africa. The grace, looks and bearing of the Felani people are outstanding, but their strict moral code prohibited anything other than unspoken admiration.

* * *

As I was detached from the parent body in Lagos with only rare visits from my boss, I found the job pleasant and undemanding except for the absence of my family. When I heard from Britten Norman that the long-promised appointment as general manager of Cameroon Air Transport was now available, I was hesitant about accepting. In my reply I said that I should have to have my wife and three of my children with me, an expense I was doubtful that they would agree to. But they did, and by the end of the year I once again had the problems and responsibilities of management. Until now Britten Norman had concentrated on crop spraying which was managed by Gerry Fretz. They only had one twin Apache aircraft which was owned by the Elders and Fyffes company. CAT maintained this and were allowed to use it for charter when it was not needed by E and F. A new twin Aztec was bought to coincide with my appointment.

At Bota, where I was now to be stationed, our hangar, administrative offices and stores were situated at the foot of Mount Cameroon. One end of the airstrip was at the base of the mountain, the other almost in the sea. The area is said to have the third highest rainfall in the world and I soon realized that my experience of bad weather flying might have influenced my appointment. With no navigational aids at Bota and a minimum at Tiko, where we had to land if customs were involved, it was vital to know every tree and rock nearby in order to operate safely. We had a compound of well furnished bungalows which housed the pilots, engineers and one male expatriate assistant who was a godsend. Unfortunately, when Africanization was forced upon us, his employment was terminated, and I was cursed with three local assistants who together could not manage his work. This meant that I had to spend much time correcting inevitable errors and discovered that the so-called cheaper local labour was in fact far from cheap. With the indigenous engineering assistants in the hangar it was a different story. I had been able to engage the top graduates of the British Training Centre which had been withdrawn not long before my arrival.

Shortly after I arrived at Bota, Gerry Fretz, a pilot who ran Britten Norman's crop-spraying unit, took me to the capital, Buea, a small town with one reasonable hotel which was the main drinking place for local bigwigs and expatriates. As I entered the bar I noticed a line of black-faced gentlemen sitting talking before I was introduced to the manager André Schoofs. Immediately there was a cry from the line, 'Not Joe Patient 139?' As I turned I immediately recognized my fellow squadron associate Ulric Cross. I discovered that I had also met André (a Belgian) at Great Dunmow when he was waiting to be dropped behind enemy lines. The outcome of all this was an evening to remember. Another cause for celebration was the arrival of my family within a few weeks.

Lucy and I were invited to dine with the Prime Minister, Foncha, who was anxious to develop an area known as the Mamfe Overside. This was basically a political move as the commercial possibilities were meagre. He had no idea of the huge costs of operating aircraft and thought that a few vegetable products from this pathetically poor and remote area would be a sufficient return. I promised to look into it. Then he said, 'You know there are diamonds up there?' He was convinced that the British knew where they were but would not reveal the source. I had heard this story before but of course it was nonsense. It would have done me no good to tell him so.

When I next met my directors I told them all this and they considered buying a STOL (short takeoff and landing) aircraft for use in the many undeveloped areas of the Cameroons. When the weather was bad, as it often was, Nigerian Airways would offload passengers and mail at Calabar. On these occasions I would stand by, knowing that anxious parents would charter me to collect their children. When the weather was really bad I would get customs to come to Bota, knowing that I could get into Bota with as little as a hundred yards' visibility. The only other pilot I would allow to fly with restricted visibility was Bill Bond who joined us later. The offloading of mail at Calabar caused many problems. The local handlers piled each lot of mail and freight on top of previous lots, so that those at the bottom often arrived several weeks later. All this encouraged me to seek a scheduled service between Douala and Tiko.

The high standard of living of the French expatriates was an eye-opener. I had first experienced this in Libya when I visited a French oil rig. The finest foods and even roses were often flown from Paris to Douala, whereas our own supplies depended on infrequent and spasmodic shipping, with the local stores almost bereft of the most basic of foodstuffs. As I flew frequently to Douala I was often besieged with requests for items unavailable in Bota which I rarely bought because they were so expensive. Having a haircut in Bota cost me 2s 6d but in Douala it would be the equivalent of £2.

The most popular recreation at Bota was probably fishing. Many expatriates owned boats and I bought one of the fastest from an enthusiast who had installed and modified an engine from a Ford Anglia which had been written off. I must confess that I do not have much patience for fishing, and after a short period of trolling, mainly for barracuda which abounded and were good eating, I would open up for the thrill of speeding.

207

Nearby was Casement Island, so named because Roger Casement, an Irishman who was executed for spying during the First World War, had been detained there. It was quite a long haul across to Fernando Poo, an island where drink and other things were much cheaper. But as the customs were often difficult, we preferred to meet one of the many fishing boats from there. Apart from dispensing the huge prawns which were plentiful, once you got to know the fishermen they would pass over brandy and cigarettes for a small consideration. We often flew charters to Fernando Poo but had to clear customs at Tiko on the return which rather took the gilt off the gingerbread.

On seeing French colonial administration at first hand, I soon recognized that, in contrast with the British, the French were much more subtle and successful. All Ministers were indigenous and were treated as Frenchmen, with their children going to school in France and with top salaries and allowances equivalent to those of French Ministers. Because the job was too good to lose, they had to do as they were told by their 'advisers' who were, in effect, the real controllers. Then, as the Minister signed everything, should things go wrong, he was the scapegoat and perhaps replaced, while any anger would be directed by the people at their own man and not at the French Government.

The East Cameroon had its dissidents and terrorists, but the summary treatment of those caught was final – their heads left in a prominent place in the village centre. Any place known to be harbouring a criminal was simply surrounded by troops and the headsman given an ultimatum to deliver the culprits, failing which the whole community would be wiped out. Drastic when viewed from present times but effective. A few bullets were good economics against long-drawn-out trials, lengthy prison maintenance and high lawyers' fees.

*　*　*

To help the members of our compound I proposed flying north to Bamenda, where there were cattle, and buy a whole cow. I had friends there who were prepared to butcher it and cut it into suitably sized portions. The idea was welcomed so I went ahead. The result for me was disastrous. The meat was excellent and much less expensive than it would have been locally, but everybody wanted the best cuts and we were left with more offal than we wanted and the cheapest cuts. To add insult to injury, not all the money was forthcoming. I finished up well out of pocket and more than a little disillusioned.

Father Denis Healy, a young and dedicated priest who ran a mission school in a remote area, told me that many of his pupils had been forced to give up schooling for the sake of just a few shillings. I called a meeting of the expatriate staff and said I would match their contributions. The result was niggardly so I augmented the amount and put the children to school for a year and continued to do so until leaving the Cameroons.

Many of the missionaries were frequent visitors to our home for a meal, a chat or to relax for a short while from the arduous bush life with a glass of brandy. One worthy Dutch Father who had spent over thirty years as a missionary confessed that he would be happy with his life's work if he knew he had truly converted one African. He had his doubts about this, admitting that most converts were 'saved' for the perks.

The Bishop of Buea seemed to time his visits to us when the avocados were ready to be picked and returned after a meal with a basket full. I had one visit from him out of season, requesting my help. Father Denis was in confusion with his faith. His Lordship, knowing I was a friend, asked me to look after him for a few weeks for contemplation and rest. I readily agreed and, the family being away, much midnight oil was burnt during discourse between us. We were equally amazed by the disparity of our lives. An honours graduate at college, he was a babe as far as the real world is concerned. When discussing poultry, I could hardly believe it when I mentioned capons. He asked, 'What is a capon?' My final memory of this amiable and good-looking but disturbed young priest, who thanked me for looking after him, was when I drove him to the airport, I pressed a gold sovereign into his hand with the comment, 'This is to remind you of the worldly things we have discussed'. I could see that when he looked at it he thought it was a halfpenny.

In November, 1962, the company bought a Dornier 28 STOL aircraft as we were under pressure to open up the very isolated areas of the north, particularly the Mamfe Overside where Foncha had interests. I had to go to Germany to collect the aircraft and for conversion to type. I was greatly impressed by German efficiency. After leaving me at the hotel, they told me that a car would be waiting for me at 0700 hrs. with the conversion laid on for 0800 hrs. When I arrived at the factory, I was surprised to find the managers in their offices as well as the rest of the workers – the norm apparently. There, and later in Lagos, I flew the necessary tests and obtained the endorsements which qualified me to check and convert my other pilots to the Dornier.

Although I had made a recce to the Mamfe Overside area I had not yet found a place which could be prepared as a landing strip. Through the British Consulate I was put in touch with a DO (District Officer) who had supervised the area. I told him the minimum requirements for the loaded Dornier to take off and land and he felt sure that he knew a place near a village which could be made suitable by felling some trees. Although it was a five-day trek through a densely wooded area to get there, he was willing to see what he could do as he knew the people and their language. Several weeks later I received a letter, literally carried in a cleft stick by a runner, giving the approximate position and telling me that after a certain date he would make a smoke fire for one hour at noon each day. The map of the area lacked detail so on the appointed day I took another pilot with me as lookout. As there were no distinctive landmarks by which to make reference, I did a timed run and then, just as I was about to start a square search, we saw smoke rising from the jungle. It could have been just a camp fire but it turned out to be the right place.

The length of runway I had asked for had been prepared, but the trees at each end of the strip made the approach too steep. I made a 'touch and go' but did not land, as first we wished to arrange for the local chiefs to meet us to discuss the future commercial possibilities. I dropped a message to the DO, asking him to lop the trees at each end and add a few yards if time allowed, and also to arrange a meeting with the chiefs the following week. This was done and, when I landed bearing a few gifts for the chiefs, the most bizarre experience followed. It was one I shall never forget, even if I live to receive the Queen's telegram. A huge crowd of natives surrounded the plane almost before I had stopped. I switched off the engines because I was afraid someone might get killed. The aircraft was later manhandled back to the end of the strip and, despite guards being placed on it, I was fearful for its safety as most of the inquisitive population had never before seen an aeroplane.

My companion and I were carried shoulder high like heroes, surrounded by bare-breasted damsels chanting and dancing to drums, whistles and many strange instruments. It seemed to go on and on, but eventually the chiefs were ready to receive us. The most extraordinary sight awaited us, and it was difficult not to burst out laughing. A Victorian frock coat, green with age, was proudly worn by one, while another, who seemed to be a senior chief, sported an equally old brass fire brigade helmet. The rest were similarly adorned with treasured garments. Through an interpreter I explained the necessity for the flights to be commercially viable and told them that the Prime Minister supported the plan. After I had described the advantages of tools, medicine, fuels and food which could be brought fresh from the coast, I asked one fire-helmeted chief what would be the first priorities for them. His immediate and succinct reply 'whisky' astonished me. When the next one requested beer I realized what children they were. These were some of the leaders shortly to be given the government of their country.

It was difficult to find a return load which would cover just the cost of the fuel, but I was determined to help. The DO had shown me the huge boulders which had been removed, the ironwood trees cut down with machetes by the children, and the levelled ground which had been tamped down by the villagers dancing on it night after night. He had taken photographs of this mammoth task performed without any machinery, and I was happy to let him have a quantity of machetes for his helpers which I had originally brought for barter purposes.

After all the discomfort which he must have suffered for the last few weeks, the least I could do was to give him a lift back to civilization, followed by a good meal and a booze up at the club. Before we left he arranged for an agent to collect local handicrafts and red peppers which grew in profusion in the area and which was the most likely produce to pay for part of the venture. When I returned three weeks later I was saddened to hear that in that short time over a score of young children had died of measles. I couldn't help thinking of the requests for whisky and beer.

During one particularly nasty storm when I was working in the office, almost deafened by the incessant clatter of rain on the corrugated iron roof, I was surprised to hear an aero engine. None of ours were flying because of the poor visibility so I was amazed to see a small aircraft emerging from the mist when I went out to investigate. It was sheer luck for the French pilot, who had been caught out by the sudden storm. With his home base at Douala completely clamped down and running out of fuel, he had made a dash for Bota just skimming the waves. A godsent drift of the low clouds just at the crucial time had revealed the runway for a few moments. I took the young man home to lunch, the beginning of a long friendship with Michel during which I learnt a great deal about the East Cameroon. When I later went to the capital Yaounde to seek permission to operate a scheduled service between the Cameroons and other isolated regions, I was glad of my new friend's local knowledge. Cameroon Air Transport had to expand or fail but before we could justify the purchase of a larger aircraft we had to prove that it would be fully utilized.

I had two meetings with the director of civil aviation, with Michel in attendance in case my limited French let me down. Every possible and unreasonable objection was raised to every route and suggestion put forward. My frustration showed and the second meeting ended in a decidedly frigid atmosphere. Michel hinted that, if I offered advantages to Air Cameroon, the company whose interest they were protecting, I would make some progress. But I decided on a different tack. As I was on good terms with the area manager of UAT I suggested operating a scheduled service to coincide with their jets to and from Paris. UAT (the French Union Transport Aerien) agreed to absorb all of my proposed full fare within their own, with CAT becoming booking agents for UAT. This would inevitably divert much of the traffic coming from the UK via Lagos and Calabar. With my application now supported by UAT (French interests) the reaction was immediate and I received a cordial invitation from the director of civil aviation to renew discussions. As a result I was able to start a scheduled service, albeit limited at the beginning. The DH HS 104 Dove was the obvious choice for our new plane and I now felt that we could justify buying one.

I received in person a request for a first class return ticket to London from a trade union official. Knowing the finances of his small union would be limited, I suggested he travel tourist and save £100. Expecting an argument perhaps based on prestige for a TU official, I was flabbergasted when he said, 'Ah, but when you travel first class, they give you a nightstop bag (£1).' It had taken me many years to get an inkling of the workings of the Arab mind but I was for ever being surprised by the African.

It was then September, 1964, and Prime Minister Foncha had been elected Vice President of the United Cameroons and the Hon Jua became a popular and respected Prime Minister. He was much easier to talk to and had once said, when I suggested employing an African pilot, 'When that happens, I'll walk.'

On a business trip to the UK I advertised for a pilot and interviewed Bill Bond together with his German wife, Rosemary. Her family had been badly treated and she herself abused by the Russians. Bill had met her while working on the Berlin airlift. He had been shot down during the war, suffered severe facial injuries and made a POW. I took an immediate liking to them both and employed him, although his references were non-existent. He was a fine pilot (though a little hairy) and one of the few who could cope with the weather problems of the Cameroons during the wet season.

The Dove we had bought from Dan Air was soon ready to be tested. I was pleased with it and, after day and night check flights, carried out the ferry flight to Tiko without difficulty. After performance checks by the French Bureau Veritas at Douala, I flew Prime Minister Jua plus eight ministers to Yaoundé on 7 May. While waiting to take them back I made a route survey to Ebolowa-Sangelima-Djoum-Abong Mbang-Yaoundé. Now that we had a scheduled service with a promise of further routes we had to get another Dove. I took leave due to me while the Dove G-AKSR was prepared.

I would endeavour to time my business trips to England to allow for a day or two in Paris. I was able on this occasion to arrive on 14 July. Bastille day is an exhilarating experience which does not pall with repetition, but on this occasion the company of an attractive and warm-hearted woman made the year a very special one. We met quite by accident while dining in a good restaurant. We both sat at single tables, but when our eyes met we instantly gelled and celebrated the usual festivities together. I was a little embarrassed the following morning to be greeted in a most friendly manner by her 12-year old daughter and son, aged 14. I cannot imagine an English child of intelligent age behaving as if it were the most natural thing to meet for the first time a man emerging from their mother's bedroom to share the fresh coffee and croissants.

I renewed my instrument rating at Gatwick on 19 July and air-tested the plane on 21 July. Management at Bembridge wanted to inspect the aircraft so I flew it there on 6 August and at the same time picked up spares that had been collected for our rapidly increased number of aircraft in the Cameroons.

When I got back my chief engineer told me that a specialized micrometer essential to the maintenance of our aircraft but virtually useless for anything else had disappeared from the locked stores. I called a meeting of all the staff and told them that if the tool was returned I would do nothing more about it. Nothing happened and I was wondering what to do when it was suggested that I should contact the local Gulla Gulla (witch doctor) man and tell the staff of my intention. Within three days the micrometer had been put back, dirty but undamaged in the locked store room.

A large snake was sitting in the centre of the runway one day when

I was about to take off from Tiko. As I taxied towards it, it reared up threateningly. I passed over it three times before losing sight of it. I had a very uncomfortable feeling that somehow it might have climbed into the undercarriage bay, although there was no way it could have climbed into the cabin. When I landed I very hesitantly investigated but there was no sign of it.

The crop-spraying pilots under Gerry Fretz saw to it that we had a plentiful supply of bananas. They would bring any stem which was not quite up to the standards demanded by E and F, for consumption in the compound. The amount grown and discarded was enormous and at one time a drying plant had been built to use the waste. But it was not a success. Having never seen bananas grow, I visited a plantation and travelled on the small-gauge railway necessary owing to the huge distances involved and was intrigued and surprised at the various stages of growth, which at one juncture I thought suggestive of the phallic symbol.

Although Gerry Fretz had made me most welcome, I felt he resented the fact that he wasn't in charge. At that time he had only flown single-engined aircraft, but some time later I gave him some dual experience at his request and he was able to get a twin rating and endorsement.

We were alerted one day to search for a plane piloted by the son of the Duke of Hamilton which was overdue in bad weather and suspected of crashing into Mount Cameroon. It was difficult to get exact details about route, destination and number of passengers. We carried out quite an extensive search without result before the Duke of Hamilton arrived to discuss possible alternatives, impressing on me that his son was an experienced pilot. I was asked to make a detailed search of the remote areas either side of his intended route where a crashed plane might be difficult to see. There was atrocious weather at the time, but we made every effort to find the plane. We had no success, but we were warmly thanked by the Duke.

*   *   *

African commercial pilot's training was going to be sponsored by both the American and British Governments and I was asked to make

215

assessments and recommendations. Whenever space permitted or an air test was required I took Boniface (my African No. 1) and later two young engineering trainees with me, who I thought might be bright enough to cope with the many academic exams. After fitting dual controls, I gave all three some flying instructions. I reported that the reaction of Boniface (who was the eldest) was very slow and I doubted whether he would qualify, but the other two were quite capable of learning and seemed intelligent. I need not have bothered. The nepotic and despotic attitudes of the area decreed that my No. 1 should be sent to the UK for training.

Boniface returned a few weeks later and resumed his duties in the office. I commiserated with him on failing to complete the course, but he was most emphatic that he had not failed but was waiting to resume later. To have a flying course interrupted for anything other than ill health is most unusual, so I went to the British Consulate in Buea where I read the letter from the chief instructor at the flying school, whose final remarks were, 'In view of the fact that this pupil wishes to become a commercial pilot, it is in the interests of all concerned that his course be discontinued.' Although confronted with this, Boniface still insisted that he hadn't failed and I was sent for by John Ngu, the African government director, who concurred with Boniface and asked me not to raise the matter again.

I was later told that Boniface had been sent to the US on a sponsored course for pilot training. Before that, he had applied to the company for a loan to buy a large car. I resisted the idea, as I knew he would be unable to repay the loan from his salary. I also queried his need for a large car. I discussed this with a UK director, Desmond Norman, who was visiting, and after talking it over with John Ngu, Norman asked me to agree. I was genuinely annoyed as I was usually left to manage without interference. I felt my authority was being undermined. The reason for the large car soon became obvious. Shortly after the loan was granted, it could be seen on the streets acting as a taxi.

Towards the end of my time with CAT the pressures of Africanization presented many problems and cut deeply into the viability of many companies. The loss of one efficient expatriate could never be compensated for by three or more indigenous staff. When returning from a business trip, I often found a change or increase in local staff, authorized by John Ngu. I gave one such girl a bunch of flight vouchers to count, expecting her to come back with the answer in a few minutes. Getting impatient, I went to find her tapping them laboriously one by one on an adding machine. I protested to John Ngu that she was completely useless to our organization and I was astonished when he upheld the waste of time and paper in using a machine for such a simple job. Even after protesting to my UK directors, I was unable to dismiss her, although she was surplus to an already overstaffed office and to any of my requirements.

As the manager of a company with British interests there were good reasons for my visiting the UK regularly, especially as that excellent French airline UAT allowed me to fly there and back first class when space was available, without any cost to Cameroon Air Transport. Imagine my surprise when, while I was away, it was suggested that the company could be run more cheaply if I was dispensed with. About the same time I discovered that some of my African staff had been paying to keep their jobs. Obviously I wanted to sack the founder of this protection racket. Within a few days the main local newspaper had a front page headline 'Patient must go'. This was followed by a most extraordinary account of the villainy I was supposed to have perpetrated beginning 'This negrophobist maniac . . .' and going on to relate how I had squandered huge amounts of the company's money on orgies, extravagant travelling and the like.

I went to see Ulric Cross, who advised me that this was undoubtedly libellous and that, to retain my respect, I would have to sue. I consulted a barrister who was sympathetic and willing to proceed with what he called 'a simple one', if only we could get it to court. Meanwhile I discovered that the person I wanted to discharge was related by marriage to Vice-President Foncha. I realized that with the big guns against me I might have problems so I sent Lucy and the children home. Apart from Bill Bond's open and visual declaration of support, I found that many who had enjoyed my hospitality now avoided me at the club. After Bill left, almost the only one who continued to show any friendship was my licensed engineer Jack Jones.

* * *

By this time West Cameroon had voted in a plebiscite to join French Cameroon instead of Nigeria, which would have been a more natural choice in view of language, custom and law. However, a consensus of opinion indicated a fear of being taken over by the progressive neighbouring Ibo tribe of Nigeria. My anticipation of trouble was soon realized when I was visited by armed French Cameroon gendarmerie who were extremely arrogant and threatening. At the time of their visit to my bungalow I was looking after Jack Jones' Alsatian dog, and they accused me of threatening them with it. I don't know how much of this harassment I could have endured but fortunately, due to my own friends in high places, my case soon came to court.

To justify their claim of my 'negrophobist' attitude the opposition called umpteen witnesses, a few of whose faces I recognized. They alleged that I had been rude to them in different ways, in some cases years before. One stated that I had refused to let him get on an aircraft but showed preference to white passengers. The simple fact that the whites had tickets and he did not did not seem relevant to him. Another had been refused a job with the company despite having a letter from his village chief (a relative) to say that he was qualified. The fact that the lad was illiterate, and in any case we did not need any additional staff at the time, seemed not to matter to the Counsel who produced this witness. He was obviously clutching at straws.

To support my own case I was able to produce several photographs of parties in my home of myself and my children playing with mostly black children including those of our servants – hardly the characteristic of a negrophobist. In addition, the contribution I was making towards the support of native children at school was difficult to refute. I could have called many more to support me, but my barrister advised against it as he considered that the case was won, and those

I called might have been subjected to discrimination and victimization later. The only thing in the libel which might have been closer to the truth was the 'maniac' accusation, insofar as I had flown in very bad weather and might have risked the lives of my passengers. I produced evidence of my specialized meteorological training and operations, but they seemed a little taken aback when I said that I was not worried about my passengers' lives but was very concerned about my own. I would not dream of risking that because, if there was an accident, the probability was that I would be the most likely person to die.

The allegation that my DFC was phoney could only have been advanced by someone whose own decorations were in that category. I regret that I produced in court the original telegram which is only sent to the recipients of immediate awards, as this telegram was retained by the Court together with other documents and photographs.

The case was tried by Mr Justice Gordon, a distinguished West Indian friend of Ulric Cross. I am sure he thought the charade was a waste of time, but I suppose justice must be seen to be done and it was only a few days before my character was vindicated and damages awarded to me. The amount was far short of that claimed and a lot less than it cost me to fight the case. It was, however, explained that, had the award been greater, I would have finished up owning a printing press, a situation obviously unacceptable to the powers that be. I was content to leave it at that. I was told that for a white to win a case against an indigenous company with strong political ties, in an African court with African advocates, was in itself a major triumph.

In view of the unpleasantness of those last few weeks (to put it mildly) I was glad to leave but sad that my hard work in building up a charter company with one aircraft, against strong opposition, into a scheduled services airline had to be discontinued because I had on principle rocked the boat.

10

Sierra Leone

Luton Airport may not sound a very glamorous base after the exotic names of my overseas stations, but I certainly met some interesting people while I was working there. Once again I was on charter work, this time for a subsidiary of Sir Robert MacAlpine. This often meant trips to various parts of the country where we would have to wait while our passengers transacted their business. With perhaps just a couple of hours, a visit to the meteorological office, submitting a flight plan, the airport restaurant and a good book would leave little time for boredom.

Transporting celebrities formed the major part of our work. Owners, trainers and jockeys from Newmarket were frequent passengers. The owners and trainers were understandably tight-lipped about their horses' chances but after a while some of the jockeys when alone and clear of the aircraft might hint that they were only there for the ride or perhaps just worth a place bet. The exception was the great man himself, Lester Piggott. He was always wordless and expressionless. He could have had five winners or none at all, but there was no sign of this, even though other passengers would be talking about it. Even when I flew him to Deauville and was a fellow guest on the owner's yacht, he seemed completely detached.

Quite the most objectionable person I have ever flown was Mary, of the well known Peter, Paul and Mary group. This trio was on a tour of the UK with frequent shows and a tight schedule.

Understandably they dashed off as soon as possible after landing as cars were waiting, but one morning at Boston, when I was waiting to take them to Birmingham, Peter, Paul and the lighting technician and manager arrived in taxis and were most affable. One of them gave me a complimentary ticket for their performance that night. I was surprised when Mary arrived in a Rolls Royce and, without a good morning smile or any sign that we existed, got into the aircraft. We were well on our way when the technician told me that an important piece of equipment had been left at Boston and asked me to radio for it to be sent by fast car to Birmingham. We were out of range with Boston by this time but, against the rules I contacted RAF Cottesmore and managed to persuade them to pass the message back to Boston. I later received acknowledgement and was able to reassure my passengers. I was therefore more than a little peeved when, on arrival at Birmingham, she went off alone in her limousine without so much as a glance in my direction. I asked the others if she was always so high and mighty. There was no reply, but the lifting of their heads and eyes skywards spoke volumes. The aircraft was due for inspection, so I contacted Luton and was told to exchange aircraft next morning. At the same time I asked for another pilot to carry on from there as I thought I might blow my top. I must, however, grudgingly admit that the show was most enjoyable (although I nearly did not go) and what amazed me was the warmth and bonhomie pervading their very professional performance.

Shortly after that episode I had to land at RAF Cottesmore to pick up the Duke of Norfolk and fly him to Goodwood. What a difference. The weather was foul, even for me, and from all the reports and with the very limited aids at Goodwood I suggested that it would be safer to divert to Gatwick where I would arrange for a car to be waiting. It was teeming with rain when we arrived at the VIP tarmac where the airport manager was waiting with a Daimler, yet the Duke went to the trouble of walking round the aircraft to thank me and shake my hand.

I read in a Sunday paper that Air Vice-Marshal D.C.T. Bennett was planning to take a Dove aircraft to war-torn Biafra in order to rescue children. Because of my recent experience in Nigeria, I went to see him at Blackbushe airfield and offered my services, as I knew far better than he all the possible landing places between Lagos and Calabar. He thanked me and asked if I could arrange to leave with him in two weeks' time. I was astonished when my employers refused my request for unpaid leave for this mercy flight, and so indignant that I resigned. A few days later Bennett asked me to go and see him again. He told me the trip was off because, when the sponsors told him that only Catholic children were to be evacuated, he scrubbed the whole trip. He was sorry that I had lost my job through my wish to help and gave me fifty pounds out of his own pocket. I was interested to see that Bennett had arrived at Blackbushe in an aircraft he had designed himself and drove away after our meeting in a car he had also designed.

*   *   *

My luck now turned, I had a letter from Bill Bond asking if I would be interested to take over his job in Sierra Leone as he was going to emigrate to South Africa. It could not have come at a better time. The trauma of my last few months in the Cameroons and now the Bennett disappointment had not only left me unemployed but depressed and discouraged.

An interview at the London office of the Sierra Leone Selection Trust (SLST) ended with me being told to get a Heron endorsement. I did this during November, 1968, with Captain Firmin at Coventry. I was met at Lungi (Sierra Leone) by Bill Bond who wasted no time and sat me up front for a trip to the mine at Yengema. I was housed in the company VIP house until Bill and Rosemary departed and I then took over their bungalow. My first meeting with Harry Parker, the general manager of the mine who had accepted Bill's recommendation of me, went smoothly and I left his office feeling that once again all was well. And so it turned out. What was to be my last flying job, and one which demanded a high standard of pilotage owing to the terrain, the weather, short runways and lack of navigational aids, just suited me. Lucy and two of my children were able to join me, and I think I can say that my stay in Sierra Leone was the most contented of my life.

The hangar, stores and offices at Yengema airfield were not elaborate but they were practical and solidly built. The loo, however, was a thing of beauty and quite out of character with the rest, having been specially constructed for the visit of the Queen and Prince Phillip in 1961. It was of course called the Royal Flush.

When flying frequently in a prescribed area, particularly when there is a dearth of navigational aids, almost every outstanding tree, rock or patch of water is committed to memory so that a blind approach can be made to the runway in safety. Once, when I was coming back from Lungi, the visibility was below normal and it was pouring with rain. I had Bert Lewthwaite, a supervisor in charge of earth-moving equipment at Yengema and Tongo, with me en route for Tongo. A little weaving about became necessary so as to stay clear of the low clouds. When I took a map out and spread it on my knees, Bert noticed it was upside down and became extremely anxious. Thinking that I might be lost, he leant across and asked if we had a problem. 'Yes,' I replied. 'The windscreen leaks.'

One of my duties was to hand in and collect passports for endorsements and residence visas. Being nosy, I would glance at them and was full of admiration for one 'gentleman' who had discreetly altered his passport entry of 'miner' to the immediate promotion of 'mining engineer'. However, the entry lacked the office stamp and initials mandatory to alterations of official documents. With such ingenuity I was not surprised to hear later that he had been appointed General Manager (GM).

*　*　*

Lucy and I have many fond memories of Sierra Leone and the little incidents that used to make us laugh and now remind us of those happy days. A five-foot cobra was a most unwelcome visitor to our bungalow one day. Even at a distance, the sight of one this size is very intimidating. Perhaps rather rashly I borrowed the cook's machete and with a dustbin lid held in front of me in a gladiatorial manner I forced the snake to retreat along the path. At intervals it would rear up facing me in a terrifying manner, and on one such occasion I took a wild swing at it and to my great surprise cleanly severed about nine

223

inches of its head and neck from the rest of its body. My servant wanted to claim the body for food but I refused and hung it over a low branch, where even a few hours later it was still quivering and covered with bluebottles. Despite this, it had vanished the next day.

At about the same time a nest of cobras was found near Ken Harvey's house. He decided to get rid of them by pouring petrol down the hole and lighting it. Whether this disposed of the snakes was never known, but the flash-back nearly disposed of Ken. He was lucky not to suffer permanent injury but it put him out of action for a time.

Playing golf one morning, I was on the backswing of my second shot when I doubled up in pain, having been struck on the wrist by a ball driven by Steve Skelchy, who had recently won a long driving competition. Almost within seconds my hand was twice its normal size. I was rushed to Tony Freeman (our Doctor) who declared no bones broken but 'hand in a sling' for a few days.

Unfortunately I was scheduled to fly that afternoon and it was one of the more important flights, with not enough time to go by road or arrange a chartered aircraft from Sierra Leone Airways in Freetown. Although feeling groggy, I knew that if I sat in the right-hand seat I could handle the throttles with my left, so I arranged for Bill Adams, who often sat in front with me, to fly straight and level. The flying for the next few days was reduced to essentials only. After a week I found no difficulty in driving an aircraft but it was several weeks before I could drive a golf ball with comfort.

During the frequent coups, the government radio had no military music to play except records of British military bands. These were played for hour after hour while we tried to find out what was going on. Inevitably this music became known as 'music to coup by'. One of these take-overs occurred over a public holiday weekend and the military came to the mine on the Monday. Tony Hall and the general manager, Harry Parker, discussed security and invited them to the Yengema Club for drinks. Ranged along the bar was a line of security officers whom Tony introduced as Major this or Captain that, while Harry ducked along to the end and introduced himself as Sergeant Parker, Home Guard!

Reminiscing one evening in the club, I mentioned that, as a lad when I went swimming, the first thing I did was to swim a length under water. A young security officer, himself a good swimmer, voiced the inflammatory comment, 'You might have done it then; you couldn't now.' I bridled and replied with, 'I could do it fully clothed.' Those nearby, suspecting a bit of fun, began to take sides; the outcome being a £5 bet. I was sober enough to realize that the new shoes I was wearing would suffer more than five pounds' worth of damage if wetted. Also, I was sure that if I quoted this as my objection, they would waive the wearing of the shoes. The young man just managed to swim the length, but I continued three-quarters of the length back, relieving the cocky young man of £5.

I had never played golf seriously until I went to Yengema where I was able to play almost every day. I would drive off 200 balls and play them all back to a green. I found a great deal in common between golf and snooker. I know of no other game where a stationary ball is struck with a rigid instrument. Just as in snooker, you can top, screw back, apply both left and right side on the ball while aiming at a hole, not forgetting the miscue (shank) and the fluke (rub of the green).

Marian and Mike Houghton, the Barclay's Bank Manager at Koidu, were given honorary membership of the Yengema clubs – Mike being an avid golfer and bridge player. We were friends but there was keen competition between us. Although a sound bridge player, he would on occasion make some outlandish psychic sacrificial bid which cost us dearly. Remarking that if he agreed to play to a system I had developed successfully with an associate during my RAF days, I would be willing to play with him against any others for large stakes. Cam Sturgeon (our golf bandit) a dour Scot, challenged my statement and a match was arranged. I wrote the system out and discussed it before starting to play. Despite Cam's almost contemtuous insistence that it would not work, his ancestry came to the fore when he opted for a modest stake. We won and he most grudgingly admitted that it seemed to work.

Mike challenged me to a golf match. At that time I had not qualified for a handicap and for a £5 bet he offered me the maximum ladies' handicap of 36. When I accepted, he then said that, playing off a ladies' handicap, I must play dressed as a lady. I countered this by insisting on playing off the ladies' tee which added to my advantage. Lucy's clothes were too slim for me so I borrowed a skirt, blouse and bra from Pet Fisk (a more generously proportioned lady). Two avocado pears filled the ample cups and with a ribbon in my hair I took my stance on the 1st ladies' tee at the weekend. Those in the club house wondered who the Amazon newcomer was. In spite of the severe handicap of hitting a long ball with two avocado pears wanting to go in different directions as I swung, amid much amusement I managed to win.

Mike had been looking after a minature Dachshund for a colleague who had asked him to find a good home for the dog. My natural liking is for big dogs but I accepted 'Otto' who became one of the family. He was a most intelligent animal who perhaps had been badly treated, for he had all the attributes of a negrophobist. The Watsons, who were close neighbours, had one of the same breed but which took a different stance when performing acts of nature. We usually took our dogs with us when playing golf and I contrived to follow the Watsons and Tina when they played. By tying Otto to my golf trolley I had a power-assisted conveyance for my clubs. Sad to say, poor Otto (to my knowledge) was never allowed to have his wicked way with her.

Another golf match was between Brian Walsh and I during a violent thunderstorm and downpour. In a few moments we were sopping wet, but the rain was warm and we proceeded with slippery clubs and only stopped when we were putting on the sand (greens) and with laughter saw our balls floating past the hole and off the putting surface.

It seemed a shame, with all the verdant grass in the camp, that the putting greens were sand, a situation I tried to improve. There being no turfing tool, I designed one and the blacksmith made it. Thus armed, the best patches of grass were raided, cut and transported to a selected area for the Camp's first green. It was perhaps for this and other assistance that I had the honour of being the first honorary life member of the Yengema Golf Club.

226

One day a native woman found a large diamond near the base of a tree outside the lease. In a very short time the tree was destroyed and the nearby area dug up. It is perhaps a good thing that the natives did not realize that this valuable bauble was found on the surface and not dug up. A bird which abounded in the area was the hooded crow, a bird closely related to the magpie and jackdaw which are attracted to shining objects. Obviously places within the lease might just occasionally reveal such objects, and crows would not have the same difficulty as humans in entering a heavily guarded area like a diamond mine. Once their sharp eyes had spotted a shining object they would pick it up and later drop it accidentally from their nest or from high branches. Had any indigenous person thought that one out, there would have been a race to climb trees and the crow population in West Africa would have been decimated.

The uninitiated, given a selection of small pebbles with a few uncut diamonds among them, would discard them for more attractive stones. The normal smaller stones look like a pair of pyramids joined at the base. In the cutting, the stone is normally divided near its widest point, which then becomes the top facet of two diamonds. In Freetown I was shown the sorting office where small groups of uncut diamonds were spread into different colours and sizes. I pointed to a stone and remarked that it was a different colour to those that surrounded it, resulting in a senior sorter being called, who confirmed my comment. The manager remarked that if I could see that shade of difference, I was wasting my time as a pilot and should be in the sorting office.

Jim Proudfoot was a popular Scot who needed no encouragement to play his bagpipes, especially at Burns or Caledonian Society dinners when he would pipe in the haggis. On one such occasion, having done his duty, he placed his bagpipes upon a chair well away from the gathering. Jeff Stewart staggering from the toilet a little 'Brahms and Liszt' flopped upon the chair which contained the treasured musical instrument, completely demolishing the chanter resulting in an exchange of words which was neither complimentary nor in keeping with the brotherly gathering and cannot be reproduced verbatim.

227

It was even suggested that a few pipers should be employed to wander about the bush at night playing their weird and wonderful laments, as this would scare the daylights out of the superstitious natives and reduce the illicit diamond mining fraternity far more effectively than the expensive security force.

★   ★   ★

We were all admirers of our Chief Security Officer Leslie Marsden CMG., who,by his quiet manner and words of encouragement, roused the maximum effort from his subordinates and the utmost respect from his peers. Leslie was unfortunately promoted to be Resident Director in Freetown. A vicious anti-Marsden campaign resulted in Leslie leaving the country. The gutter press that day headed their front page 'Marsden CMG kicked out'. We all felt the loss, especially when his replacement was Brigadier Michael Harbottle, whose last job had been with the UN forces in Cyprus. His attitude to subordinates might have been fine had he confined it to Cyprus. My first brush with him happened shortly after landing at Hastings one afternoon. I cannot remember whether Harbottle addressed me as Captain, Joe, or Patient; it doesn't matter. But what he said did: 'We will take off at 0830.' My immediate response 'We won't' rather shook him. When asked the reason I went to great pains to tell him that there were regulations governing hours of rest that are mandatory relative to hours being on duty, irrespective of hours flown during the period. I went on to tell him that I had occasionally broken those rules in the interests of the management but under no circum-stances would I accept an order to do so. 'Had you said, "Can we get away at 08.30." I would have agreed and not bored you with the technicalities.'

Michael Harbottle tried hard to be popular but could not quite overcome what I call an abrasive manner. He let his hair down on one occasion at the GM's barbeque by dancing round the lawn with his 'convenient wife' to the music of 'The Sugar Plum Fairy'.

Brigadier Harbottle further annoyed me when he wrote a book *The Knaves of Diamonds*, which was his version of the greatest diamond robbery of all time, by referring to me as 'Birdie Stapleford' perhaps

228

because I was either in the air or on the golf course. Although there was nothing derogatory about me in the book, in fact the opposite, there could be no confusion. There was only one Heron pilot on the mine during his period in Sierra Leone. However, my name is Joe Patient and he could have easily contacted me as well as Leslie Marsden and not put me in the category that he expressed in the 'Author's Note' – 'Where the cap fits let him wear it.' Had he contacted me, I could have enlightened him, particularly at his astonishment expressed on page 88, at the 'non coup broadcaster' among other details of the whole nightmarish charade.

There was a degree of satisfaction for me that the Great Diamond Robbery occurred with Brigadier Harbottle in charge and not Leslie Marsden. Bill Bond and I had discussed at length the probability of such an event and were surprised that it had not happened before. However we rather thought that it would take the form of hi-jacking the aircraft. Neither we nor the security officers were allowed to carry guns, so there would be no question of doing other than what we were told if there was a pistol at our head. It would be a simple matter, with no radar cover of the area, to pick us up, force us to fly and land at any of the many remote and isolated airstrips, or even in open country or on beaches in Sierra Leone or, more probably, Guinea or Liberia where there would be waiting get-away cars or canoes or the hijackers would simply vanish into the bush. There would be no problem in rendering the aircraft and radio unserviceable and it could be days before we found a village with any means of communication. A search and rescue operation in such a large area with so little to go on would be unlikely. We discussed the further possibility of the diamonds being put into a strong sack and our having to fly to a clearing where they could be dropped to associates some considerable distance from where we would be forced to land. Although the security diamond transports were supposed to be secret, even to the pilot until shortly before take-off, I invariably knew when one was to go. Therefore, if I could work it out, there must have been many who could do likewise and inform those who had no right to know, but who needed this vital information for their nefarious plans.

When the inevitable robbery took place, it was in such an open manner that it could only have occurred with connivance at the very highest level. Alternatively the actions were carried out by simpletons. But the main actor in the farce was a very level headed and successful Lebanese entrepreneur.

On 13 November, 1969, I was briefed to wait for the helicopter to arrive with the security officers and a consignment of diamonds, drop off a passenger at Tongo and then proceed to Hastings in the usual way. Apart from Harbottle and his security escort, there was an indigenous passenger with rather a supercilious air, who was a reporter with the Broadcasting Corporation and had been visiting the mine for material. When we arrived at Hastings I circled the field until the security vehicles were in sight and Harbottle had given me the OK to land. I came to a halt in the normal parking area and switched off (the passenger having previously been briefed to remain in his seat). As I was getting out of the cockpit, Harbottle and the escort had just got clear of the aircraft when all of a sudden shouts, screams, gunfire or firecrackers were all around us. I looked out of the window and saw the security officers being attacked by a horde of natives with a couple of 'off whites' in the background waving guns (one appeared to be a Sten gun) and vicious-looking clubs. I rushed back to the cockpit, switched on the radio and transmitted a Mayday call to Lungi airport telling them to contact the police. While this was going on, I glanced back at our passenger who had at the first sound of violence cowered down into his seat and had turned a rather light and pasty shade of grey. The whole action lasted less than two minutes, the parking area being cleared in that time apart from the two dazed unfortunates wandering about, and then a few people running from the hangar with belated assistance.

Meanwhile I got airborne again in an effort to find and follow the two get-away vehicles but it was a hopeless task with so much bush closely surrounding the airfield. After I had landed without sighting anything, there came a tedious report to the police who took everything down in longhand.

For weeks afterwards passengers from Yengema, myself included, were searched for diamonds, even to the extent of removing footwear. It was of course a red herring ordered by the government. It may have deluded a few of the local populace but as more than one of the offenders had been recognized and named, this action was ludicrous. Then there began a bitter tirade by the local papers against the diamond companies in an effort to divert attention from the obvious. One newspaper, however, began to insinuate that the government was implicated, with dire results for their premises.

About a week later I was called again to Freetown to make a statement to the police. This time, however, in addition to the statement (once again in longhand) I was questioned at intervals by a senior police officer who seemed to want me to say things in a different way. I quickly made it clear that there was very little to add to my previous statement. But he implied that I had contradicted myself. My demand to see my original statement was brushed aside with 'It doesn't matter.' I went to the meeting before noon and left well after eight p.m., hungry as well as angry.

I was astonished when the trial eventually took place and I was not called. I probably knew as much about the robbery as anyone, and could easily have been thought to be implicated. In view of the blatantly 'fixed' trial, this was obviously why I had not been called to give evidence by either the prosecution or defence. On my next visit home I was offered £2,000 for my story of the diamond robbery which of course I refused. It would certainly have cost me my very comfortable job. By the time I eventually left Sierra Leone, the story was old hat.

There are inevitable highlights in any expatriate's experience of life in a country as remote as Sierra Leone but, in addition, the day-to-day existence in a busy job within a tightly knit community is seldom dull and the social life never seems to drag, so that one returns home when it is all over with a host of memories of people and places, many happy, some less so, but it is a good life for those who can adapt – as Lucy and I always could.

*   *   *

In many parts of Africa the 'fetish' area or place exists under different

231

names. In Sierra Leone it is the Poro Bush. This area is taboo to all except the witch doctor and has a peculiarity endemic to the mining area of Yengema in that it is conveniently moveable and mysteriously appears near areas with diamond-bearing potential. The trespass of these areas involves penalties. Michael North was arrested for having entered a Poro Bush and the demands for his release caused some chuckles. It took a lot of wrangling with local bigwigs to get Michael released. The ransom note demanded all sorts of items – one being a Sea Horse (a rare item 200 miles from the sea) and a White Cock. This caused quite some speculation in the interpretation. Fortunately the matter was resolved out of court before it had been established whether the Cock referred to was a farmyard animal or the appendage of some unfortunate expatriate. So the matter was closed without loss of face, or anything else.

In February, 1969, I was unfortunate to lose my briefcase (or had it stolen) on a trip to Freetown. This caused a great deal of inconvenience as it contained my log book, vaccination certificates, passport and worst of all my well-worn teddy given to me by Joy twenty-six years previously. My flying details I could obtain from my monthly reports, another passport from the High Commissioner in Freetown, with no more bother than a statement, a form filled and a couple of photographs. A shot or two of vaccine no one is going to cry about, but I was very upset about my teddy. When the GM's daughter, Julia, heard, she was kind enough to obtain a substitute for me which I have to this day.

In April, 1970, the Heron was almost due for a Check 4 overhaul which could not be done locally. Arrangements were made through the London office to have it carried out by Scottish Aviation at Prestwick. Meanwhile Dave Veitch, our aircraft engineer, and I would take our holidays. To save fares it was agreed that both our families would accompany us, but at the same time we would make it a leisurely trip. At Bathurst, Gambia, we were most impressed by the warm welcome and the cleanliness of the place, which was particularly noticeable when compared with its less clean West African neighbours. By getting up early each morning we were able to see a little of each place we stayed in; we would leave after lunch and fly through the normal siesta period. Casablanca was memorable for an outstanding reason. During a visit to the huge Souk, we were followed by one persistent fellow who made pertinent enquiries about my daughter Eleanor as to how much I would accept for her. I had received many such offers for my other daughters in Egypt, Jordan and the Lebanon, but they had all been discreet enquiries from persons known to me. This was my first and only open-air proposition.

When we got to Gatwick we all felt the trip had been a success and went our various ways. The following day I flew my 'baby' to Prestwick and returned home for my holiday. All travel had to be coordinated with the London office. One of the treasures there was Margaret Dawson whose help with the arrangements (often at very short notice), the many complexities of international currencies and travel formalities, not only for the employees but for wives and often unaccompanied children, was quite invaluable. You were always met with a friendly smile and your problems were listened to sympathetically over coffee. When you left you felt relieved, knowing that everything that could be done would be done.

When I joined SLST Harry Parker had impressed upon me that any social flying requested was entirely at my discretion to carry out. These flights, invariably at weekends, consisted of cricket, rugby, soccer and golf teams, the latter usually with wives, playing or otherwise, to compete at other mines or to the Capital, Freetown, with occasional trips to neighbouring countries. During the whole of the time I was in Yengema, despite having to refrain from alcoholic refreshment on those trips, I only refused on one occasion.

It appeared in the flying programme that the rugby team would be flown to Freetown, without this having been referred to me. I took umbrage and told the secretary to amend the flying programme and inform the rugby club secretary to make other arrangements. Gordon Percy, the team captain, asked me to reconsider, but I refused. During the same week at a party, while dancing with Sheila Sturgeon (whom I liked), she also pleaded with me to fly the team.

I found this more difficult but still said 'No'. Later while playing golf, Mike Wallen who was acting GM, came to speak to me. Before he had a chance to speak, I queried, 'Is it about the rugby team?' When he replied, 'Yes,' I explained the reasons for my refusal and then said, 'Mike, if you order me to fly the team on Sunday, my resignation will be on your desk on Monday.' Mike left with: 'OK Joe I understand.'

The various parties spoke volumes for the hosts, from the local beer, cheese and peanuts – not always restricted to the less well-off– to the champagne and Cordon Bleu goodies. At one of the very senior (infrequent) do's, the murmur of 'Who's cheating on the entertainment allowance' could be overheard. In contrast the parties given by the 'Three Musketeers', three men who, with their wives, formed a close-knit group and seemed to enjoy a standard of living that was blatantly in excess of anything that their salaries from the mine would have made possible and so was an inevitable source of speculation. The extravagance of their parties was notorious, only matched by the obvious not 'off the peg' clothes and jewellery of their spouses, who were frequently seen spending as if there was no tomorrow. How to entertain so suddenly, so frequently and so lavishly on relatively junior salaries did not need a Sherlock Holmes to make a reasonably sound calculated guess. However, it is not for me to criticize, for I certainly enjoyed their hospitality.

When the time came round for leave, finding a replacement for just one month was always a problem. Unless the pilot had worked in the area before he would need about a week to be shown the different mines and ports of call and to learn how to handle the security diamond run. Many of them, who were used to long runways and a surfeit of navigational aids, found that the landing strips were short, some very short, and that navigation aids consisted of a few topographical features seen en route if you were lucky with the weather. It was not a job for the timid.

On 16 December, 1970, I once again flew to Lungi to pick up my relief pilot, Captain Wild. Fortunately he had filled in for Bill Bond before so it was a formality giving him a route survey the following day which ended with him dropping me off at Lungi for my flight to the UK. We wasted no time on my return. He flew the Heron into Lungi and, after clearing customs, I flew the aircraft back to Yengema via Hastings where I picked up additional passengers. There were others returning from leave on the same aircraft. They were pleased with these arrangements as it saved us all the tiresome road journey to Freetown. Some had availed themselves copiously of the alcoholic beverages on board and were taunting me because I could not join them. They stopped, however, when I threatened them with a bumpy ride. The following year I could not get Captain Wild and was worried about my replacement. He took six and a quarter hours and thirteen landings before I felt happy with him, against the two and a half hours with Captain Wild.

An episode still chortled about merits inclusion. John Wright and Barry Budinger were Assistant Superintendents of Police, but in our security force. John was a stalwart of the rugby team, with the stature of an all-in wrestler with a beer gut, and a person you would not like to meet in a lonely place on a dark night, but whose appearance belied his humourous and generous nature. Barry was an Adonis by comparison and both were favourites among the ladies of 'dat place'.

Returning to Motema from a session at the bar in the Yengema Club, John conducted a check of the Police Station records. Not believing what he had read, he asked Barry for confirmation of the neatly worded entry: one baboon – large, dead – held accused of a GBH (Grevious Bodily Harm) assault on one Pa Mansary of Nimikoro. Knowing that baboons normally occupied more southerly latitudes, John went outside to see 'dat ting' which turned out to be a very big chimpanzee.

Pa Mansary, working in his rice field, heard a noise behind him, but, expecting his wife with his midday 'chop' took no notice until he was grabbed, at which Pa, realizing that it was not the soft caress of Mama Mansary, screamed for help and was badly mauled during his attempts to get away. The animal was killed by farmers with machetes. With a possibly mortally wounded Pa Mansary on their hands, the farmers felt the need to prove the facts to ever-doubting police, so, bundling both Pa and animal into a taxi, took them ceremoniously into Motema.

The police treated the case with due deference (the accused being unable to deny the charge) and it was not until the victim had been admitted to Koidu Hospital and was off the danger list that 'dat ting', which by now was rather smelly, got a decent burial.

On one occasion, when my licensed aircraft engineer had gone on leave, his replacement was running the engines on test preparing for an after lunch take-off. I was playing golf at the time and, listening to the engines seemingly at full throttle for rather excessive periods, I was sufficiently worried to stop playing and drive to the airfield to see what was going on, just in time to witness the fourth engine being belted at full throttle by someone who could not possibly have had any real experience. I did not wait for him to finish but signalled to him to shut down. I immediately asked the general manager to send this moron back whence he came as I would not fly the aircraft if he had touched it. When the difficulty of getting another engineer was raised, I offered to supervise the maintenance myself and get any necessary signatures when required from my licensed engineer friend in Sierra Leone Airways. My solution was agreed and everything went smoothly during the engineer's leave.

Included in my monthly report to head office in London was an explanation indicating the additional work carried out by myself and staff. I always tried to include a little humour in the reports and included: 'Have you heard the story of the three most useless things in the world? I will not bore you with the first two, but the third is "a letter of thanks from the management".'

I had problems in September, 1971, when I flew the President, Dr Siaka Stevens, with his entourage to Liberia to see President Tubman who later, with a great blaring of sirens, returned to the airport to see the Doctor off. I had been warned of their return and decided to do a run-up check, when to my consternation I found that one of my starter motors was unserviceable. To obtain a replacement would have meant a night stop or even longer, the thought of which was not attractive. Also, the embarrassment of letting the government down would have been thought by some to be deliberate, such was the suspicious attitude towards the mining company at the time. I had no knowledge of the length of runway required for a three-engine take-off on the Heron, but from my test experience felt that I had adequate runway length to perform this with safety, relying on the airflow to rotate the propeller and so start the engine. However, it would not have been wise to try this with all aboard and I did not know how long the departure ceremonies would take. If prolonged this would result in the engine overheating which of course I should have to keep running. My only safe recourse was to make the three-engined take-off and then cruise round, having arranged with flying control to inform me when the party was ready to leave. This was done and I returned the Doctor and his entourage safely. They thanked me for the trip without so much as a question about the unorthodoxy of the procedure.

Being one of the SHODS (Senior Heads of Department) with possibly the most free time on my hands, I was elected chairman of the Yengema Club committee. The mine had three clubs, the Golf, Rugby and Yengema Social, the last being the main meeting place, with its billiards room, table tennis, games, dance area and swimming pool, all conveniently close to the bar.

One of my first problems as chairman was delicate. There were always a few local girls hanging about outside the club and the committee had received complaints from wives (who may have received knowing looks from 'les girls') asking that the problem be dealt with. How can you prohibit walking past an open verandah close to a normal thoroughfare? Many were daughters of respected locals and one of the more popular was the daughter of the Ambassador to the United Kingdom. To get rid of them was going to be very tricky. A wrong move could cause an international incident. The local press were only too willing to stir up trouble between the mine and the government. Not even the management representative could offer any solution other than a notice posted in the club asking that members should not encourage, just ignore, any girls loitering near the club.

The entertainments committee put on an excellent cabaret show in the club. I was able to train a chorus line of a dozen ladies dancing a Cha Cha Cha which was well received. The evening was only marred by the hypersensitive objection to a mimed version of Al Jolson.

When any social events were planned, one could always rely on the unstinted assistance of Ray and Georgie Whacker who were unashamedly true cockneys. They were not always invited to the upper echelon parties, but it was always refreshing to have them to ours. Furthermore their two children, together with Danny Drummond's daughter, were probably the best behaved children to visit the mine.

There are so many other incidents and people worthy of mention during my stay in Sierra Leone and other outposts of the British Empire and elsewhere, but unfortunately space forbids.

Various entertainments and social evenings were laid on when directors and other important folk from the London office were making their rounds. On these occasions I would usually fly to Freetown to collect invited guests, both indigenous and expatriate, who frequently added others to their invitation on some pretext or other. Knowing this, I ensured that the total coming by air was not the full complement of the aircraft. With imagined discrimination so rife, should I have had to off-load anyone, as I valued my job, it would have been expatriates. Juma Sei, the chairman, invariably accepted invitations to these affairs but was afraid of flying, so travelled slowly for many hours in his Mercedes. He had the nasty habit of taking home with him whatever food or drink was left in the Rest House, on one occasion taking the table linen as well. It is believed that he was eventually sacked by the President for this.

Apart from the head office VIPs, the visitors to the mine I remember most clearly were Haile Selassie, the Marquess of Lothian, the Dutch Ambassador and his wife, Graham Greene, almost every High Commissioner from the nearby countries and quite often Siaka Stevens.

Another was a party of British MPs touring the country. I was to pick them up and bring them to the mine before taking them the next day to Freetown. I took one of my cleaning lads with me to put the steps out, etc. After waiting several minutes this 'shower' ambled out to the aircraft with bottles of beer in their hands, looking like a bunch of winos, jackets slung over shoulders, one with his shirt hanging out and needing a shave. I was ashamed, particularly as my cleaner said, 'Surely these cannot be British MPs?' Fortunately they were the only passengers scheduled for the next day. Judging it nicely for time, I did my run-up of the engines as they arrived at the hangar and, on the third engine, contrived to make it splutter. After shutting down, I advised these 'gentlemen' to take the car (a rather long and un-comfortable ride) as it looked like an engine change. This the GM immediately arranged. I told the engineer to remove the engine cowlings and, as soon as the cars had left, I suggested that he change the set of plugs and all would be well. In 32 years of flying, this was the only occasion that I felt justified in deliberately putting an aircraft unserviceable.

On St Valentine's Day, 1972, there was great excitement at the mine. The third largest diamond ever known was found. Mr K.O. Williams (engineer) and Mr W.D. Adams (security officer) were the first to spot this huge 2½ by 1½ inch stone weighing half a pound. We flew this discovery to Freetown where it was shown to Dr Siaka Stevens who named it the Star of Sierra Leone. Estimated to be worth a million pounds in its uncut state, it was eventually sold to Mr Harry Winston who has handled many of the world's famous diamonds. The 'Star' was broken down into eleven stones weighing 328.14 carats, the largest being 143.2 carats. This was later re-cut to produce another six stones reducing the final total of cut diamonds to 238.48 carats from 968.9 carats of 'virgin stone'.

An unusual feature of Sierra Leone is a hill of virtually solid iron ore situated at Marampa. The mine there held an open tournament on 18 March, 1972, and I flew a golf team there to compete. As it included a nightstop, I was able to partake of their generous liquid hospitality. In view of my unmerited handicap of twelve I, needless to say, was completely outclassed, but came away with a necktie to commemorate the event.

Like many millions who play 'Goff' (as pronounced by the 'U' people) I have never made a hole in one – but I have by accident managed an almost certainly less frequent phenomenon. With a long drive at Yengema, I faded a ball very close to an out of bounds area. Not being sure and not wishing to walk back, I played a provisional ball which went in the same direction. We found both the original and the provisional balls touching.

*　　*　　*

Lucy and I were concerned about the two youngest of our children and felt it was time for us to return to the UK to make a real home for them. I told the general manager of our decision and suggested that I should resign, send Lucy home, but stay on myself until another pilot could be found. I was replaced by Captain Elmes who arrived on 30 May, 1972. I gave him as much flying, information and introductions as I could over five days, ending with a diamond security run.

*　　*　　*

The wonderful send off I received from my many friends almost made me regret my decision to retire from flying, but I knew that it was now time for me to return to the country of my birth. I had flown for thirty-two years, mostly in senior and executive positions; I had worked hard but I had also enjoyed my leisure activities up to the hilt. I had always been a gambler and had been successful on many occasions, both socially and in undercover situations. In short, I had led a very full life.

But the more settled period I was looking forward to did not materialize. Risk-taking in the antique business can be every bit as nail-biting as some of the hazards of flying, and my experiences of that trade remain to be told. Successes and catastrophes in other ventures were equally unforeseen, as were the sometimes life-threatening problems of my own health. I am, however, a great survivor.

One on my greatest personal pleasures continues to be the all too rare occasions when Lucy and I meet Norry and his charming wife. We share many yarns and memories of the past, remembering especially the irrepressible humour of Tommy Forsyth, the quiet

240

humility of Johnny Baker and the outstanding qualities of many comrades who shared a joke, a game of billiards, or general high jinks in the mess. Many of them did not survive.

Norry and I also exchange a good deal of leg-pulling about who is going to live the longest. This is perhaps especially poignant when it takes place between two men who shared such dangers, and could so easily have died together fifty years ago.

Index